ELECTRIC EUSTON TO GLASGOW

ELECTRIC EUSTON TO GLASGOW

O. S. NOCK

ACGI, BSC, DIC, CEng,
FICE, FIMechE, FPW Inst
Past President:
Institution of Railway
Signal Engineers

LONDON

IAN ALLAN LTD

First published 1974

ISBN 0 7110 0530 3

Published by Ian Allan Ltd, Shepperton, Surrey, and printed in the United Kingdom by
The Garden City Press Limited, Letchworth, Hertfordshire

CONTENTS

PREFACE

Many years hence when railway historians are studying the evolution of the British railway system in the last quarter of the twentieth century, and have before them little except the bare facts of what was and what was not done, they could well be excused for jumping to quite a lot of wrong conclusions, and for falling into much criticism of the top management and of the Government departments that held the purse strings. But in providing me with data on which to base this book my railway friends at the Board, and in the London Midland and Scottish Regions have told me enough of the background story over the seven frustrating years since the Euston–Liverpool–Manchester electrification was completed to enable me to lift the veil in one or two places, and show that it was not plain sailing; that the delays, the changes of plan and of emphasis, were not the result of railwaymen on the job 'not knowing their own minds', and not eventually doing all that they might have done. The vision was there from the outset – nay, even before the Liverpool–Manchester project was completed. Far-sighted railwaymen, high ranking in all the different disciplines, saw the way ahead clearly enough; but I suppose it was no more than natural that those who controlled the national finances did not put the same emphasis on railway modernisation.

The electrification of the West Coast main line north of Weaver Junction has therefore to be studied against a background quite different from those of great British railway projects of former years. The well-worn *cliché* 'Times have changed' applies to no facet of our national life and economy more than to railways; and the administrators of today, struggling month after month, year after year to get the electrification project authorised could, if they knew their railway history, occasionally have looked back wistfully to the time when the board of the London and North Western Railway could decide, 'just like that' as it were, to go ahead with a great project like the goods lines beneath the whole complex of the Crewe north junctions, or still more so, when the Midland could decide on their own to build the Settle and Carlisle line. But in one respect times have *not* changed. It is now just about a hundred years ago that John Bright, the great Quaker and Radical politician uttered the historic words:

> "Railways have rendered more services, and have received less gratitude, than any other institution in the land."

Those same words could have been spoken, with equal justification by any senior officer of the British Railways Board at any time during the last ten years!

It is to present something of the mammoth job railways are continuing to do, and continuing to deserve the gratitude that remains so elusive to them, that this book has been written; and although I expect the majority of my readers will be those whose interest in railways is friendly, there will no doubt be critics, if no more than of parts, or details of the scheme. One high ranking railway officer, who has been a close personal friend for many years, was a little apprehensive that certain passages in Chapter 3, where I had discussed possible side-effects from the continued need to work the Liverpool and Manchester–Scottish expresses by diesel as far as Preston, would open the floodgates to the critics, despite, as he kindly put it, your 'carefully chosen words'. But those who would criticise for criticism's sake will find a way in through the most closely-knit defences; and I have endeavoured to show how carefully and constantly the overall scheme was trimmed and tailored so as to make it eventually acceptable to those who controlled the purse strings. Now it is finished we have a magnificently integrated 'new' railway, embodying engineering techniques that in each branch are second to none the world over, and of which advantage is being taken by a highly rationalised and imaginative pattern of traffic operation.

At the time of final proof correction the 'Electric Scots' have been running for just a month. They are not only fulfilling all that was expected of them but they are indicating quite clearly that the electrified network has possibilities far beyond the present time-table. On the opening day, May 6th, the first down express, the 07.45 from Euston, clocked into Glasgow in 5hr 8¾min with four intermediate stops en route, at Watford Junction, Preston, Carlisle and Motherwell. These accounted for a few seconds under 12min, but two stops for adverse signals took another $4\frac{1}{2}$min, so that the actual running time was only $292\frac{1}{4}$, and the net 285min, the latter an average of $84\frac{1}{2}$mph. On the same day the Royal Scot ran on time on its five-hour schedule, but during the first week of operating the all-electric schedules some astonishing individual feats of locomotive performance were achieved, of which the most remarkable and significant that has come to my notice was on one of the down expresses from Birmingham, loaded to 11 coaches. This train passed Tebay at 90mph and then proceeded to accelerate on the 1 in 75 of the Shap Incline to 95mph!

When we have in Great Britain locomotives that will take a train of 390 tons up a gradient of 1 in 75 at 95mph it is indeed time to begin talking of a new era in railway travel. My own first journeys on the five-hour Royal Scot yielded net running times of 18 and 19min below schedule time, showing running averages of 86 and $86\frac{1}{2}$mph over the 401.3. For the moment such evidence of locomotive capacity will be kept in reserve for recovery of time lost through incidental delays; but improvement to the 'new' railway is increasing. In the logs of the track testing special detailed in the final Chapter of this book it was noted that the speed limit round the Wolverton curves was specially raised from 80 to 90mph for the tests. It has now been raised to 100mph for ordinary traffic. Again, when electric traction was first introduced south of Crewe we were all duly impressed that the new locomotives took their trains up the Madeley Bank at 87mph. Now that gradient of 1 in 177 is taken at 100mph as a matter of course. So progress continues in every facet of the railway.

This has been a fascinating book to write. While in collecting data for 'Britain's New Railway' I was dealing with the officers of a single region, this time there have been two, with the co-ordinating influence of British Railways Board headquarters. It would be impossible to mention by name all those who have kindly given their time to supplying me with information, indicating lines for my personal observation in the field, and inviting me to join in some of their inspections. It was perhaps inevitable that a vast and ever-growing weight of paper would pile up before the project was finished, and I am very grateful to the staff of the Press Office at BRB Headquarters for acting as a central 'post office' on my behalf, and for arranging the various travelling facilities with which I was favoured while on the job.

I would like to thank my good friend Derek Cross for putting at my disposal a magnificent selection of his photographs, and Mrs C. Boyer for her careful work in preparing the signalling plans.

Silver Cedars
High Bannerdown
Batheaston
Bath

O. S. NOCK
October 1973

1: *HISTORICAL INTRODUCTION*

In any study of the West Coast main line of today one cannot be other than conscious of the tremendous historical background – a background as impressive in the singularity of purpose with which the entire route north of Preston was built, in its first Engineer, and in the way it blazed the trail of high-speed travel even before the nineteenth century was out, as in the developments since the groupings of the British Railways in 1923 that have led gradually to the present time. Unlike so many of the present trunk routes of Great Britain the line northwards from Preston, not only to Glasgow and Edinburgh, but right on to Aberdeen, was conceived as a single project. It is true that the actual construction was carried out by a number of different companies, but there was one basic idea behind the whole. Of all these railways Joseph Locke was the guiding hand as Engineer, and all the early locomotives bore the unmistakable imprint of Alexander Allan.

In the days of the early planning George Stephenson was consulted over the route north of Lancaster, and still thinking in terms of avoiding heavy gradients he proposed crossing Morecambe Bay and proceeding up the Cumberland coast. This would have put Whitehaven, and eventually Barrow, on the main line to Scotland, though at that time Barrow scarcely existed. It would have been a long way round – a northern counterpart of some of Brunel's routes down in the West Country. Fortunately however Locke would have none of it, and planned a much more direct route through the mountains. He had no inhibitions about gradients, though he certainly did have about tunnels. Perhaps it was the experience of having to complete Vignoles's grim, unfinished task at Woodhead that influenced his future practice. Certain it is that if, when north of Oxenholme he had gone straight ahead up Long Sleddale, instead of climbing on the shoulder of Hay Fell and swinging round to the right towards Grayrigg he could have got to Penrith on easier gradients than going over Shap. But it would have meant a summit tunnel under Gatesgarth to get into Mardale.

But if Locke bequeathed upon the locomotive department of the LNWR, and its successors a bugbear in operation that was not finally dispelled till British Railways began using two Class '50' diesels for the day Anglo-Scottish expresses in 1970, the legacy that the Caledonian inherited from him was even worse, though at Beattock the terrain made the long gradient almost inevitable. Great was the controversy in Scotland as to whether the line from Carlisle to Glasgow should be carried northwards from the border through Nithsdale or Annandale. To many influential Glaswegians the claims of Nithsdale, putting Dumfries and many thriving smaller burghs on the main line, were overwhelming. So they might have been if Glasgow had been the only ultimate goal in Scotland. But the men of the Grand Junction, who were, after all, the driving force behind the construction of the West Coast route north of Preston, had a much wider field in view. There was Central Scotland, and beyond that Perth, and Aberdeen. Above all there was Edinburgh. The Euston Square Confederacy, as the West Coast alliance was sometimes called, had even in those early days a strong antipathy towards the Hudson group at York; and although at the time the Caledonian was projected the Great Northern had not come into being the West Coast were intent upon getting a direct line to Edinburgh in opposition to anything that might eventuate on the other side.

With all this in view a route through Annandale and Upper Clydesdale was a 'must' for the Caledonian, and it was in the trijunct layout of Carstairs that the first sods were cut in its construction – to display complete impartiality, one towards Glasgow, one towards Edinburgh, and one towards Carlisle – simultaneously! When completed, thus far, the West Coast Route from London to Edinburgh measured 399·7 miles, and 401·4 miles from London to Glasgow, by the Caledonian of course north of Carlisle. So far as Edinburgh was concerned, competition with the East Coast was definitely 'on'. It was perhaps significant that right into the twentieth century the Edinburgh sections of the Anglo-Scottish expresses from Euston had preference to the extent that on those services where the combined trains were divided at Crewe, to provide easier haulage tasks over the mountain sections, the Edinburgh portion preceded the Glasgow.

The potentialities of the West Coast route for serving Scottish areas north of the Edinburgh–Glasgow axis were exploited from an early date by the inauguration of the celebrated 'Tourist' express serving stations on the Highland line as well as Aberdeen. It is ironic, however, that travelling habits and some operating features of the day should have been pin-pointed by a misfortune that befell this train at Wigan on August 1st, 1873. Some of the essential safeguards of fast train travel today were then in no more than a rudimentary form. While the merits of having a brake applied to every vehicle in a train were recognised there was profound difference of opinion as to how the job should be done. The London and North Western Railway was then using the Clark and Webb sectional chain brake, and with this, if any part of the train became detached from the engine that part was completely bereft of brake power, other than anything the rear guard could apply by hand.

On this particular night, when tourist traffic to the Highlands was building up in readiness for the commencement of the grouse shooting season, the train consisted of no fewer than twenty-five coaches, all four-wheelers. Many of them were family saloons privately chartered, and accompanied by horse boxes, and all marshalled indiscriminately. This itself throws an interesting light on the problems then faced by the operating department. The train was drawn by two engines, and was running through Wigan station at about 50 mph when the driver of the train engine felt a jerk. Looking back he saw sparks flying from the rear, so he stopped as soon as the primitive brake equipment would permit and walked back, to find to his astonishment that he had only seventeen vehicles on. What actually caused the extraordinary and disastrous accident was never fully established, but for some reason the sixteenth coach became partially derailed at some facing points at the entrance to the station. It was a family saloon, followed immediately by a luggage van, which latter was completely derailed, swerved to the left and demolished a shunters hut. But the couplings held, and the station staff had the terrifying experience of seeing this important express go speeding through the station with the sixteenth coach partly off the road, and the rear van – or what they thought was the rear van – swaying and lurching about on the ballast. Still more extraordinary was the fact that both vehicles were completely re-railed at a crossing north of the station, and when the driver walked back they were standing correctly in line, as if nothing had happened!

The couplings had, however, broken between the seventeenth and eighteenth vehicles, and six of the last eight vehicles, derailed and with no brake to check them ran wildly in all directions – one indeed, crashing through a parapet wall and landing on the roof of a factory. Without going into any details as to the way in which these light wooden coaches smashed up, and of the resulting long and grievous casualty list, there was naturally a most searching inquiry as to how the derailment of the sixteenth coach could have been caused, and suspicion fell upon the nearby facing points. At that time they were not fitted with a facing point lock, and all inquiry centred upon the possibility of their having been moved accidentally during the passage of the train. The occurrence was considered serious enough for a Court of Inquiry to be set up, quite apart from the ordinary inquiry by the Board of Trade Inspector. Although nothing was eventually proved the circumstances were such as to show clearly what risks were involved at facing points. Wigan, in 1873, did for the practice of facing points protection what the terrible runaway train collision at Armagh was to do for continuous automatic brakes sixteen years later.

Preston achieved notoriety in a different way. Before the introduction of corridor coaches and dining cars the routes over which long-distance daytime expresses were operated made arrangements for stops to be made at certain intermediate stations where there were dining rooms for passengers to obtain lunch, or other refreshments. From a very early date Swindon became the luncheon stop on the Great Western line to the west, while on the Anglo-Scottish routes the staging points were York on the East Coast, Preston on the West, to be followed by Normanton on the Midland, when that company inaugurated its through Scottish services in 1876. At Preston the lunch interval was originally twenty-five minutes on the morning express from Euston to Edinburgh and Glasgow; but when competition with the East Coast began in the summer of 1888 the North-Western authorities unkindly expected the passengers' digestion to co-operate in the speed-up. Indeed the shortening of the lunch interval from twenty-five to twenty minutes represented a bigger percentage cut than the acceleration in running times imposed upon the locomotive department!

The introduction of dining cars robbed Preston of its one-time importance to the through traveller, and in the early years of the twentieth century more and more trains began to pass it without stopping at all. The separate Liverpool and Manchester Scottish expresses provided the connections to and from the Lancashire towns, and after World War I even the famous afternoon 'Corridor' expresses ceased to stop at Preston. It is remarkable how the 'wheel' of traffic development can come full circle, for in the new timetables of May 1974 Preston will come into a limelight such as it has never previously enjoyed. Before leaving the Preston of 'lunch interval' days, however, it is interesting to recall that the railway race of 1888, in which the 'lunch' participated, arose from a reduction of fares on the East Coast Route – or rather by making available to third class passengers a fast express service hitherto only available to first and second class travellers. With both East and West Coast routes carrying third class passengers on their 'crack' Anglo-Scottish express the disparity in journey time to Edinburgh that had previously existed – nine hours by the East Coast and ten hours by the West Coast – was no longer acceptable. When time-cutting began, the efforts of the East Coast to retain their superiority in speed led eventually to the 'Race'.

The modern technique in locomotive designing that has made possible the planning of schedules on the basis that trains of twelve coaches can be hauled up the 1 in 75 gradient of the Shap Incline at 90mph, and will require a slight application of the brakes to observe the permanent speed restriction of 80mph for about half a mile over the actual summit at Shap, inevitably causes one to reflect upon the locomotives that have run the rails in past years between Crewe and Glasgow, and of the men who designed, built, and operated them. In the latter part of the nineteenth century the engine designing practice of the Caledonian Railway was probably unsurpassed anywhere in the world. It is astonishing to find in lands many thousands of miles from Scotland how far the influence of Dugald Drummond spread. In their simplicity, in the correctness of the principles built into them, and in the enlightened thinking that accompanied their development his 6ft 6in 4–4–0s of 1884 were among the most advanced locomotives in service at that time. This achievement on Drummond's part received world-wide recognition, in the way he was consulted by overseas engineers, and not least by the princely salary he received from the Caledonian Railway.

I have stressed the point of simplicity in design. In this Drummond differed from his equally striking contemporary on the LNWR at Crewe – Francis W. Webb. Drummond claimed that with a truly scientific design of cylinders and valves there was no need to go in for compound expansion, as Webb was doing; nor need one have vast boilers to provide steam for high power output. In the development of his principles Drummond built two of his otherwise standard 4–4–0 engines, in 1889, with boilers carrying a pressure of 200lb per sq in, instead of his usual 150lb per sq in, and on test, in regular express passenger service he obtained an output of 850 indicated horsepower at 37mph (33 per cent cut-off) and the astonishing figure of 940ihp at 51mph (27 per cent cut-off) in 1889! These were outputs considerably in advance of anything required at that time, and pressures of 150lb per sq in remained customary for some little time after. It is interesting to speculate upon how Caledonian locomotive practice might have developed had Drummond not been tempted by the prospect of the locomotive constructional business in Australia. The sad vicissitudes in his subsequent career have no part in the West Coast saga. His successors at St Rollox took his superb 'engine' layout, and put progressively larger boilers on, achieving an outstanding initial success, in the 'Dunalastair' 4–4–0s, that was eventually to lead them into a blind alley; but not before J. F. McIntosh had been greatly honoured by having his 'Dunalastair II' class adopted as standard by the Belgian Government.

In view of the kind of performance expected from the new electric locomotives it is interesting to recall details of some of the fastest runs north of Carlisle in the nineteenth century. These were made on the Tourist express during the summer of 1896, with 4–4–0 locomotives of the first 'Dunalastair' series, on a train then running non-stop between Carlisle and Stirling. With trains weighing 170 to 180 tons behind the tender, that is little less than half that of a twelve-coach train of today, there were recorded occasions when Beattock station, 39·7 miles from Carlisle, was passed in 37–38min, and Beattock Summit, a further ten miles to the north, passed in 53½min from a dead start. It was customary with that train to pass Carstairs in a time averaging 60mph from the dead start – and that in the summer of 1896. One could, however, discourse for whole chapters on the past achievements of steam locomotives of both the Caledonian and LNW Railways, and not less those of the LMS. Here it must suffice to mention no more than four further notable feats with steam, to set the stage for what is now possible with electric traction.

Just as the Caledonian established some records for high power output in the nineteenth century so the North Western pushed the British record up to new heights in some dynamometer car trials just before World War I. The 'Claughton' class of four-cylinder 4–6–0 introduced in 1913 was not what its designer, C. J. Bowen-Cooke, originally intended. It was to have had a considerably larger boiler. But the civil engineer of the day could not accept the increased dead weight per axle, even though the cylinder layout eliminated hammer blow entirely. So the design as it took the road was something of a compromise. But when skilfully handled, as was the rule with the LNWR top link drivers and firemen of that era, the 'Claughtons' were capable of outstanding feats of power output, and on the trial run of November 4th, 1913, with the train now so well known as The Royal Scot, a load of 360 tons was taken, over Shap Summit, 109·6 miles, in 110¼min from the dead start at Crewe. Eight records of indicated horsepower taken between Carnforth and Shap Summit gave, successively, 1,504, 1,407, 1,494, 1,526, 1,669, 1,606, 1,593 and 1,496ihp. The maximum value of 1,669, attained in the approach to Tebay at 69mph remained an outright British record until the Grouping in 1923.

The time to pass Shap Summit was of course considerably slower than that of the little 'Precedent' class 2–4–0 *Hardwicke* on the last night of the Race to the North in 1895, when the time was 101½min, and the 'Claughton' *Ralph Brocklebank* on the test run of 1913 had no need to dash down to Carlisle like *Hardwicke* did on her racing record. But against these LNWR feats I may quote my best recent time in the 'two-diesel' era on the Royal Scot, when we passed Shap Summit in 86½min from Crewe. For the ultimate in steam we turn naturally to the work of the Stanier 'Pacifics' and one run made in the late autumn of 1936 has a particular interest today. On this occasion not only was the entire distance between Euston and Glasgow covered non-stop on two successive days, but the run was brought down, for the first and only time with steam traction, to under 6hr.

The fires of competition between the East Coast and West Coast Routes to Scotland were beginning to crackle more openly in that autumn of 1936. The East Coast had already shown its hand so far as speed was concerned when the Silver Jubilee express was put on in 1935, with a 4hr run to Newcastle. Only 124 miles separated Tyneside from Edinburgh, and at a continuation of the same standards of speed a service between London and Edinburgh in the level 6hr seemed an easy possibility. It is true that the distance involved was less than from Euston to Glasgow, 392·7 against 401·4 miles, but West Coast supporters hoped that if the East Coast did table a six-hour run from Kings Cross to Edinburgh the West Coast would reply with an equally quick time from Glasgow to Euston. By that time in railway history the emphasis on the West Coast Route had definitely centred upon Glasgow.

During the period of restricted train service during World War I many limitations on choice of route were imposed. From London the only through bookings to Edinburgh could be made from Kings Cross, and so far as Glasgow was concerned the morning service from London was from St Pancras via the Midland route to St Enoch, and the afternoon service from Euston. After the war, in due course, these restrictions were removed, and Euston once again had a good service to Edinburgh. When The Royal Scot train was introduced in 1927 it included a completely self-contained restaurant car portion for Edinburgh, and the overall time from Euston was the same to both Scottish cities. It was from 1937 that the balance began to swing more pronouncedly in favour of Glasgow, though in overall time not to the extent that West coast supporters had hoped.

The trial runs of November 16th and 17th, 1936, had certainly raised expectations to the highest pitch. With the Stanier 'Pacific' engine No 6201 *Princess Elizabeth* and a seven-coach load – roughly equal in tonnage to the rival *Silver Jubilee* a non-stop run over the 401·4 miles from Euston to Glasgow was made in 353½min, 6½min inside the level 6hr; and on the following day with an extra coach added, the return journey to London was made in 344¼min. The average speed from end to end was 70mph, and the intermediate 'laps' were run at 65·9mph from Glasgow to Carlisle, 70·5mph from Carlisle to Crewe, and 72·4mph from Crewe to Euston. The 'flying' average over the 364·5 mles from Carstairs to Wembley was 73·3mph. But having regard to the longer distance to be run, and that the speed was higher than anything previously scheduled regularly over the West Coast Route, the time of the new 'Coronation Scot' express of June 1937 was made 6½hr. There was every intention of further acceleration once the service had thoroughly settled down. But war came again two years later, and in the event 6½hr was the fastest time to be scheduled between Euston and Glasgow with steam traction.

World War II brought restrictions in travel that were even more severe than those of 1914–18, all the more so in that they were imposed from the outset, and intensified by the very strict black-out regulations, and the interruptions of service by air raids, and long diversions when parts of the line had been damaged. It is difficult to guess what might have happened if war had not come in 1939. Both East Coast and West Coast routes were in keen competition in providing increasingly attractive travel facilities; and so far as motive power was concerned the LMSR had prepared in outline the design of a very large 4–6–4 streamlined express passenger locomotive which was intended to surpass by a considerable margin the maximum performance characteristics of the 'Coronation' class streamlined 4–6–2.

It was one of the ironies of the war situation that not only the West Coast main line, but the whole LMSR and the railways of Britain generally lost a tremendous amount of prestige in 1939–45. That this was cruelly unjustified is almost beside the point, and in viewing the situation in retrospect it is hard to see that it could ever have been otherwise. But as this situation which existed in 1945 and became accentuated in the ensuing six or seven years, weighed very heavily against railway development in Great Britain, and reacted strongly against the first measures taken towards modernisation, it is important to look back to the war years and see how this extraordinary situation developed. It began in the last years of peace, when the four main lines railways of the grouping era launched the historic Square Deal campaign, in an attempt to secure the passage through Parliament of new legislation freeing them from many restrictions in the fixing of rates and fares that were urgently needed to put them on a competitive basis with other forms of transport.

For reasons that need not be enlarged upon here the Square Deal campaign got a 'bad press', and despite the then recent speed achievements of both the East Coast and West Coast routes the railways did not stand high in popular esteem in Great Britain. With the outbreak of war and with the consequent restrictions on private motoring and the rationing of petrol, more people than ever before were compelled to do their travelling by train. It was a new experience for many, and in crowded, dimly-lit carriages, on trains drastically decelerated and frequently delayed still further, that new experience was not one to endear them to railways in general. It was nothing to those who had to endure wartime travelling conditions to know that the railways were stepping up their throughput of freight by an almost fantastic extent. For security reasons during the war publicity regarding railway achievement had necessarily to be couched in the most general terms, and much of it fell upon deaf ears.

Towards the end of the war, when American troops were here in their hundreds of thousands they also experienced the railways of Britain in the least glamorous epoch of their history, and without fully appreciating the reasons for the lack of lustre there were undoubtedly many occasions of unfavourable comparisons. Although the floodtide of dieselisation had not yet hit the American railways, the output of new locomotives from the La Grange plant of General Motors was already high, and there is no doubt that a good deal of unofficial propaganda for the diesels took place. The American loves something new, and the sleek, gaily painted cab-nosed units fairly caught popular imagination. Some of it undoubtedly rubbed off on to British commentators, and some of the blame for the lack-lustre state of the British railways was pinned upon the old faithful steam locomotive.

Commercial interests were not long in taking up the cause of the diesel, but in the meantime a shocking misjudgment by one department of the Government of the day threw a savagely realistic light upon the economic background to any possible railway developments. The Ministry of Fuel and Power gave such enthusiastic acclaim to the small-scale, limited-objective plan of the Great Western Railway for converting a number of locomotives from coal to oil firing to launch an overall scheme on national lines, in order to reduce the demand for coal—then something of an embarrassment to the Government. Expenditure on a vast scale was authorised for conversion of locomotives and installation of oil-firing plants, and it was only when some £3m had been spent that everything came to a grinding halt. The Treasury had pointed out that no foreign exchange was available to purchase the necessary oil. This not only made still-born the national plan for oil-firing of steam locomotives, but it postponed indefinitely any ideas of modernisation that involved the use of diesel locomotives. And it was only when this situation showed some signs of easing that the first phase of railway modernisation was projected.

2: *THE SEARCHING PRELIMINARIES*

The success of the first stage of the West Coast main line electrification, between Euston, Birmingham, Liverpool and Manchester, was immediate and immense. The public flocked to travel. Passenger receipts soared; but even before the last link was completed and fast electric trains were running over the most southerly 82 miles of the 'new railway', between Rugby and Euston, railwaymen and industrialists alike were urging upon the Government of the day the desirability of continuing the programme to its logical extension. Its eventual success was already apparent, though not perhaps to the degree actually achieved when the fast express trains were running into Euston. But in the execution of the great scheme a vast amount of technical experience had been accumulated; the capital value of plant in use was enormous, and on these grounds there seemed every justification for extending the work northward and securing the financial and sociological advantages that appeared within grasp, in connecting the five largest cities in the country by one closely integrated high speed electric railway.

Delay would inevitably result in the dissipation of those assets, both human and material. Costs were almost certain to rise, and a hiatus of no more than two or three years would mean a virtually fresh start. Unfortunately such practical considerations represented only a small proportion of the factors that had to be taken into account. It is regrettably easy for those who do not have the responsibility for making decisions to proclaim what ought, or ought not to have been done at some critical moment, and I always recall the words of a scholarly but entirely non-technical writer on Scottish affairs who once asserted: "The Highland Railway should have been one of the first to adopt electric traction, and it will never give satisfactory service until it does so." At the outset therefore I feel it is necessary in this book to glimpse a little of what went on before the extension of the London Midland electrified system was finally authorised.

Although nearly four years were to elapse before that authorisation came, matters did not stand still out on the line. It was clear that the predominant factor contributing to the great success of the Euston–Birmingham–Liverpool–Manchester scheme was speed, while cleanliness, regularity and punctuality of service were major contributory items. With the tremendous physical upheaval that necessarily accompanied the up-grading of the main line already modernised – the virtual building of an entirely new railway over the tracks of the old one – it was evident that comparable disturbance would take place in the north if the necessary civil engineering work were undertaken in one concentrated 'crash' programme. Therefore, in the course of routine renewal and maintenance work a modest programme of upgrading was introduced, to enable speed limits to be raised, individual items of route rationalisation to be carried out, reballasting of track, and re-alignment of curves and certain junctions. On the London Midland part of the route sufficient work had been done by the winter of 1969–70 for some substantial acceleration of the West Coast express service in 1970.

But while railway engineers had been steadily and unobtrusively paving the way a vast amount of study and cost investigation had been in progress at the highest levels. That the entire project of 'Route Improvements and Electrification' was to a large extent a financial exercise is evident from the opening paragraph of a lengthy report prepared by the British Railways Board, dated April 1968. It reads: "The present proposal for route improvements and electrification is a development of the trunk railway network to improve the commercial position and to lead to a less costly and less labour-intensive service. This report concludes and recommends that authority should be given for an outlay of £54·6m for implementing the scheme as soon as possible."

The project as then submitted to the Minister of Transport – as the office was then known – was in two parts, indicating the separate costs and the resultant savings expected. The first part was summarised as 'Route Improvements', and included resignalling throughout, and provision for improved service, and accelerations, using double-headed diesel-hauled trains between Crewe and Glasgow. The second part provided for electrification to be carried out concurrently with the route improvements included in the first part. The costs submitted to the Minister were based on the assumption that authority would be given some time during 1968, and that the entire project would be completed in four years. The report of the Railway Board emphasised the need to act quickly in view of the growing challenge of civil aviation, and of the approaching completion of the M6 motorway. As a result of the route improvements outlined it was proposed, at that time, to raise the average speeds of the main line passenger trains between Crewe and Glasgow from under 50mph to 70mph. The report included these significant words: "The need to strike soon in this part of the market is very apparent, and given the necessary authority this can be achieved in 1972."

Even without the prospect of improved service and electrification the physical situation on the West Coast Route north of Weaver Junction was becoming yearly more critical. The track alignment was little changed from that required in the days of steam traction. Curves and junction layouts involved the permanent imposition of many speed restrictions; but it was particularly in respect of the signalling that improvement was most urgently necessary. Apart from a short length of colour light signalling north of Carlisle installed at the time when the mechanised marshalling yards at Kingmoor were constructed, and the main lines through Wigan (North Western) station, the entire route from Weaver Junction to north of Motherwell was still equipped with manual block, and semaphore signals. Between Weaver Junction and Carlisle (Citadel) there were no less than seventy-five manual block posts, plus eighteen colour light intermediate block signal sections. In the years before World War II much had been done to improve the sighting of all isolated distant signals, by replacing semaphores with colour lights, and on certain of the severe inclines in the North Country colour light intermediate block signals had been installed on the ascending line to improve line capacity in locations where speed was normally low. But the mixture of semaphore and colour light signals was obviously unsuitable for a high speed route. Furthermore, not only were the majority of the interlocking plants overdue for renewal, but by 1968 a permanent difficulty had developed in obtaining signalling staff.

The question of 'route improvement' also included proposals for eliminating surplus track capacity. The changing pattern of traffic over this route gave many points for consideration, not only in removal of sidings and connections at the sites of country stations now closed, and in former steam locomotive yards, and freight reception roads, but in rethinking the whole strategy of train working in the areas. Clearly the project could be made more attractive financially if by funnelling additional traffic on to the modernised route others could be closed, and considerable savings in operating expenses effected. Attention naturally became centred on the historic Settle and Carlisle line of the former Midland Railway, which it was considered could be closed completely, while traffic over the former Glasgow and South Western main line between Gretna Junction and Kilmarnock was expected to be so much reduced that this could be converted to single track. The Minister was advised: "These reductions can be completed in 1972–3, within the expected time scale of the Surplus Capacity Grants."

The improvements in train service, as then foreseen, were as follows:

Service	*Av. speed in 1967 mph*	*Av. speed in 1972 mph*	*Through trains each way per day in 1972*
Euston–Preston	61	72	10 and over
Euston–Blackpool	53	60	6–9
Euston–Carlisle	61	76	3–5
Euston–Glasgow	58	75	6–9
Birmingham–Glasgow	45	68	3–5
Liverpool–Glasgow	44	68	6–9
Manchester–Glasgow	41	67	6–9
FOR COMPARISON			
Kings Cross–Newcastle	62	62	10 and over
Kings Cross–Edinburgh	63	63	3–5

The report concluded by summarising the costs of the various alternative proposals, and also setting out the estimated effects of deferment. An interesting conclusion was that if deferment was enforced the least damaging arrangement would be to defer both route improvement and electrification together, but for the shortest possible time. It was emphasised that a staggered programme of construction was very undesirable, although some essential renewals could not be deferred. There was a very significant item so far as route improvements were concerned. The capital outlay for route improvement, as proposed in the main scheme, was £29·4m, whereas the very minimum needed in routine renewals would involve an outlay of some £14m – at 1968 costs—spread over the ensuing eight years. The financial effects of deferment of the main proposals, including electrification, in the estimated reduction in the resulting cash surplus were quoted as £4m, if completed one year later than proposed, that was in 1973 instead of 1972, or up to £10m if another two years later.

While noting the advantages to be gained with route improvement and the continuance of diesel traction, the report summarised the following points in favour of full electrification:

(i) Further improvements in freight services, particularly for faster trains such as Freightliners.
(ii) Substitution of electric multiple units in some local services to give lower operating costs or better service quality.
(iii) The potential savings of up to £12m in buying new diesel locomotives.*
(iv) The avoided complexity and cost of multiple working of locomotives and provision of electric train heating if diesel traction is continued. And in turn the provision, on the train, of a relatively unrestricted power source for developments in heating, air conditioning, power operated doors and the like.
(v) The use of indigenous fuels, or in the future any conventional fuel for generating electricity.
(vi) The improved environment by reduction of noise and fumes, but offset by the visual intrusion of the electrification structures.

The budget as recommended for acceptance by the Government was thus:

Route Improvements	£29·4m
Electrification of the Route	£20·7m
Partial Immunisation of subsidiary lines	£0·2m

* If the line was electrified some Class 50 diesel-electric locomotives made surplus could be transferred elsewhere and save buying new locomotives that would be otherwise needed.

30 Electric Locomotives		£3·3m
Optionally 10 additional locomotives		£1·0m
	Total	£54·6m

In view of its historic interest mention must be made of the detailed proposals in connection with the Settle and Carlisle line. The complete closure was recommended between Horton and Newbiggin. These fragments, at either end, were to be kept open in consideration of quarrying activities. Between Horton and Newbiggin the track was to be lifted, and the land disposed of, though in that area doubt was expressed as to whether any ready purchaser would come forward! But perhaps a more surprising move was the proposal to close the 'Little North Western' line, between Settle Junction and Carnforth. The line between Wennington and Morecambe had already been closed in 1968, but as later chapters of this book relate the whole position regarding the former Midland lines north of Skipton has changed. It is equally so with the Glasgow and South Western main line between Gretna and Kilmarnock.

Following the submission of the report, there were many goings and comings, and meetings between Ministry of Transport officials and representatives of the British Railways, and nearly a year went by before any sign of definite action emerged. The Minister was certainly in a difficult position. The Government of the day was in severe economic difficulties. Following devaluation of the currency a pledge had been given to minimise capital expenditure on development works, and the 'electrification' part of the proposals of May 1968 seemed undoubtedly to fall within that category. In March 1969 the Minister wrote to Sir Henry Johnson, then Chairman of the BRB, pointing out the difficulties in coming to a decision. He said that the case for rationalisation was a good one, and hoped that the proposals would not come within the classes of expenditure vetoed by the post-devaluation pledge. In his opinion the case for full electrification was less strong in any case, and that a decision could not be expected before the early months of 1970. He quite frankly admitted that while there was every prospect of the 'route-improvement' or rationalisation scheme being approved very soon, the ultimate decision on electrification could go either way.

This of course presented British Railways with the very situation they wished so earnestly to avoid—namely a staggered programme, if indeed the second stage was authorised at all. But there was an added complication, of which the Minister himself was keenly aware. If electrification was eventually adopted, the signalling would require to be immunised against the effects of stray alternating current from the traction supply. The signalling scheme included in the overall proposals for route improvement was completely in readiness for electrification and therefore included immunisation, at a cost of some £2m for the LM Region alone. The very real chance that electrification might not be approved posed an awkward situation. If work went ahead on signalling as then planned there might be an abortive expenditure of £2m on something that was not wanted. If on the other hand it was to be omitted, much re-design work would immediately be required, with a consequent delay of four to six months before contracts could be placed. Worse than that, if work on the route improvement project was sanctioned on a non-immunised basis, and early in 1970 the electrification itself *was* authorised, everything would have to be switched back again!

An 'immunisation working party' set up at the request of the Minister, and including representatives from the British Railways Board, the Ministry of Transport and the Treasury, did not resolve the problem, and when in April 1968 the Minister was able to authorise the route improvement project the BRB invited tenders for the signalling work on two alternative bases—with immunisation, and without. While work on the track continued through the summer of 1968 the signalling tenders were submitted, and BRB did everything possible to strengthen its case for full electrification. With signalling renewals overdue on many parts of the line it would be most undesirable to postpone the placing of the signalling contracts beyond November, and by then it would be necessary to decide the crucial question—with or without immunisation. As an article in the *Financial Times* in October 1968 remarked: "Indeed, the £30m worth of track and signalling improvements have been regarded as Hobson's choice if present operations are to continue." There was an ominous ring about those last words, implying that unless something was done soon deterioration in service was inevitable.

Inevitably much discussion took place, both inside the Ministry of Transport and the Railways Board, and outside, on the possibilities of alternative forms of traction. It was argued that putting two diesel-electric locomotives on certain daytime expresses would cost far less, and yield time savings as great as electrification. More seriously, attention was drawn to the Advanced Passenger Train project on which a recent decision had been taken for British Railways and the Ministry of Transport jointly to spend £10m developing and testing prototypes. Could not this gas-turbine train be used instead of ordinary electric traction? Against this the BRB argued that the APT could be driven equally well by electricity, or in any case introduced first either on the London–Newcastle, or London–South Wales routes. In retrospect it seems that most of the extraneous arguments advanced against full electrification north of Weaver Junction envisaged little improvement except the acceleration of the existing train service. Proposals such as those to close the Settle and Carlisle as a through route now look rather odd in view of what is to be told in the very next chapter of this book, and the application of electric traction to the *status quo* between Weaver Junction and Glasgow, and its prospects led the *Financial Times* to comment further:

"Electrification will yield considerable competitive benefits, not so much in still faster journey times – only a further 20 minutes would be saved on the Glasgow–Manchester run – but in costs and profitability and thus in scope for competitive pricing. This is important, for rail traffic north of Weaver Junction is split very roughly half and half between freight and passenger, and time savings, although highly desirable, are not perhaps as useful as price flexibility for a freight service that is already able to offer overnight delivery."

The original submission by the British Railways Board in April 1968 had a trenchantly worded section entitled, 'The Quality of Electrification':

"In this part of the report it is appropriate to summarise some factors surrounding a proposal for major railway electrification.

"Revitalising the essential trunk railway routes is a necessary continuing process. As a feature of this modernisation, excluding financial criteria, it would be everyone's judgment that electrification is the 'best' traction system, wanted by the users as much as by the operators.

"The quality of service provided by it is internationally recognised. Great prestige is attached to the New Tokaido

Line and the electric railways of Europe. The United States, formerly wedded to diesel traction, are investing gigantic sums of money in suburban and inter-city electrification. Our own electrifications in this country have been conspicuously and rapidly successful, indicating recognisable benefits to the community greater than those seen by the individual as directly affecting his pocket.

"However, limitations of financial resources and the need for a profitable business outcome make action desirable only in those areas where application of these criteria also gives a satisfactory result. As a business entity the railway can only quantify those aspects of benefit which it can turn into revenue or reduced costs. The study described in this report demonstrates the outcome on a section of trunk route having the highest priority for electrification."

The tremendous pace at which the pattern of railway service has evolved around the peg of astonishing success of the Euston–Liverpool–Manchester scheme, is revealed by the fact that no hint seemed to be forthcoming in all the BRB arguments for electrification in 1968–9, of the positive revolution in passenger train service that would be wrought as a result. As will be told in the next chapter the foundations for this revolution were laid in 1972, with the far-reaching timetable changes affecting existing electric services through Birmingham and Wolverhampton. Another point that was not made, perhaps with good reason, was that the diesel locomotives on British railways generally had not proved so reliable as had been expected when the Modernisation Plan was launched, nor so economical to maintain.

Then, when the question of whether to immunise or not was still unresolved, and the ultimate outcome of electrification or not was an uncertain as ever the Prime Minister of the day chose that difficult period to change his Minister of Transport, substituting Mr Fred Mulley for Mr Richard Marsh. It goes almost without saying that the new Minister had very little previous experience of transport matters, and did not mind admitting it in public; but at the time he took office another factor was becoming apparent. It was what has sometimes been called 'the sparks effect'. An independent market research was conducted into public attitude towards electrification taking fully into account the fact that so far as acceleration of service was concerned the same advantages could be provided by Class '50' diesels using two in multiple. This research revealed, against all logic, that the public still had greater faith in electric traction, and, as *The Railway Gazette* expressed it, "were prepared to back their preference with cash at the booking office window". This expression of public preference, added to all the financial and technical arguments put forward by the British Railways Board, made the case well-nigh irresistible.

In view of the change in Ministers of Transport it was perhaps not surprising that for several months a great silence centred over St Christopher House. The British Railways Board had no inkling of what was happening. Some thought that the silence was a good thing, but the pessimists were just about giving up hope. But then, on February 23rd, 1970, came the long hoped for news: electrification was authorised, but with so little preliminary advice of the decision that BRB did not know until a few hours before the public announcement what the outcome would be. It had taken about seven years in all to secure this decision because, as previously mentioned, the first tentative proposals were made well before the Euston–Birmingham–Liverpool–Manchester scheme was completed, in an attempt to secure continuity of effort. And so at last the most searching investigation ever conducted into the viability of a railway electrification project was at an end, and railwaymen, engineers and operating men alike could get on with the job! Euston–Glasgow in 5hr was now definitely on the agenda; and the optimists were pointing out that this was programmed with no maximum speeds higher than 100mph. Already there was talk—outside official railway circles I must add however!—of speeds up to at least 110mph and possibly 125 being authorised before the new timetable was introduced in May 1974. This, of course, was wishful, and rather impracticable thinking; but I have quoted the suggestion to show how the welcome announcement of the authorisation of the scheme sent a wave of buoyant optimism through the railway world, and its many well-wishers. 'Sparks-effect' indeed!

Furthermore there was no waiting for electrification to accelerate the service. In the preliminary discussions much had been made of what it was possible to do with a pair of Class '50' diesels, and in the summer service of 1970 some substantial improvement of the timings between Crewe and Carlisle took place. Even with many of the earlier speed restrictions remaining it was possible to schedule runs over the 141 miles in the level 2hr, and between Preston and Carlisle, 90 miles, in 75min. With a clear road I have seen the latter section done in 66½min, with two Class '50' diesels and a twelve-coach train. However, I must not dwell on this interim period, except in the pleasurable anticipation it gave of the kind of service we might expect when full electrification was completed.

3: *THE PHILOSOPHY OF ACCELERATION*

The electrification of the Euston–Birmingham–Liverpool and Manchester lines of the London Midland Region, completed in 1966, demonstrated above all else two fundamental facts of transportation. The first was that with scientifically designed electric locomotives very fast schedules could be readily maintained, and the second was that the public likes an electrified railway. I am not suggesting that equally fast times could not have been maintained with other forms of traction. Given a much larger and heavier unit, or combination of units, the same standards of speed could have been attained with diesel electric locomotives; and if all the available knowledge and design techniques had been employed it would not have been impossible to design steam locomotives capable of equivalent performance. But with either alternative form of traction the entire significance of the success of the work so remarkably consummated in 1966 would have been lost. It was in every sense of the expression 'the sparks effect'.

The introduction of the 'AL6' electric locomotives put the London Midland Region in possession of motive power units that were able virtually to eliminate the effect of gradients anywhere south of Liverpool or Manchester with trains of up to twelve coaches. They could run at the maximum speed of 100 mph on the 1 in 330 gradients of Robert Stephenson's original London and Birmingham Railway, and accelerate a train of this magnitude to over 90mph on the 1 in 177 gradient of Madeley Bank. Start-to-stop average speeds of over 80mph could be scheduled with confidence, and a pattern of service developed that in frequency and consistency of high-speed running brought an almost sensational increase in passenger travel revenue. Furthermore, the engineering excellence built into locomotives, track and overhead line equipment resulted in a very high standard of reliability.

At the same time it must be conceded that the geographical

circumstances were very favourable to transport by rail. Journey times of about $1\frac{1}{2}$hr from London to Birmingham, city centre to city centre, and $2\frac{1}{2}$–$2\frac{3}{4}$hr between London and Liverpool, London and Manchester were of a duration with which the civil air lines could not compete and while individual circumstances and a little 'bending' of the speed limit might enable expert motorists to come somewhere near such times from their homes to the places of their business in one or other of the northern cities, the hazards of bad weather travelling on motorways would still be inclined to load the argument in favour of railways. In the seven years that have elapsed since the completion of the first section of the electrified London Midland lines one could certainly expect some improvement in performance of the electric locomotives, with a resultant further cutting of journey times, and faster uphill running.

At the same time, however, the circumstances north of Liverpool and Manchester were somewhat different. The train service between those cities, and equally that from Birmingham northward to Glasgow and Edinburgh has never been particularly attractive to the man who is in a hurry; and although application of the same standards of locomotive performance to those now well established southwards to Euston would make possible substantial cuts of running time, in the north, despite the historic physical obstacles of the Shap and Beattock Inclines, speed is unfortunately not the only factor contributing to the overall time possible between Manchester and Glasgow, for example. The present project does not include for electrification of the connecting lines from Liverpool and Manchester to the West Coast main line, nor of that from Carstairs to Edinburgh. Changing of locomotives will be necessary, for the present at any rate, together with combination or separation of certain train formations at junction points en route.

Although it is anticipated that the journey time between Manchester and Glasgow, for example, will be reduced to 3hr 29min there is no doubt that for many business men the private car will remain an attractive alternative. The ease of access of the M6 motorway to most of the favoured residential districts around both Manchester and Liverpool would give a northbound traveller a 'flying' start, compared to that enjoyed, or endured, by his counterpart starting northward from London. Against this, of course, the railway could undoubtedly claim a greater reliability, as an all-weather proposition, and the undoubted advantage of offering relaxed travel, with the opportunity of attending to business en route. Nevertheless it has been clear to those planning the new train services that competition is likely to be keen in this particular section. It could equally be so in the longer distance between Birmingham and the Scottish cities. Also, in a journey time of around 4hr the competition of air travel, so successfully met by the established railway services southward from Liverpool and Manchester, could remain an important factor.

All this may sound a slightly pessimistic view of what the electrification to Glasgow may bring forth, until – and it is a heavily underlined 'until' – one comes to examine the services that are to be introduced. This chapter is necessarily being written some time before the new schedules are absolutely finalised; but I have had the privilege of seeing the draft timetables, and of discussing many implications of them with the respective officers of the London Midland and of the Scottish Region. Although the points on which I am now to comment may not be precise in every small detail the timetables are, at the time of writing, sufficiently finalised for their import to be discussed authoritatively. The vital point to appreciate at the outset is that it has not been a case of adding a Scottish addendum, as it were, on to the existing electric services from Euston, but virtually recasting the entire West Coast main line timetable. The foundations of it were laid in an exercise of skilful forward planning in the summer timetables of 1972, in which New Street station, Birmingham became the nodal point – the 'Grand Junction' – not only of the West Coast, but of the important connecting services to the North-East and South-West of England.

In the previous chapter I touched briefly upon the time-honoured situation in which all the principal railways in England tended to point towards London, and that cross-country routes tended to come off second best when it came to timing express passenger services. In the present context, the steady improvement in speed over the West of England main line of the former Midland Railway received a forceful 'shot in the arm' when the important decision was taken to establish first class connectional links at Birmingham with the West Coast route, and to change completely the earlier pattern of electric service from Euston, and onwards from Birmingham to the north. The practice of continuing London–Birmingham expresses to Liverpool or Manchester, via Wolverhampton and Crewe, was discontinued, and instead the half-hourly service of 100mph trains from Euston terminates either at Birmingham or Wolverhampton, and an entirely separate service of regular interval departures from Birmingham leaving hourly, at five minutes before the hour, provides the northward link. Far more than this the regular XX55 departure from Birmingham has become the central feature around which the entire West Coast main line service has been planned. It is not only the West Coast route that hinges up on this XX55 service from Birmingham. To provide the rapid, reliable, cross-platform connections at New Street station, the cross-country trains running south-west to north-east across England, and equally those from the south-west to the north-west, have been so closely interwoven that any disturbance of the timings at New Street would have repercussions on the *East* Coast main line, north of York, and at Bristol, Cardiff and still farther afield.

Forward from Birmingham the northbound departures alternate to Liverpool and Manchester. Some of these trains originate at Coventry, while others originate variously at Bristol, Cardiff, Southampton, and Plymouth. At Birmingham they provide excellent connections into the through Birmingham–Scottish expresses which leave New Street mostly at five minutes past the hour. From Bristol there is an unbroken sequence of arrivals at New Street at forty to forty-five minutes past the hour, to feed into the XX55 departure. This service with its inviolable departure time, and that of the Birmingham–Scottish trains, governs the timing of the purely Birmingham service from Euston, run at half-hourly intervals throughout the day. Those arriving before the SW–NE and SW–NW connectional group leave Euston at ten minutes past the hour, while the XX40 departure arrives in New Street just after the Scottish departure. Neither of the London services have any connectional significance except, of course, from Coventry. It is purely a case of line and platform capacity at New Street.

So far none of the timetable features mentioned had any direct bearing on the principal Anglo-Scottish services; but the establishment of XX10 and XX40 departures from Euston to Birmingham has led to a new philosophy so far as the other departures from Euston are concerned. The success with which the signalling on the main line south of Crewe has been able to cope with high speed trains running at close headway has led to the arrangement of the off-peak 100mph expresses in what are termed 'flights', of six trains in succession at close headway, thus:

XX40	Birmingham
XX45	Glasgow
XX50	Liverpool
XX55	Manchester
XX00	Carlisle – or North Wales – or Blackpool
XX10	Birmingham

All these trains, except the fifth of the series, are booked to pass Rugby (82·6 miles) in 59min from Euston. It is interesting to hear Officers of the London Midland Region referring to this time-tabling as an 'off-peak' service! After the XX10 Birmingham there is certainly half an hour's break to give space for fast freights. 'Off-peaks' or not, there are eighty-five '100mph' expresses on the line between Euston and Rugby leaving between the hours of 07.40 and 19.40, a service density surely without parallel in the world, seeing that freights and semi-fasts have also to be accommodated. On some Friday evenings the departures from Euston from 16.25 to 19.00hrs total 24, or an average headway, for 2½hr, of 6½min! Most of these trains are booked to pass Rugby in 56min, a start-to-pass average of 88½mph.

So I come to the Anglo-Scottish service with electric haulage throughout. Timetable paths have been prepared for hourly departures from Euston for Glasgow at forty-five minutes past the hour, with overall times of between a level 5hr and 5hr 9min. At the moment of writing some of these are conditional, or 'dated' trains, but it is hoped to operate a regular hourly service as traffic develops. There are, apart from the speed, certain very interesting features about the timings. The first two down trains, the 07.45 and 08.45, call at Watford Junction to take up passengers; but from 10.45 the first stop of these Glasgow trains will be at Preston, reached in 154½min for 209 miles, an average speed of 81·5mph. Preston to Carlisle will be run in 68min (79.4 mph), and Carlisle to Glasgow (102·3 miles) in 79½min, 77·6 mph. The overall time of trains making two stops is 5hr 9min, or 77mph inclusive of 6 min standing time. The 10.45, which will retain the name 'Royal Scot', will call only at Preston, and reach Glasgow in the level 5hr. The average speed from Preston to Glasgow, 192·3 miles, will be 79·2mph.

Before looking into more detail of the timings north of Preston I must mention a very interesting new Anglo-Scottish service, the 09.35 from Euston, which is a through Restaurant car express to Inverness. It runs via Birmingham, and with the 10min earlier start from London, and a call at Watford Junction takes up the standard 'Glasgow' path at Stafford. With subsequent stops, in the electrified area at Crewe, Preston, Carlisle and Motherwell, the arrival at Inverness is at 19.45hr. The return working starts at 10.30, and reaches Euston, via Birmingham at 21.04. It will be extremely interesting to see what patronage is accorded to this enterprising service. The up train has the very fast standard working allowance of 65min start-to-stop from Carlisle to Preston, an average speed of 83·2mph. So far as I know this is the first time the up run over this section has been timed faster than the down, though this is accounted for by insertions of recovery time.

Turning now to the philosophy of the new arrangements, the service suddenly and generously lavished upon the town of Preston commands immediate notice. Including trains at present 'dated' there are eight runs from Euston at average speeds of between 81 and 84mph, and no less than seventeen trains at around 80mph forward to Carlisle. In addition to those originating from London there are those from Birmingham, Liverpool and Manchester, all of which run forward separately from London trains from Preston onwards. With no more than marginal variations either way it can be said that one can travel from anywhere up and down the West Coast main line at an average speed of around 80mph, providing one keeps 'under the wires'. The following are some examples:

Journey	*Distance miles*	*Standard non-stop speed mph* Down	Up
Preston–Crewe	51·0	83·8	77·5
Preston–Carlisle	90·1	79·5	83·2
Carlisle–Carstairs	73·5	78·3	77·5

The variations between the down and up directions are due to varying interposition of recovery time.

The speed situation changes considerably, however, when connections have to be made off the electrified line. Both Preston and Carstairs are cases in point. Even where through trains are concerned, such as Liverpool and Manchester to the Scottish cities and the Euston trains to Blackpool, engine changing is involved, and with the present arrangements at Preston it is not going to be a speedy business. It has always been a different matter at Crewe, where engines have been changed on the Anglo-Scottish expresses from the very inception of the route – well over a hundred years ago. There are conveniently sited shunting necks, and one can change from diesel to electric, or vice versa in 5min, if necessary. At Preston the anticipated time of changing is more than double this.

One can fully appreciate the need to have minimised the capital cost of the new electrification, and for the seeking of means of retrenchment in other directions to reduce operating expenses that could offset the cost of electrification as a whole. Consequently no attempt was made to include in the West Coast scheme the important fringe, or feeder lines. I shall describe in a later chapter how the modern signalling controls have been extended from the new power boxes at Warrington and Preston to include a considerable number of feeder lines, chiefly because this process will result in major reductions in operating expenses; but the philosophy of acceleration is not in itself an argument for electrification of a line, and today – for a time at any rate – the important feeder lines from Manchester to Euxton Junction, from Liverpool to Earlestown Junction and from Preston to Blackpool have not been placed under the wires. The three sections represent route mileages of 25·8 (via Bolton), 18 miles, and 16·2 miles, to Blackpool Central. These three sections, through busy areas, would have represented an additional 26 per cent on the total route mileage of the complete West Coast scheme as authorised, and because of their physical and traffic natures would probably have involved a higher percentage increase in total cost.

The trouble with such seemingly tempting additions is that it is difficult to know where to stop. The Liverpool–Scottish trains will be using the historic Liverpool and Manchester Railway line as far as Parkside Junction, and it is almost unthinkable that only the western section of this famous pioneer link should be electrified. If on the other hand justification were sought for electrification between Liverpool and Manchester on its own account, the former LNWR route would probably not be favoured. As a short inter-city electrified link one fancies that the old 'Cheshire Lines' would find the strongest justification; and this would not be to the advantage of the Liverpool–Scottish service. At one time, at the height of activity on the former Lancashire and Yorkshire Railway, it could have been argued that the Manchester–Blackpool route, with its intense holiday and commuter traffic would have been ideal ground for electrification, and the general policy of that company in days before World War I seemed to be pointing towards such a development. Today however, the situation is entirely changed, and electrification would certainly not be justified on the basis of the local traffic.

It is interesting nevertheless to analyse how the leaving out of the Manchester–Euxton, and Liverpool–Earlestown sections are going to affect the overall journey times between Lancashire and the Scottish cities. Take the case of the 'crack' 07.53 Manchester to Glasgow: the overall time of this train, 3hr 29min, giving an average speed of 65mph is vastly better than anything available before electrification, but it takes a very long time really to get going. There is some close timing in the early stages with the 07.48 Liverpool to Edinburgh. The two trains arrive at Preston at 08.38 and 08.43 respectively; there is 'cross-platform' interchange between the two trains, affording fast service from Manchester to Edinburgh, or Liverpool to Glasgow with only one change of carriage, and departures, under the wires, are at 08.51 and 08.56. The station times are 13 and 13min respectively, while locomotives are being changed. In this particular instance, however, a virtue is made out of necessity, for the cross-platform interchange between these two trains could not be reasonably cut below five minutes nor could the running headway out on the line.

The effect of diesel haulage from their respective starting points and station time at Preston however is to mean that 58min have elapsed before the Manchester train is 31 miles on its way, and a full hour and 8min before the Liverpool is away from Preston. The two trains have made average speeds of only 32, and 38mph by the time the wheels begin to turn under the wires; thenceforward, the Manchester, with only one stop, makes the splendid average of 77mph from Preston to Glasgow.

The Edinburgh, with stops at Lancaster, Carlisle, Lockerbie, and the engine changing stop at Carstairs still managed to average 64mph from Preston to Waverley. It is tempting to speculate upon the psychological and commercial effects of the slow starts to these Lancashire–Scottish journeys, and perhaps even more so of the effect coming at the latter end of a corresponding southbound journey. One can indeed ponder upon what might be done if the line was electrified throughout. With electric standards of running it ought to be possible to reach Preston in 25min from Manchester, instead of 44½min and to be under way again in the level half hour. This would clip 25min off the journey, and provide a 3hr service from Manchester to Glasgow, at an average of 74mph. It would still be possible to provide the 5min of cross-platform interchange by turning the Liverpool train on to the slow lines at Balshaw Lane, and running the two trains parallel from Euxton Junction, and arriving simultaneously at adjacent platforms in Preston station.

All this may seem dangerously near to 'teaching one's grandmother' . . . But I do know how the grand conception of the West Coast electrification scheme has been trimmed to save costs, and I feel it is only right to point out a few of the side-effects that have resulted from this very necessary diplomatic parsimony. One can only hope that the success of the major part of the scheme, which is proving so beneficial to travellers from London and Birmingham, may result in authorisation of extensions to these very important feeder lines. At the same time the philosophy of acceleration can be applied to the personal and individual side of travelling. Not every Lancashire business man bound for Scotland might find it convenient to make Liverpool Lime Street or Manchester Victoria his starting point. Where early morning starts and late evening arrivals are concerned one has always in mind the successful examples of Hampden-in-Arden, Runcorn, Watford Junction and Wilmslow, as stations of the 'Parkway' character, centred in a catchment area for potential business travellers.

Neither in the South Lancashire industrial area, nor in Scotland, however, do there appear to be ready-made equivalents of the four stations just mentioned, except to point out that nearly a million people live within a 16-mile radius of Preston station. Apart from smaller places one has only to mention Accrington, Blackburn, Blackpool, Bolton, Chorley, Darwen,

Leyland, Lytham St Annes and Southport, all of which could well provide potential customers for the electric railways. I know that British Railways are keenly aware of the competitive power of the M6 motorway, which is so easy of access from all the centres of population that I have just mentioned. But even to the most intrepid of travellers, the motorway, as an all-weather proposition is not an ideal start to a busy day; the alternative of a relative short drive into Preston, and then a comfortable breakfast in the train, and the reasonable certainty of a punctual arrival in Glasgow soon after 11.00hrs or in Edinburgh not much later, should tempt many to venture 'under the wires'.

Later in the day of course, the city terminal departures naturally come into their own, and that is where an 'all-electric' journey would have its undoubted advantages. At the risk of being accused of over-stating the case, there is another point where the inherent advantage of railways could be forcibly emphasised, and that is in the availability of alternative routes. An electrified line from Preston to Manchester, including the link between Victoria and Piccadilly stations would provide an all-electric alternative to the main line. In the ordinary way railways, with a network such as exists in Great Britain, have the facilities and the record of being able to extricate themselves much more quickly from situations when one route is temporarily blocked, than other forms of transport. Again it is the philosophy of speed, and acceleration that can burnish up the 'image' so effectively when a difficulty or emergency is quickly resolved.

Seeing what a vast mileage of increased high speed service is being provided by the extension of the electrified line from Weaver Junction to Glasgow it might seem rather ungracious to yearn for still more – especially as I am very mindful of the struggle the British Railways Board had to secure authorisation of the scheme at all, as described in the preceding chapter. And in referring to numerous improvements the connection to and from the West of England must not be forgotten. It will now be possible to travel over the 387 miles from Bristol to Glasgow in only a few minutes over the level 6hr, making an overall average speed of 64mph. Inevitably the connectional time in Birmingham cannot be of the briefest, and allowing for the various other stops the running average is approximately 70 mph. It is interesting to recall that in pre-grouping days a through carriage service was operated on the 10am up from Glasgow, for Bristol, but this was routed via the regular North to West line of the joint GWR and LNWR services between Liverpool, Manchester and the West of England, from Crewe via Shrewsbury, Hereford and the Severn Tunnel. It is in the cause of acceleration, and of the connectional pattern developed in Birmingham that the Severn Tunnel route has no more than recently been abandoned as a North-West to South-West trunk route, in favour of the Midland line south west from Birmingham.

4: THE ROUTE: WEAVER JUNCTION TO GRETNA

Weaver Junction, the technical zero point of this great project, was virtually unknown to the travelling public until a few years ago, and the simple turnout taken with little reduction of speed coming immediately after the crossing of the River Weaver itself on a lofty viaduct was not such as to attract any attention. Yet it holds an important place in railway history quite apart from the notoriety recently piled upon it. The original way from London to Liverpool was to follow the Grand Junction Railway to its very end, north of Warrington where it made a triangle junction with the Liverpool and Manchester Railway at Newton Junction now called Earlestown. In 1869, however, the new direct line to Liverpool was opened. This crossed the Mersey at Runcorn, but it was in the junction with the main line just north of the deep valley of the Weaver that history was made. As far as can be traced this was the first instance anywhere in the world of the use of a 'fly-over'. The up line from Liverpool was carried over the down and up main lines on a viaduct, and curving round to the right descended and trailed into the up main line at 'Weaver Junction', just short of the high viaduct. Thus was avoided, at one and the same time a conflicting route, and a diamond crossing with the down main line. Lately the name has led to the colloquial use of the sartorial slogan 'Weaver to Wearer' for the electrification project, and although the changes in operating strategy consequent upon the completion of the project start at Crewe, or even farther south, an examination of the line itself can appropriately begin at Weaver Junction.

The West Coast main line is here still on the route of the historic Grand Junction Railway, and near the site of the former Preston Brook station the projected line of the railway intersected, on the skew, the Duke of Bridgewater's Canal. An aqueduct had to be constructed and the railway taken underneath. Because of the skew location and the width of the canal the railway underpass was quite a long one, and since Joseph Locke designed it with each of the railway tracks in a separate arch opening, it seemed like a short tunnel to the ordinary traveller. So indeed it was described in Coghlan's *Iron Road Book* of 1838 – "Tunnel 110 yards long". Actually Coghlan was considerably out in his reckoning, for the original aqueduct was 90ft long along each track, while the canal itself was no less than 40ft wide. There was a two-fold problem here for the civil engineers. Re-alignment of the track was necessary to permit of higher speeds, and greater headroom was needed for electrification. The centre pier of the aqueduct was removed. This made possible the required track slues, for re-alignment, and it reduced to a minimum the increased depth required. The problem was also eased by the agreement of the canal authorities to a reduction in the width of the canal to 20ft.

Nevertheless a difficult problem remained, that of keeping both railway and waterway open while reconstruction was in progress. In similar circumstances in previous electrification schemes, either the canal was closed and the aqueduct rebuilt at the actual site, or a new aqueduct was built alongside and in due course rolled into its final position. At Preston Brook, however, neither of these alternatives was acceptable. It was necessary to reduce the closure of the canal to an absolute minimum and so the new aqueduct was constructed over the part of the canal that was to remain, and was on completion lowered into position on to previously prepared bored piles, topped by a pile cap placed behind the existing abutments. While the new aqueduct was being constructed the portion of the canal eventually closed was used for water-borne traffic. The accompanying drawings show the original, and present elevations on the London face of the aqueduct, in each case looking at right angles to the line of the canal. The plan view shows the general scheme of reconstruction, and the extent to which the railway tracks have been slued.

In a very few miles beyond Preston Brook the line enters the railway complex of South Lancashire, where in a distance of less than 30 miles there are intersections with no fewer than four cross-country lines of considerable importance as well as junctions leading to areas that are sources of staple traffics; even in this area of strict rationalisation of route there are branch lines that it has been necessary to retain. This South Lancashire area is one of sharp intermediate gradients on the main line, and one that was frequently subject to speed restrictions of a semi-permanent nature over sections of the line where the ground was unstable because of the effects of underground colliery workings. Furthermore, many of the junctions were laid out with facing turnouts on curves, that necessitated a generally moderate rate of speed. On one of the fastest ordinary runs in the history of the LNWR it was not possible to cover the 27 miles from Warrington to Preston in less that 26min; and even in all the excitement and risk-taking in the Race to the North in 1895, the time over this section was not reduced below 24min – an average speed, pass to pass, of 67½mph. Such a speed, over an appreciable section of the route, would have been quite unacceptably low for modern requirements.

A great deal of track improvement has been necessary to enable the standard timing for high speed express trains to be established at 24min, for the 34·5 miles from Weaver Junction to Preston, involving an average speed of 86·2mph pass to stop. Even so, it has not been possible to eliminate entirely locations where speed restrictions formerly existed. There is Winwick Junction, for example, where the present main line diverges to the right from the original Grand Junction line proceeding to its northern extremity, and Golborne Junction, where the present direct link in the main line, after passing beneath the track of the Liverpool and Manchester Railway, joins the original northward connection from Parkside today used by the Liverpool–Scottish expresses. At both these locations, despite careful re-alignment, the local geography is such that the speed limit has not been raised to more than 70mph at Winwick and to 80mph at Golborne. Only by quite inordinate expenditure could this have been pushed higher.

Wigan (North Western) is another difficult locality. The station is at high level, with the tracks just north of the platform ends crossing the former Lancashire and Yorkshire line at Wigan, Wallgate. There is a considerable curve to the north, counterpart of the curving approach from the south, and although the tracks through the actual station are straight, those curves, and the difficulty of further improving the alignment has resulted in another short length of restriction to 70mph. North of Wigan, however, drivers have a clear run to the outskirts of Preston. This, however, is one of the most sharply graded stretches south of Carnforth, with speed having to be recovered

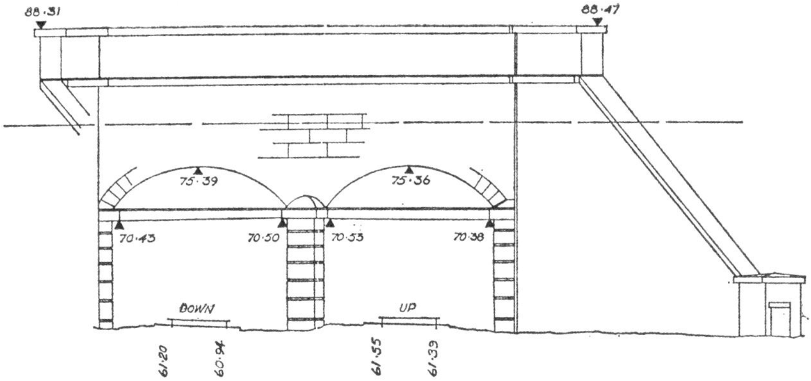

Bridgwater Canal Aqueduct: *Above*: original elevation on London face, and *below*: new elevation.

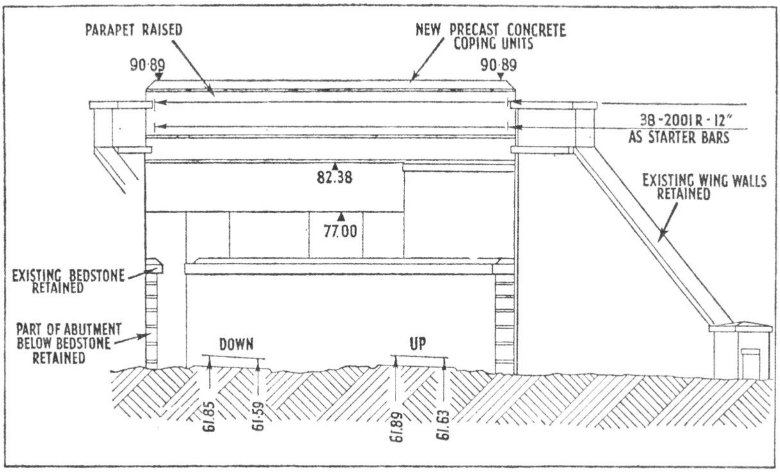

from the Wigan '70' up the 1 in 104 gradient of the Boars Head bank. On one of my recent journeys, with two Class '50' diesels speed had not risen to more than 75mph by the time we topped the 1 in 104 gradient and passed over the site of the one-time junction at Boars Head. This used to be the starting point of an LMS alternative route to Carlisle via Chorley and Blackburn to Hellifield and the Settle and Carlisle line. But the sections from Boars Head to Chorley and Chorley to Cherry Tree are now closed and the track lifted in places. The present alternative route diverges at Farington Junction, and takes the spur to Lostock Hall Junction on to the Preston–Blackburn line. I have more than once travelled by night

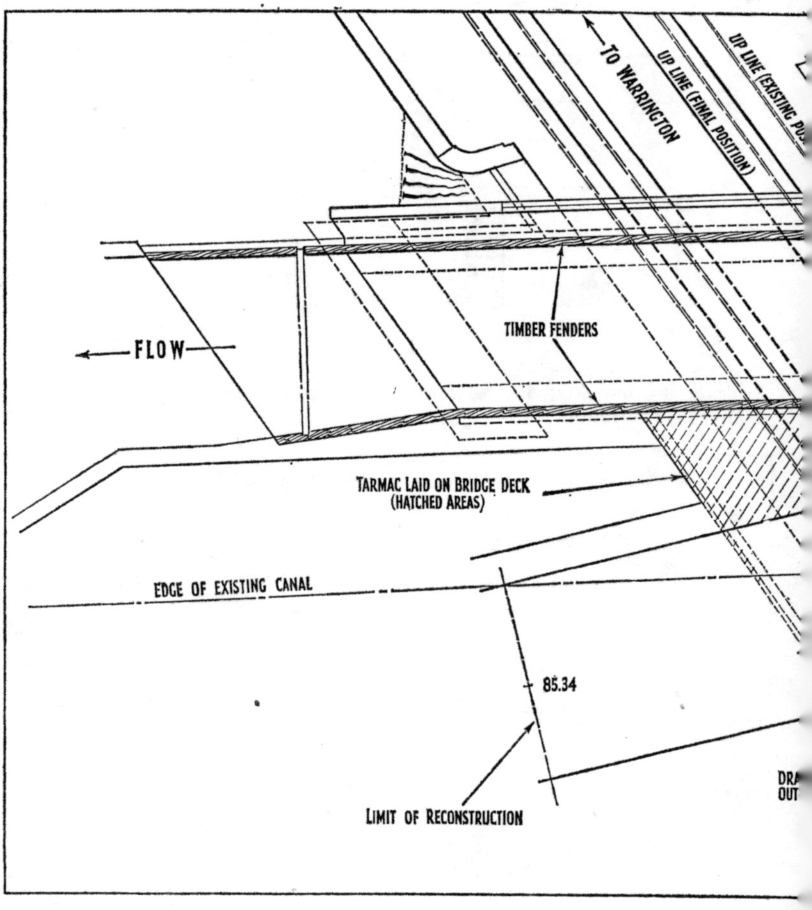

Bridgewater Canal Aqueduct: Plan of reconstruction.

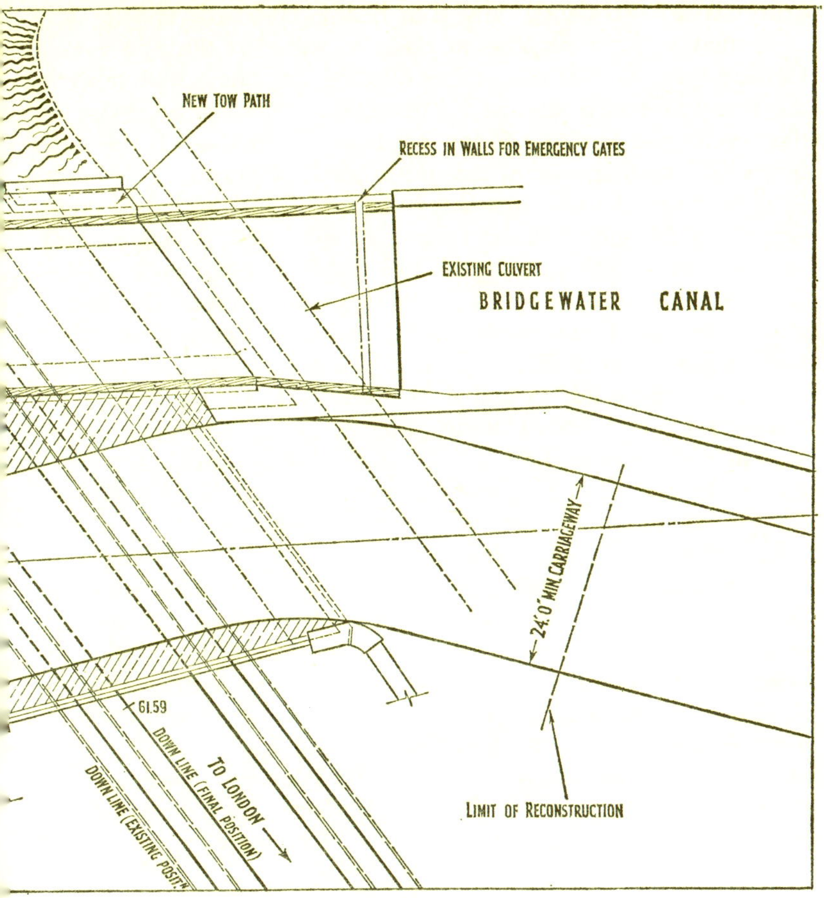
NEW TOW PATH
RECESS IN WALLS FOR EMERGENCY GATES
EXISTING CULVERT
BRIDGEWATER CANAL
24'0" MIN CARRIAGEWAY
61.59
DOWN LINE (FINAL POSITION)
TO LONDON
DOWN LINE (EXISTING POSIT.N
LIMIT OF RECONSTRUCTION

expresses to Scotland, via the Boars Head diversion and awakened later in surprise to find we were on the Settle and Carlisle line, instead of passing over Shap. The speed limit is the full 100mph from just north of Wigan; but one imagines that even with the new Class '87' electrics on the job the new trains will not regain the 'ton' until north of Standish.

The line used to be quadruple tracked from this latter point right into Preston; but the closing of the intermediate stations at Standish Junction, Coppull and Balshaw Lane and the increased capacity of the remaining two has removed the necessity for the additional tracks. A new junction has however been laid in just to the south of the site of Balshaw Lane station, so that four tracks are available at Euxton Junction, where the former L&Y line from Chorley, Bolton, and Manchester comes in, while $1\frac{1}{2}$ miles to the north the station at Leyland is retained, for use by the Manchester–Preston diesel multiple unit service. So far as junction connections are concerned the southern approach to Preston remains much as previously, with regard to the main line. The route rationalisation affects the former L&Y lines, as shown in the plan on page 109. Before referring in more detail to the route alterations to the north of Preston station other works necessitated by the electrification must be described.

There are first of all the modifications involved to many overline bridges. On the London Midland section of the complete electrification scheme, between Weaver Junction and Gretna Junction, no fewer than 219 bridges have required altering in some way or another. North of Lancaster in particular, where the magnificent stone bridges built by Joseph Locke have blended marvellously into the landscape of the fell country a problem in amenities was presented to the engineers of the present day; because even the humblest overbridges carrying secondary roads, or even occupation farm crossings were, without exception, works of art. I can imagine some readers begin to think, 'if the Doric Arch was pulled down in the cause of modernisation why bother about a few small bridges in a sparsely populated countryside'; but public opinion towards the environment in country districts has become very strong, and those who built the M6 motorway through the Westmorland hills were required to spend considerable sums towards the rehabilitation of the rugged landscape of the district, once the job was finished. So it has been with the new electric railway.

With the need to raise many bridges to provide the necessary clearance for the overhead wires an interesting constructional procedure was devised, for use not only in the amenity conscious regions of the north country, but throughout the Weaver–Gretna section where applicable. At Newton Heath works, Manchester, and at Taunton concrete works complete arch sections were pre-fabricated in reinforced concrete, each section being 2ft 3in wide. The units were designed to be of such size and height as to be capable of being lifted into position by a road crane, working from the roadway. This technique had the advantage of enabling bridges of any required width to be built up, by placing the requisite number of arch sections in parallel; even more so, it enabled the reconstruction work on certain bridges to be done piecemeal, by closing part of the over-passing roadway, inserting half the replacement arches, and then attending to the remaining half. When skew spans were involved the pre-cast arches were formed to suit the individual location during construction in Newton Heath works, as in the interesting case of White Horse Bridge, near Barton and some 5 miles north of Preston.

Station reconstructions have take place at Warrington and Wigan, but these do not compare for magnitude or difficulty with some of the reconstructions undertaken on the electrified lines southward from Liverpool and Manchester. Even at Preston the work has not been extensive. The principal change there was to lay in such connections as would permit of either-direction running on every track through the station. The curve at the north end has been an obstacle to fast through running for over a hundred years. The speed restriction for non-stopping trains used to be 15mph, and even with careful re-alignment and the elimination of all redundant connections it has not been possible to raise this limit above 35mph. This will not be such a serious hindrance in the new all-electric time table, because every day-time Anglo-Scottish express, whether from London, Birmingham or the Lancashire cities will be making a passenger stop at Preston. It is now only the fast freights, and certain of the night trains that will pass Preston without stopping. Neither of these latter groups of trains are timed so sharply as the day Anglo-Scottish expresses, and so the incidence of a permanent 35mph slack through the Preston area will not be serious.

About 5 miles north of Preston one of the most interesting items of bridge reconstruction has been carried out. This was the White Horse bridge that carries the A6 trunk road over the line near the site of the one-time Barton station. It was a curious piece of work for the early period in which it was built – 1844. This part of the line, the former Preston and Lancaster Railway was one of the links in the chain of railway communication to the north, inspired and instigated by the Grand Junction Railway. The road crossed the railway at an angle of 60 degrees, but the bridge itself was built square to the line, and it had to be no less than 135ft wide, and in railway terms qualified as a tunnel. The headroom above rail level was insufficient to accommodate the overhead electric wires, while it was also desirable to set back one abutment, to permit of re-alignment of the track for higher speeds. So complete reconstruction was needed. The new bridge had been designed to cross the railway at 45 degrees, but a number of factors combined to make the actual job of reconstruction unusually complex.

The local Highway Authority insisted on the maintenance of a dual carriage way 30ft wide, or two single carriage ways 15ft wide for the A6 road traffic throughout the operation. In addition to this, the original bridge carried an 8in diameter gas main, and important Post Office trunk telephone cables, while directly above the site, at a height of 31ft 6in is the CEGB's 132kV overhead power line from Blackburn. From the railway point of view it was desired to take advantage of the reconstruction to re-align the tracks to permit of uninterrupted running at 100mph. The new bridge was designed to have forty-two prefabricated reinforced concrete arch sections, made at Newton Heath works, each 2ft 3in wide by 14in deep.

The physical difficulties, and the interim requirements to keep traffic flowing both on rail and road led, through careful planning, to the establishment of a three-stage scheme of reconstruction. In broad outline, stage one involved the building of a new skew arch, just north of the existing bridge to carry the southbound traffic on the A6 road. Having relieved the original bridge of southbound road traffic, the relevant portion of the old bridge could be demolished, and excavation carried out to prepare for the new abutments sufficiently far back from the line of the old ones to permit of the re-alignment of the railway. Then the centre section of the new bridge could be positioned, and duly surfaced to form a northbound lane for A6 traffic. Finally, the rest of the original bridge was demolished, new abutments completed and the remaining arch sections of the new bridge placed into position. The conception of the changeover sounds simple enough, but some complicated detail work was involved.

First of all the southbound carriageway of the A6 had to be diverted to pass over the first section of the new bridge to be placed in position. Then the northbound carriage way had to be carried partly through the garden of a nearby private house, and the owner's greenhouse had to be dismantled to make way. Having secured the diversionary route to enable work to commence on the central section, the extreme situation became difficult as will be appreciated from the photograph on page 12 of the illustrations. The engineers had secured the space to work but they were virtually marooned on an 'island' site bounded on two sides by the teeming highways, north and south, of the A6, and on the third by the railway. All material and equipment had to cross the heavy traffic flows on the highway. In the meantime temporary bridges had to be built across the railway to carry the gas main and the Post Office trunk telephone cables.

I was privileged to ride north in the cab of one of the Anglo-Scottish expresses when the work, not only at White Horse Bridge but in many other localities, was in an advanced stage and I was impressed with the handsome appearance of the bridges that had been completed. The new pre-fabricated arches give quite a distinctive style to the numerous overhead bridges, and above the arches the facings and parapets are styled in stone facings to match the original abutments most of which remain. At present, of course, the new parts are very obvious by their cleanliness, against the 100-year-old weathered stone of the original parts. On the London Midland section of the route no fewer than ninety bridges have been completely reconstructed, and another forty have been raised bodily by between 12in and 18in. Not all these are stone structures; there were fifty of these latter, which had the original arches replaced by the new pre-fabricated sectional type, from Newton Heath and Taunton. Between Preston and Lancaster there is a northern counterpart of the well-known juxtaposition of rail and motorway south of Kilsby Tunnel, where the line comes abreast of the M6 motorway. This will be yet another of those satisfying stretches of railway where an express train can leave its road competitors standing.

Approaching Lancaster there is an instance – one of the very few – where the overall plan of a continuous West Coast main line did not keep quite in step with local activities. The Lancaster and Preston Junction Railway was, to all outward appearances an entirely independent concern, and its promoters apparently thought that Lancaster would be the ultimate goal. For having engineered the splendidly straight line from Preston, over which the modern express trains skim along at an uninterrupted 100mph, they continued down the hill into the centre of the City of Lancaster, to a terminus from which there was no convenient way out to the north. Consequently when the highly strategic Lancaster and Carlisle Railway was promoted, and Joseph Locke was appointed engineer, the first thing he had to do was to find a way through or round the city from which there was an outlet to the north, and a divergence to the left began at a point 45 chains south of the original Lancaster terminus. It passed to the left, and almost beneath the walls of the twelfth-century Royal Grammar School, and so steeply downhill, and on a curving alignment to the new station, just beneath the castle walls and on the left bank of the River Lune.

Until well into the 1930s the starting point of the Lancaster and Carlisle Railway used to be known as 'Lancaster Old Junction', with the short line to the original terminus still used for goods traffic. But the sharp divergence on to the new line, and the continuously curving alignment until the Castle Station is passed called for some reduction of speed even in steam days. It is on this station that the 'O' milepost of the Lancaster and Carlisle Railway still stands. Although the junction at the 'Old' location has now been removed it has not been found possible, even in these days of route improvement, to raise the limit above 70mph. It was not always treated with such circumspection. I have the liveliest recollections of a night on the 'Ulster Express' in 1936, which then ran non-stop from Preston to Morecambe Promenade. It was a Friday evening in the height of the holiday season and we had a load of over 500 tons, hauled by two Midland compounds. We took the 'Old' junction at an unchecked 68mph and accelerated to nearly 75mph through the Castle station. I, with many others, was enjoying a late night drink in the dining car at the time and the devastation among the crockery and glassware was indescribable! I believe the speed limit was then 50mph.

On the electrified railway Lancaster Castle station remains much as it was, except that it has now become the main line passenger junction for the Furness line. The one-time status of Carnforth has indeed completely changed. So far as the West Coast main line is concerned the 'wheel' of history has not only turned full circle, but gone off into a new circle altogether. When the Lancaster and Carlisle Railway was first built there was no junction, and few dwellings thereabouts; but a small wayside station was erected, about the size of the diminutive Bolton-le-Sands of thirty years ago, and called 'Carnforth–Tealand'. It served the hamlet of Tealand, some distance to the north. But from the opening of the main line from Ulverston in 1857 it began to assume the position of a first rate junction, particularly for mail traffic. Before World War I no fewer than nine mail trains called during the night hours. Today there are no platforms on the electrified West Coast main line, and so far as the Furness line traffic is concerned the junction is now merely that with the former Midland Line to Hellifield. As mentioned in Chapter Two this latter line was on the list for closure at one time during the negotiations towards the authorisation of the West Coast electrification scheme; but with the present extensive utilisation of the Settle and Carlisle line for freight the proposal to close the Carnforth–Hellifield line has receded.

So at a speed of 100mph the mountain section is entered. The vertical rise is 885ft in the next 31 miles, averaging 1 in 185. Such a gradient is, of course, no obstacle to the modern electric locomotives; but in the late 1840s Locke did not have the finance to drive the railway straight through the mountains as the Japanese National Railways are now doing with the extensions of their spectacular Shinkansen Line, or indeed as Sharland did thirty years later in building the Settle and Carlisle. Locke built a first class road, and a relatively fast one; but it does include a good deal of curvature on which speed is limited variously to 80 or 85mph. Until the prospect of electrification became a real one, and there were locomotives which by their performance south of Crewe would be capable of climbing the Grayrigg bank at over 90mph, the curves that Locke laid in, contouring up the hillsides, were of no consequence. Today much has been done in re-alignment to make them comfortable at sustained speeds of 85mph.

As Grayrigg summit is neared the prospect is now very much changed. There is first of all the requirement to shut off power – not as was sometimes the case in former days, when water level and steam pressure were low, and the boiler had to be pulled round in readiness for the attack on Shap proper—but because the succession of reverse curves into the Lune valley require a reduction to 75mph; and with ordinary good going the Grayrigg bank will have been climbed, at 80 to 85mph. Also, in this once-lonely mountain countryside the M6 motorway joins in from the south and runs within sight of the railway in the deep valley of the Lune between Low Gill and Tebay. At Low Gill, the old branch line from Ingleton has now disappeared, although the old viaduct across the valley can still be seen, and Tebay, once a bank engine station of the first importance as well as a junction for the North Eastern line over Stainmore Summit to Darlington, is marked by little more than the windowless building of the 'remote relay interlocking' of the modern signalling system, and the changeover point between the English and the Scottish electric control areas.

The charge through Tebay, to get maximum impetus for the attack on Shap, was always a feature of steam locomotive working in this area, and the existence of water troughs on a short length of level track near to the intermediate signal box of Dillicar added to the spectacle. With water troughs on the shores of Morecambe Bay, at Hest Bank, this second set little more than 25 miles farther on was significant. Whatever other difficulties might be experienced in climbing to Shap the London and North Western Railway made sure that their locomotives should not be short of water. It was in the 'charge' on Shap that C. J. Bowen-Cooke's four-cylinder 4-6-0 locomotive *Ralph Brocklebank* registered, in 1913, the highest horsepower so far attained by any British locomotive – a record that was not surpassed until more than ten years later. The new electric trains will pass Tebay at 100mph, and although the subsequent 4 miles of 1 in 75 of the Shap Incline will take its toll, even if no more than slightly, it will be necessary to apply the brakes to observe the speed restriction of 80mph over the actual summit.

In the last days of the diesels over this route, when use of two Class '50' locomotives has provided an engine horsepower of 5,400, the speed on the 1 in 75 gradient has usually been at least 75mph and speed restricted to 60 'over the top'. While the romantics and the sentimentalists amongst us may be inclined to whisper '*Eheu fugaces labuntur anni*' over the changed circumstances at Shap Summit, with the removal of the signalbox, and the end of bank engine working with all its interest for the enthusiast and photographer, no practical railwayman is going to shed any sentimental tears over the final conquering of this $1\frac{1}{4}$-century-old bugbear of train working, and the ending of all the toil and sweat traditionally associated with the attainment of that bleak, inhospitable summit point, 915ft up in the Westmorland fells.

The descent to Carlisle has its problems even in this modern age. Before the introduction of through steam locomotives working between Crewe and Glasgow, which meant that the surmounting of Shap was only half the total 'battle', it used to be said that once over Shap Summit drivers ceased worrying. Maybe so, as far as steam production and power output was concerned. But at the infinitely higher standards of speed that are now being established the downhill length will take longer than the ascent! It so happens that Shap Summit is precisely half way between Carnforth and Carlisle, and the diesel timing, with two Class '50' locomotives, was also exactly the same, $26\frac{1}{2}$min for 31·4 miles, each stretch including 3min recovery time. This meant that on an unchecked run, making up time, two Class '50' locomotives would have been expected to average 80mph from Carnforth to Summit, and equally 80mph from Summit down to the Carlisle stop. I have done the uphill stretch in $22\frac{1}{2}$ min on one occasion, with one coach less than the maximum load for the timing. This uphill booking will be quickened to $22\frac{1}{2}$min, 83·8mph average, with electrification.

No comparable quickening will be possible downhill. From where Shap passenger station used to be the line enters upon a very winding stretch of line, passing the limestone works at Shap Quarry and Harrison's Siding, and then in the glen of Bessie Ghyll where the speed limit cannot be raised above 75mph. There is a short length of 100mph road past Clifton and the one time junction of the Eden Valley line of the North Eastern Railway, but then comes the approach and passage through Penrith, restricted to 70mph. It will indeed be a sign of the changed times that with electrification the minimum speeds on a run from

Preston to Carlisle will in future not be at Grayrigg and Shap Summit, but in rounding the curves at Lancaster and Penrith. As at Lancaster it would have been difficult to obtain any appreciable raising of the speed restrictions in the Penrith area without an altogether inordinate expenditure, which it would have been difficult to justify on the grounds of saving in time.

Once clear of the Penrith area there is a 10-mile stretch that can be covered in little more than 6min; but then the curves once more intrude, with the sharp swing to the right at Wreay. The new speed restriction here in 80mph, followed by a length of 90mph, and after that comes the necessarily cautious approach to Carlisle. It certainly needs skilful driving and sharp acceleration from the speed restrictions to make Carlisle in $23\frac{1}{2}$min from Shap Summit. Running conditions in the Citadel station have not been noticeably changed. All through platforms can be used in either direction, but the approaches from the south, both from the Newcastle and the Midland main line, have been singled though that from the Maryport remains the same. The extent to which centralised signalling control has been applied is discussed in a later chapter. No attempt has been made to ease speed restrictions through the station, for at present there is only one passenger train northbound and two southbound that pass through without stopping.

A considerable amount of route rationalisation has been effected north of Carlisle station. The abandonment of the Waverley Route, and other lines of the former North British Railway, has made possible much simplification, and the goods lines from the Dentonholme yard now pass to the Kingmoor yard without any confliction with passenger lines from the Citadel station. The plans on pages 129 and 131 show how the changes there have been made, and also how freight traffic, except for through express services, have been kept entirely clear of the passenger station. This is not entirely a recent development, because in the pre-grouping era there were connecting lines that took the freight traffic of all the seven railways feeding Carlisle clear of the actual Citadel station area. But until World War II there was only a two-track bridge over the River Eden at Etterby Junction, and it was not until the new fully-mechanised Kingmoor marshalling yards were built that freight traffic from the north was able to pass into the freight reception area by a 'flyover', and thus avoid using a route conflicting with down traffic.

The work done in these two important schemes of improvement certainly paved the way for the recent streamlining of the layout.

It is now appropriate to make division in the description of the electrified route at the Border, rather than at Carlisle itself, because the Border is not only the division point between the London Midland and the Scottish Regions of British Railways and a division point both geographically and politically, but in a rather curious way it was a line of demarcation in pre-grouping days. The London & North Western and Caledonian Railways always worked in very close partnership. So far as the Lancaster and Carlisle section of the former was concerned they were born out of the same family attachment; and Joseph Locke was engineer of both. But for some reason, which is obviously lost in the mists of antiquity the Caledonian mileposts north of Carlisle, and extending to the Border, were of the standard LNWR pattern. The mileage was reckoned from Carlisle station, but through Rockcliffe and Floriston the tall, conspicuous LNWR posts were used, and it was only north of Gretna that the small Caledonian type came into their own, often discreetly camouflaged in the foliage of a small bush. Stop-watching, often to a bush that did not contain a milepost, sometimes gave startling, if ephemeral speed records!

Such are the physical features of the 'new' West Coast route. How it has been equipped, with electric traction supplies, and signalling, and how it is being used are discussed in later chapters of this book.

5: THE ROUTE: GRETNA TO GLASGOW

Riding north from Carlisle at the head end of a fast train one has not even reached the border before the famous bifurcation of Gretna Junction can be sighted ahead; and in thought if not in actual fact the old question is posed: which way to Glasgow? Nithsdale or Annandale? G&SW or 'Caley'? It has been told earlier how Locke settled for Annandale, but also how it was not entirely a question of geography that led to this choice. There were the interests of Edinburgh as much as those of Glasgow to be considered so far as the men of the Grand Junction were concerned, though the purely Glasgow interests of the one-time GPK&A made an extremely strong case for the Nithsdale route. The differences of opinion did not die down with the decision of the Caledonian to go up Annandale; in fact the feud – for such it became! – between the Annandale and the Nithsdale factions became one of the most deep seated, bitter, and longest sustained in the history of the British railways. It is therefore not altogether surprising that certain interests raised the old controversy again when the prospect of electrification to Glasgow arose.

One can well appreciate the arguments in the minds of the Nithsdale faction: that the G&SW line tapped more sources of potential intermediate traffic, particularly in the developing industrial districts in Ayrshire; but if any alternative to the Caledonian line were ever considered, such claims would have been passed over on the grounds of speed alone, apart from the need to provide for Edinburgh, as in 1848. And so the West Coast main line of LNW and Caledonian days has become the West Coast electric line of today. At the same time the Nithsdale route has been cast for a very different rôle, that of junior partner rather than deadly rival, with an extremely important part to play in the constructional period. At one time 'Sou' West' interests felt that this supporting rôle during the changeover to electric traction on the Caledonian was rather like asking the old line to sign its own death warrant; and indeed I have told in Chapter Two of this book how it was proposed to single the line throughout from Kilmarnock to Gretna as a cost saving contribution to set against the cost of electrifying the main line of the Caledonian. But the industrial development in Ayshire which was instanced in support of the idea of electrifying the G&SW rather than the 'Caley' route is now producing so much freight traffic that the original singling proposals have been very much watered down as I shall describe in detail when I come to detailed reference to the new signalling.

The Caledonian line presented a remarkable and perhaps unique 'constructional site'. In the 65 miles between Gretna Junction and Carstairs, apart from the market town of Lockerbie, there is now not one source of intermediate traffic. Such sidings and running loops as exist are there purely for operating purposes, not for collection or dispersal of traffic. The line passes through a mixture of pastoral and lonely upland country where the establishment of working sites of the more conventional kind could have presented some difficulties; and so, with the alternative G&SW route available from Glasgow the unusual step was taken of closing the Caledonian to all ordinary traffic during the normal daytime working hours. This left the line completely free for the engineers' work trains to proceed with the job of erecting the overhead wires. The diversion of the Anglo-Scottish expresses began on Monday, May 3rd, 1971, and to avoid as much as practicable the disturbance of timetables south of Carlisle the trains that were diverted via Kilmarnock and Dumfries were started earlier from Glasgow, to the tune of about half an hour. The first train to follow the diversion route was the 07.05 to Euston, and normal working was restored each day with the departure of the 17.30 to Birmingham, which ran via Carstairs. The night expresses were not affected. This arrangement was in operation for exactly two years and was undoubtedly a great help towards the speedy execution of the main scheme of electrification.

Naturally these temporary arrangements caused a good deal of inconvenience to travellers. South of Carlisle weekday possessions were still regular occurrences in May and June of 1973, with single line working and the delays that are inevitable in such circumstances. There has naturally been much concern over the loss of goodwill towards the railway occasioned by such delays; but seeing that a virtually new railway has been built over the tracks of the old one while normal traffic has continued to be carried the interruptions have been remarkably few. The extra time given to express trains that were diverted to the G&SW line between Glasgow and Carlisle was not a strictly comparable assessment of the respective speed potentialities of the two routes; because on the Caledonian line much had already been done to improve the track and accelerate the running, whereas on the G&SW the work done had not been a great deal more than routine maintenance. Furthermore, it was at one time not intended to retain that part of the original G&SW main line via Barrhead, but to use the longer route via Paisley. From this preliminary survey we can now proceed to consideration of the electrified Caledonian line in some detail.

One length of the G&SW line that has been singled is that between Gretna Junction and Annan, and the junction layout at Gretna has been remodelled according to the latest practice eliminating the diamond crossing, with switch diamonds previously installed on the old standard double-line junction. Then, less than 2 miles further on is Quintinshill. It was perhaps no more than incidental that the old Caledonian signal box, the very one concerned in the terrible affair of May 22nd, 1915 should have been the very last mechanical box to be taken out of service on the entire West Coast main line. I am not forgetting that between Crewe and Nuneaton there are a number of interlockings operated from mechanical type lever frames, but these latter form part of a lengthy installation of continuous colour light signalling. Until it was taken out of use in July 1973, however, Quintinshill was a purely mechanical interlocking. On the remodelled railway the long passing loops, which were also involved in the disaster of May 1915, are retained but now remotely controlled by the new power signal box at Carlisle. There is a slight inter-penetration of London Midland signalling control here, for the area of Carlisle power box extends to Kirkpatrick on the West Coast main line, and over the singled section of the G&SW line from Gretna Junction to Annan.

The continuous rising gradient of 1 to 200 from the Solway viaduct to Cove Quarry will scarcely be noticed, with the modern electric locomotives in use; but near the summit of this first incline on the Scottish part of the route is an automatic half-barrier level crossing that is equipped to the latest requirements of the Department of the Environment, prepared after the disastrous collision between a high-speed electric train and an almost stationary, and enormous transformer that was being drawn over the level crossing at Hixon, Staffordshire. The modified arrangements at Cove, brought into operation in October 1970, are the provision of a steady amber light in addition to the flashing red lights on each side; the extension of the warning period before a train reaches the crossing from 24sec to a minimum of 37sec; the provision of an 'Another Train coming' illuminated sign and the installation of additional telephones on approaches to and at the crossing. The amber light has the same meaning as that in normal three-light road traffic signals – 'STOP, unless it is unsafe to do so'. The twin flashing red signals of course mean stop.

The first sign that a train is approaching is given by the warning amber light, which shows for 5sec, and the sounding of the pedestrian warning bells. Then the red 'Stop' lights begin to flash alternately, 6–8sec later the barriers begin to be lowered, taking a further 6–8sec to reach the lowered position. A further period of about 16sec elapses before the fastest train reaches the crossing. The bells stop when the barriers are down. If another train is coming the barriers stay down, the red lights continue to flash, and a sign saying 'Another train coming' lights up, when the first train passes over the crossing. New road approach signs carry the internationally recognised 'Gate' symbol and are supplemented by a plate describing the crossing and telling road drivers to stop when the signal lights show. A new mandatory sign sited approximately 100 yards from the crossing on each approach road, is worded: 'Drivers of large or slow vehicles must phone and get permission to cross' with the added information that 'Large means *over* 55 feet long or 9 feet 6 inches wide or 32 tons total weight – Slow means 5 mph or less'. A telephone is provided at each of the mandatory road signs for this purpose and a vehicle driver who has telephoned for permission to cross must use the telephone beyond the crossing to inform the signalman when he has passed clear. There is another crossing that has been similarly equipped at Nethercleugh, about $2\frac{1}{2}$ miles north of Lockerbie.

All the former wayside stations have been closed and in most cases the buildings and most signs of them removed, so that those of us who used to log Kirkpatrick, Kirtlebridge, Ecclefechan, Nethercleugh, Dinwoodie and Wamphray will have to rely upon the adjacent mileposts if comparison between past and present running is desired. But even in this respect there is a significant change. In anticipation of possible future developments Scottish Region has re-pegged the line out in kilometres. It is, however, not general British Railways policy to introduce kilometre posts – yet! Apart from Lockerbie which is being retained as a major point for concentration of both passenger and goods traffic in this rural area, the last passenger station to be closed south of Carstairs on the Caledonian line was Beattock; and in view of its historic interest as a bank-engine station, and as junction for the one-time popular branch to Moffat the circumstances of its closure in January 1972 are worth recalling.

Passenger stops at Beattock, principally by the Liverpool and Manchester Scottish expresses, were largely traditional, and in recent times generated very little traffic. The difficulty over retaining such stops as part of the new electric service was that the station would have to be modernised, by lengthening the platforms and providing a new overbridge. It was felt that some of the small amount of traffic that was lost by the closing of Beattock might be successfully diverted either to Lockerbie or to Dumfries, and that the cost of rebuilding the station, and the time involved in the station stop could thus be avoided. There is always a feeling of slight nostalgia when some old established facility of the British railway system is ended; and in the case of Beattock one recalls the halcyon days of the old Tinto Express, which started from Moffat, and provided a 'prestige' residential service into Glasgow from Beattock and the stations in upper Clydesdale. It was sufficiently important for a top link express passenger engine to work north from Carlisle to take on its haulage from Beattock, and it was to this end that the 'Cardean' class 4–6–0 No 907 was proceeding on the fateful morning of May 22nd 1915, when she got no farther than Quintinshill.

Theoretically speaking the 10 miles of the Beattock Bank should provide no greater tax to the new '87' class electric locomotives than Grayrigg or Shap are likely to do farther south; but in discussing the design developments of the new locomotives, in Chapter Seven, I have emphasised the attention that has been given to arrangements for sanding. The Beattock Bank, particularly in inclement weather, is a place that can

ARLY DEPARTURES FROM TEAM

bove: The pioneer British main line esels, Nos 10000 and 10001 of the MS climbing Shap with the down Royal Scot', in August 1958 / *Derek ross*

Below: The experimental English Electric Gas Turbine locomotive, GT3, oil fired and with mechanical transmission descending Shap with a Carlisle–Crewe test train in October 1962 / *Derek Cross*

1

2

THE ENGLISH ELECTRIC CLASS 40s AT WORK

Above: At Penrith No 1 Junction, No D 291 on Perth express passes an Ivatt Class '2' 2-6-0, on Blencow–Penrith lime shunt, July 1964 / *Derek Cross*

Below: The down 'Royal Scot', hauled by No D 331, approaching Penrith, April 1966 / *Derek Cross*

KINGMOOR IN APRIL SNOW

Coke train, Tyne Yard to Workington leaving behind Co-Bo diesel No D 5707 / *Derek Cross*

4

TEBAY IN THE 'SIXTIES'

Above: The down 'Royal Scot', hauled by Class '40' No D 299, passes a permanent way train headed by one of the last two 'Royal Scot' 4-6-0s to remain in service, No 46140. July 1965 / *Derek Cross*

Below: In September 1963, the morning Crewe–Perth express, hauled by No D 331 is passed by a Glasgow–Liverpool express, hauled by D 299 / *Derek Cross*

CLASS 47s IN THE NORTH COUNTRY

5

Above: Birmingham–Edinburgh express near Tebay in July 1967 / *J. H. Cooper-Smith*

Below: In May 1971, the 15.55 Carlisle—Euston is leaving Oxenholme hauled by No 1825 / *J. H. Cooper-Smith*

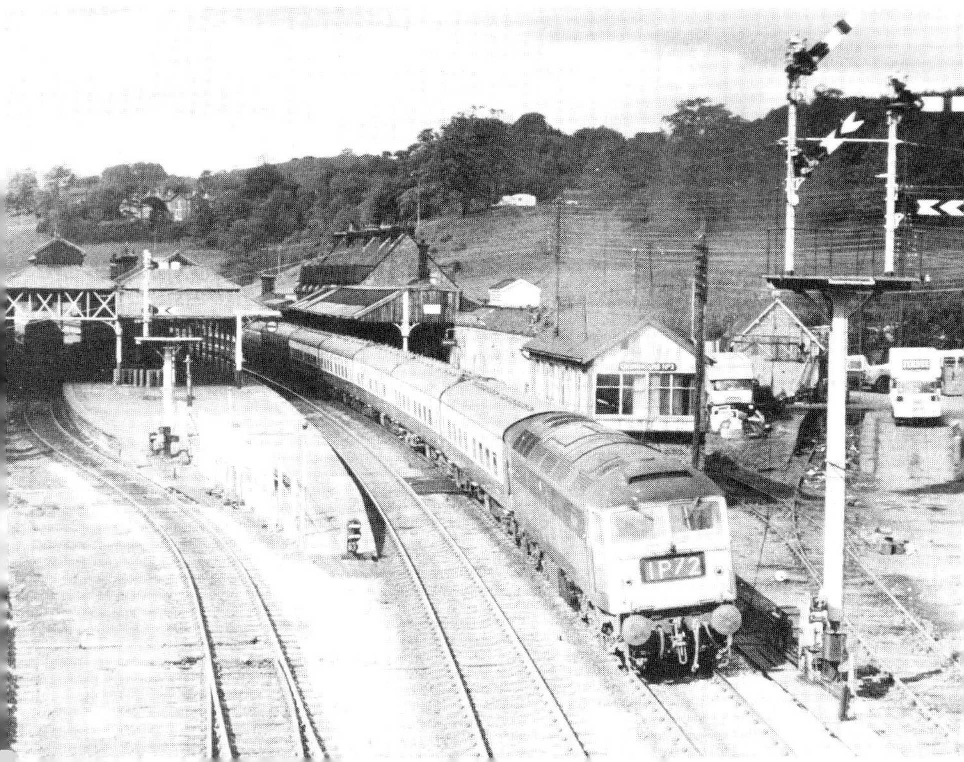

6

CLASS 40s NORTH OF CARLISLE

Above: The down 'Royal Scot' (loco D 269) passing Kingmoor sheds in April 1965, with much steam still in evidence / *Derek Cross*

Below: In April 1971, 'Nominated' Rootes container train, Solihull to Linwood, at Dentonholme North Junction, hauled by D 278 / *Derek Cros*

HE CLASS 50 DIESELS IN PAIRS

7

bove: The 15.00 Glasgow to Euston, assing Shap Summit, in June 1970. ocos 406 and 421 / *J. H. Cooper-Smith*

Below: Liverpool–Glasgow express entering Carlisle, June 1970, hauled by Nos 444 and 441 / *J. H. Cooper-Smith*

8

PRESTON IN THE TRANSITION STAGE

Above: A Class '50', No D 402, leaving with a London–Heysham Mail and Parcels train in May 1968 / *Derek Cross*

Below: Before the accelerations: the down 'Royal Scot', passing through fc the north, with a single Class '50', No D 424, in May 1968 / *Derek Cross*

9

CHANGES ON ALL SIDES!

In May 1970, with track improvements in evidence and the M6 motorway under construction, the morning Liverpool–Glasgow express approaches Tebay, hauled by Class '50' locomotives D 413 and D 433 / *M. S. Welch*

1S63

THE PICTURESQUE WAY NORTH

Far left, top: The up 'Royal Scot' threads the curves between Low Gill and Grayrigg, in June 1971, headed by two Class '50' diesels / *D. E. Canning*

Far left, bottom: The 12.05 Euston to Perth, climbing Beattock bank, just passed Greskine signal box, hauled by a Class '47' No 1849 in May 1967 / *John M. Boyes*

PREFABRICATING NEW ARCHES AT NEWTON HEATH

Above: Building the framework, and setting the reinforcing rods in position / *British Rlys*

Left: Examining the finished arch / *British Rlys*

12

RECONSTRUCTION OF WHITE HORSE BRIDGE

Above: First stage with southbound carriageway of A6 transferred to new arch, showing also how abutment has been set back / *British Rlys*

Below: View from track level, looking south, showing necessity for moving the western abutment / *British Rlys*

ꞮE-FABRICATED ARCHES
ove: Framing under construction /
itish Rlys

Below: Arrangements for lifting completed arches for skew span / *British Rlys*

14

'KEY' POINTS IN MODERNISATION

Above: Birmingham New Street, South End; electrically hauled express for Euston leaving / *British Rlys*

Below: Preston: a Class '50' locomotiv No 428 arriving with the 11.05 Eusto to Carlisle / *J. H. Cooper-Smith*

;OUTH OF WIGAN

\bove: 'Under the wires' at Varrington, June 1973. Carlisle–Villesden freight hauled by Class '47' Vo 1859, passes the 12.05 Euston to Flasgow: Loco No 430 (Class '50') / *)avid M. Cross*

Below: The up 'Royal Scot' passing Springs Branch Junction, hauled by two Class '50s', Nos 439 and 401 in March 1971 / *J. H. Cooper-Smith*

16 **ROUTE IMPROVEMENT AT CARNFORTH**

Above: Looking south before re-signalling was completed / *British Rlys*

Below: Looking north showing elimination of platforms on main line and signalling modernisation works in progress / *British Rlys*

make complete nonsense of calculations about tractive effort, adhesion factors, horsepower and such like. I have seen a superb steam 'Pacific' engine, manned by one of the keenest and most expert drivers at that shed of experts – Crewe North – reduced to the capacity of a Midland compound, by an early morning mist, that incidentally heralded a gloriously fine summer day! A remnant of former practice has had to be retained on the Beattock Bank, as on other steep inclines on the Scottish part of the new electrified line, in the form of runaway catch points. Not all the freight trains running over the line will be fitted throughout with continuous brakes, and while such trains still need to be operated catch points are essential on the heavy gradients. The implication of their continued existence are discussed in the chapters dealing with signalling.

There are running loops on both up and down sides of the line at Beattock summit, remotely controlled from the new power box at Motherwell, and similar though not quite such extensive facilities at Abington. At Symington however, of the once extensive station and junction layout nothing whatever remains. All the stations in Upper Clydesdale have gone, and the compilers of running logs of the new trains will have to choose mile posts to replace Elvanfoot, Crawford, Abington, Lamington, Symington and Leggatfoot. So we come to Carstairs, the historic starting point of the Caledonian Railway. It is probably the most changed *station* on the West Coast main line north of Weaver Junction – even including Carnforth. The problems facing the engineers in adapting the old location to new requirements were certainly complex, because a station on a curve had to be made suitable for through running at 90mph and at the same time modernised to permit of convenient passenger exchange.

The critical point in the replanning was the connection from the Edinburgh line, coming in on a minimum radius curve to make a facing connection with the up main line. Its position was dictated by the associated need to have a crossover road between the up and the down main lines, so that trains from the Edinburgh line could connect with the down main platforms. The modern practice of avoiding diamond crossings wherever possible reduced facing inter-section with the up main line to the one turn-out. Even so, the existence of the curve, and the need to have super-elevation for 90mph made the turn-out an

Carstairs station: original and present track layouts.

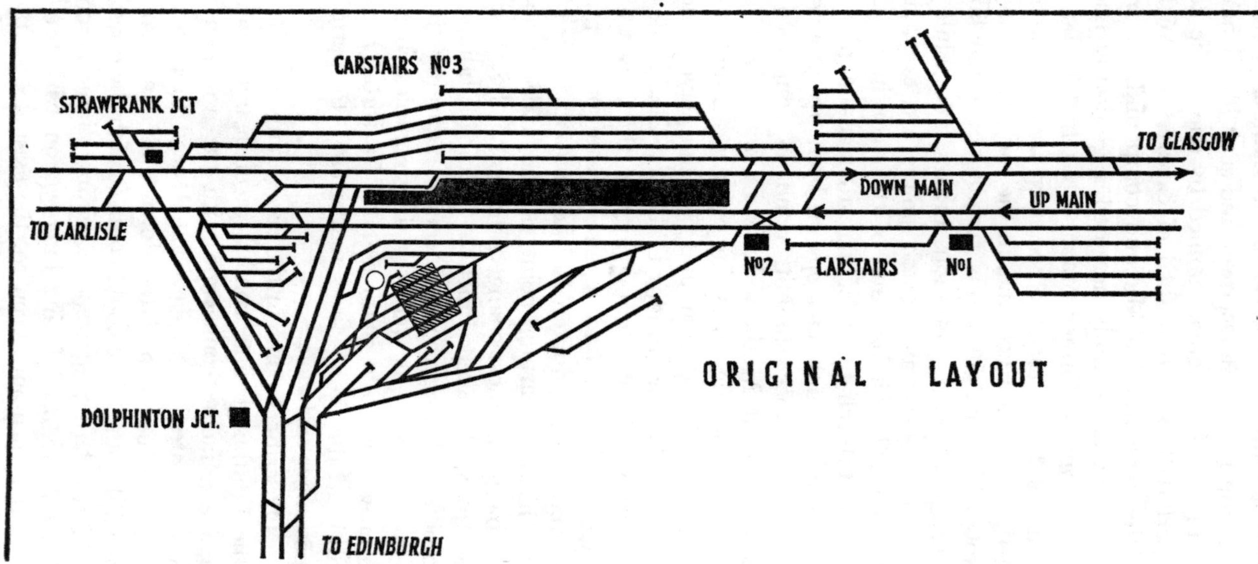

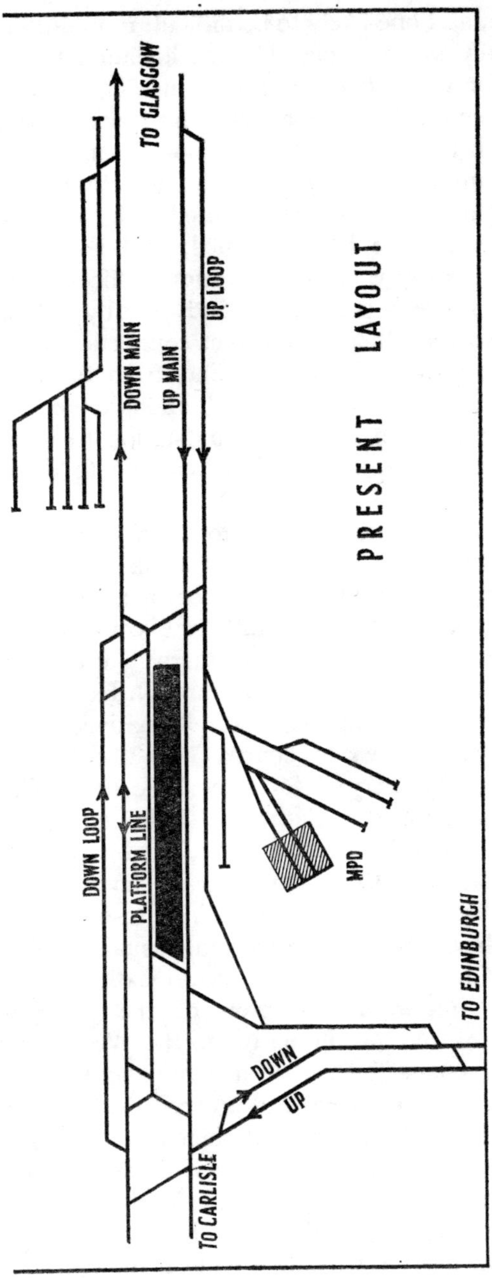
TO GLASGOW
DOWN MAIN
UP MAIN
UP LOOP
PRESENT LAYOUT
DOWN LOOP
PLATFORM LINE
MPD
TO EDINBURGH
DOWN
UP
TO CARLISLE

awkward one to design, and one likely to be difficult to maintain. It was however virtually unavoidable. The modification to the road bed to provide for through running of non-stop trains at 90mph has had another curious side effect. The track needed the deep ballasting to bring it up to modern standards, and as it would have been undesirable to excavate, to obtain the necessary depth the platform faces were raised. The original station buildings however have been retained, and there are steps down from the platforms into the various offices, with continuous railings to prevent passengers inadvertently falling down from one level to the other. The direct connection from the Carlisle direction on to the Edinburgh line, from the one-time Strawfrank Junction, has been retained, though the two purely Edinburgh expresses run into Carstairs station to make a passenger stop as well as to change from electric to diesel traction.

Passing the junction of the short branch to Lanark, and one of the few of the old stations to be retained, Carluke, we come to what could be termed the 'Motherwell complex' of lines. The map on page 142 shows the area involved, covering not only the West Coast main line through Motherwell itself, but also the alternative route from Law Junction through Holytown, and that valuable adjunct to the aggregate of alternative routes, the Hamilton Loop. There has, of course, been an electric service from Glasgow to Motherwell for some little time. This followed the eastern side of the Cathcart Circle to Mount Florida electrified at 6.25kV and then continued over the Kirkhill line to rejoin the West Coast main line at Newton. The conversion of the *west* side of the Cathcart Circle to 25kV has now provided yet another useful alternative route as used on the test runs described in Chapter 11; but the electrification of the Hamilton loop is an important extension of the Glasgow suburban electric network. As an alternative to the West Coast main line it would of course be rather a roundabout route, because a southbound train would have to proceed in the *down* direction through Motherwell station, and then take the right hand fork to regain the normal up direction to Holytown. It will be seen from the map that the spur from Wishaw North Junction on the Holytown line to Shieldmuir Junction is being electrified. On the north line electrification ends at the entrance to Mossend Yard.

Regular travellers by the Caledonian line will have been accustomed to the frequency of speed restrictions, both permanent and temporary in the area north of Carstairs, and the train-logging enthusiasts were inclined to put their stop watches away once a northbound train had slowed down for the curves at Law Junction. But as on the former LNWR line in the industrial districts of South Lancashire so it is also north of Carstairs today. With the numerous track improvements carried out the line maximum speed between Carstairs and Motherwell had been raised to 90mph by April 1973. At that time the upper limit between Motherwell and Glasgow had not been raised above the overall of 70mph at one time imposed throughout Scottish Region; but by the time the electrification is completed this will be raised to 90mph between Motherwell and Newton. There is a restriction to 80mph through Motherwell station but apart from this the only point between the Scottish border and Newton where speed will be permanently restricted to less than 90mph will be in the neighbourhood of Garriongill Junction, where the main line from Law curves round to join the non-electrified Morningside branch, that passes under the Holytown line nearby. The first quarter mile is to 70mph, the second to 60, and the third to 70mph. But the fact that apart from this one locality an express train can run continuously at 90mph to the Motherwell approach, and can regain that speed immediately afterwards is a striking testimony to what has been done to the track in this area. As the map shows clearly there is no lack of industrial connections!

In the burgh of Motherwell there were some interesting cases of bridge reconstruction. In Scotland Merry Street became known as the 'bridge of the 39 problems'. Like many reconstruction jobs on the route it was a case of providing headroom for the overhead electric wires at a location where an old stone arch bridge built some 120 years ago carried a busy highway across the main line in the middle of the town. Merry Street, for such it was named, was widened in 1905, and to render the full width of the load-carrying arch available for vehicular traffic pedestrian walkways on steel sections were added on each side. But with the gradual development of municipal and other public services the bridge was eventually carrying no fewer than thirty-nine main connections of one kind or another. These were in seven different categories, thus:

gas mains 3
water mains 3
Post Office ducts 5
electricity supply lines 19
street lighting cables 5
television relay cables 3

And one sewer made up the grand total of thirty-nine. The job was made more difficult because of the cramped site in the middle of the town which prevented cranes from being given room to manoeuvre. The problem was solved by construction of a Bailey Bridge, approached from a temporarily raised road level, which allowed road traffic to continue while the old arch below was demolished and new abutments built. In the meantime the new pre-stressed concrete bridge deck was constructed beneath the Bailey Bridge, which continued to carry the road traffic until the new bridge was completed.

There was another awkward bridge reconstruction in Motherwell only a few hundred yards northwards down the line from Merry Street. The location diagram reproduced herewith shows how Muir Street, running parallel to the track of the Hamilton branch, crosses the main line on the skew in the middle of the station. In this case the main girders, 10ft deep and of massive plate web construction, each had a clear span of more than 70ft while the overall width of the bridge structure at right angles to the roadway was 43ft. The adjustment to secure the additional clearance for the overhead electric wires was obtained by the process of jacking up, but as can well be imagined it was no small weight that had to be dealt with. The accompanying drawing shows how jacking brackets were fitted on to the ends of the main girders, so that 300-ton hydraulic jacks could be applied to lift the bridge bodily to the required additional height.

As the line approaches Glasgow so the civil engineering works became more intricate. Between Newton and Rutherglen Junction the main line runs through a succession of cuttings in a residential area, where there are a number of overbridges. It was the same problem over again – insufficient head room for the overhead wires. Following precedent, the bridges could have been raised, piecemeal, closing one half of the roadway while the fine old stone arches were dismantled, and the new ones built to the increased headroom required for the wires. In this

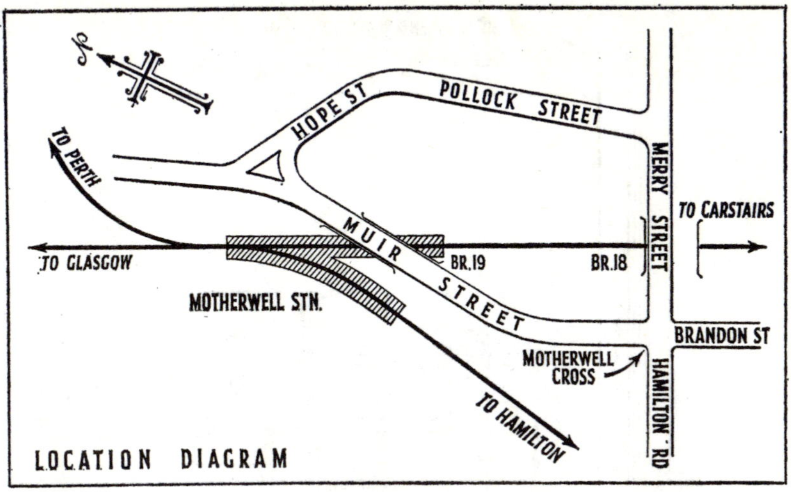

Motherwell Muir Street: location of bridge over station.

instance however an interesting alternative was decided upon, namely to deepen the cuttings, for a distance of about 1,000 yards. Although, even in pre-electrification days, this was a fairly busy line for commuter traffic there was the period of the Glasgow Fair Holiday when this traffic is at its lightest. The time had the advantage too that there was a reasonable chance of good summer weather, and so the bold step was taken of closing the line altogether, and giving the tractor-shovels 'absolute possession'. The old track was lifted; the old track foundations were scraped out, and the level deepened. For a few days the line looked like a 'railway conversionists' dream, with no track in sight, and lorries, tractors and such like producing a beautifully smooth level road bed through the cuttings. In the meantime of course all railway traffic was routed via Mount Florida and Kirkhill. The pictures on pages 21 and 22 of the illustrations show the unusual appearance of the Cambuslang cuttings during this operation, and also a fine impression of the stone overbridges which it would otherwise have been necessary to demolish.

The passenger stations have been retained at Uddingston, Newton, and Cambuslang, and then after emerging at the western end of the cuttings there is the interesting rearrangement of the tracks inwards from Rutherglen Junction.

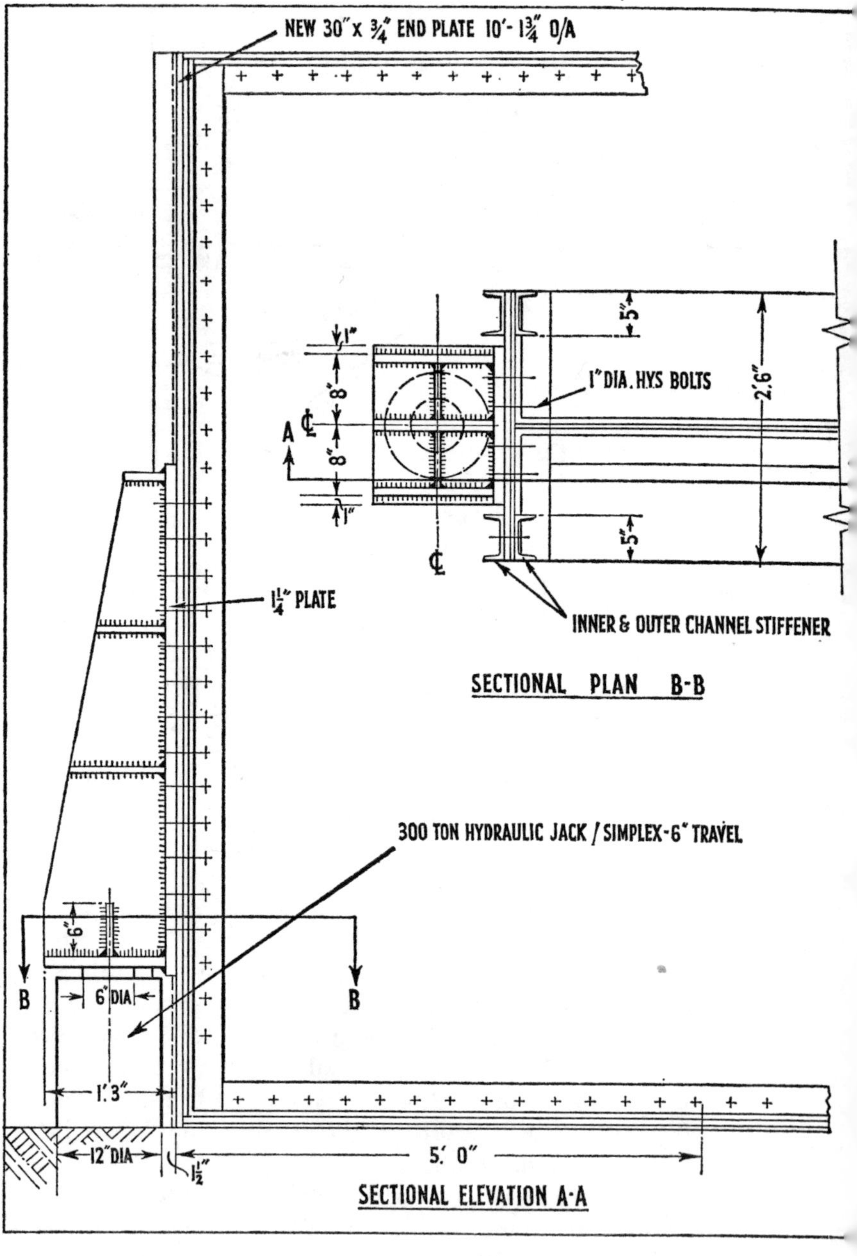

Motherwell Muir Street bridge: detail of jacking brackets and additions to main girders.

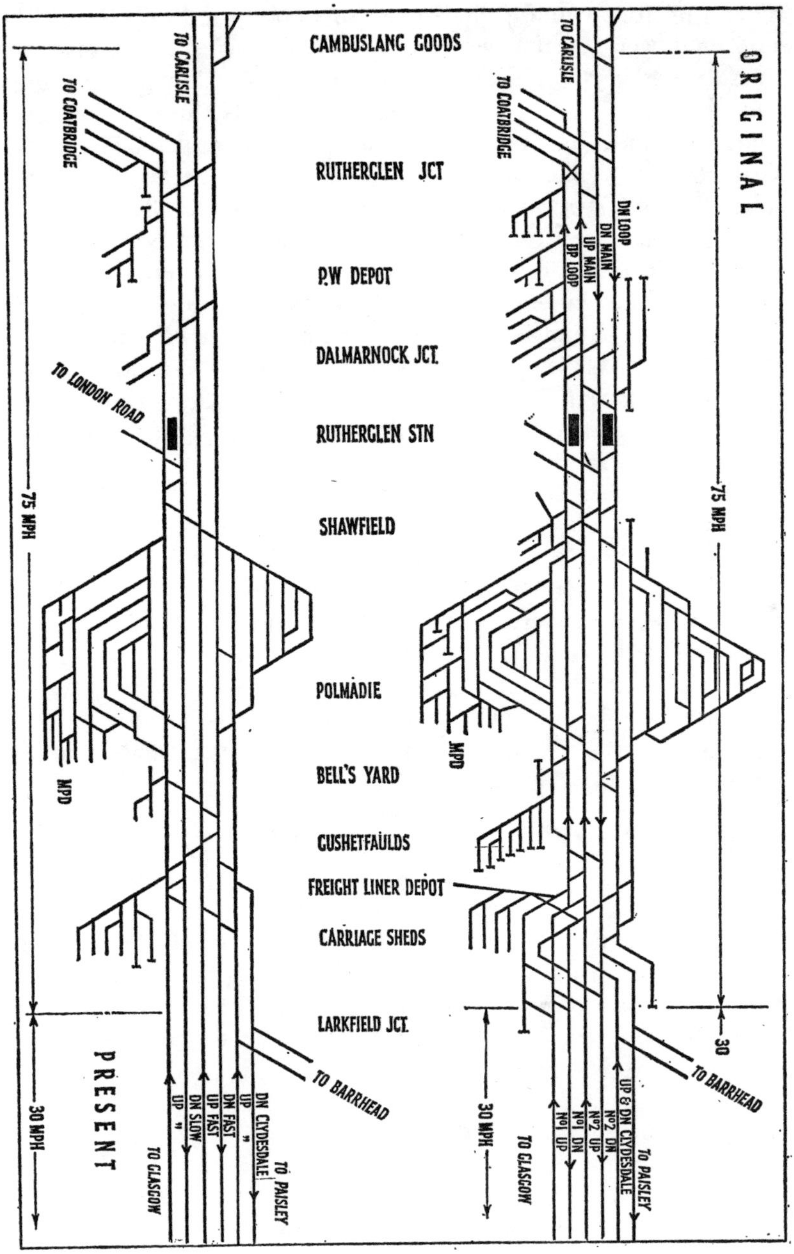

Cambuslang–Larkfield track rationalisation; original and present arrangements.

There are four running lines from this point, and originally the fast lines were in the centre, with platform faces for all four lines at Rutherglen station. This has now been changed to bring the two fast lines together on the south side, and to provide platforms only on the slow lines at Rutherglen. Then, at Gushetfaulds Junction there begins the central Glasgow 'complex' of the former LMSR lines south of the Clyde. While this is certainly not quite so complicated as it was there is still a fairly intricate pattern, as indicated on the map on page 145. The only appreciable change from former days is the elimination of St Enoch passenger station. The former G&SW line across the Clyde, to College Goods station, and its connection to the old North British line is still in use, but of more concern to the electrification of the West Coast main line, apart from the accelerated express passenger services into Glasgow is the freight traffic from General Terminus, where there is a heavy import of iron ore. This is destined for Ravenscraig steel works, Motherwell, and behind this is a tale to be told.

The natural route for this traffic would be through West Street, as can be seen on the map, and on to the West Coast main line at Gushetfaulds Junction; but in the Eglinton Street, Gushetfaulds, West Street area there is some complicated engineering. The line from Terminus Junction to Gushetfaulds runs not only beneath the main passenger line from Central station to the G&SW main line, and to the Cathcart Circle and the Kirkhill line, and additionally beneath the G&SW line from College Goods, but also under a perfect labyrinth of main highways; and just when the resources of Scottish Region were being extended by all the incidental effects of the changeover to electric traction on the main line they were unlucky enough to sustain a partial collapse of the 120-year-old West Street tunnel, which has involved closing that part of the line entirely during repairs. In this difficult period the heavy iron ore trains from General Terminus, bound for Ravenscraig, had to be taken southwards over the Muirhouse spur to Strathbungo Junction, had their direction reversed there, and hauled back to Langside Junction, and thence round the spur to Gushetfaulds. It was a tedious and time-consuming operation that Scottish Region could well have done without in the changeover period!

But West Street was far from being the only civil engineering headache in this area. From Gushetfaulds Junction the quadruple tracks of the West Coast main line curve round northward through the Eglinton Street tunnels before rising to the level necessary to cross the viaduct over the Clyde and into the Central station. In those twin tunnels, with two tracks in each, the clearance was as insufficient for the overhead wires as in so many other locations north of Weaver Junction. In view of the intricate pattern of highways above, not to mention many buildings, raising the roof of the tunnels was out of the question; deepening as in the Cambuslang cuttings would have been a very difficult job; but fortunately a novel solution was available to the engineers of Scottish Region. This is the so-called 'slab track', with which British Railways have been experimenting for about five years. A trial installation is in service between Nottingham and Grantham. It is being used on various railways abroad, including sections of the Shinkansen high speed railways in Japan. Its immense attraction so far as these Glasgow tunnels are concerned is the reduction in depth it makes possible. The Eglinton Street tunnels, like the unfortunate neighbouring one at West Street had concrete inverts under the ballast, and the accompanying drawings show how the conventional form of permanent way was modified to incorporate the new technique.

The first task was to remove the rails, the old ballast, and top 6in off the existing invert before a specially adapted concrete paver moved into lay the new track. At Eglinton Street the tunnel that will eventually carry the 'slow' lines was tackled first, and completely closed to traffic. From the 'paver', which is a unit similar to road laying machines, wet concrete is fed into the front, and as the machine moves forward the concrete is profiled to the required shape, proceeding forward at the rate of about 1 yard per minute. On the top of this base which is about 12in thick, accurately aligned profiles are laid on which the running rails are set. Quite apart from the advantages it afforded in the reduction of height, and thus solving the headroom problem for the overhead electric wires, it is generally expected that slab track will probably result in very much lower maintenance costs. It has been stated that the 'life expectancy' will be about fifty years. Each of the Eglinton Street tunnels was closed for about four months during which time the new track was installed. This track was of particular interest to me personally, because not long before visiting Glasgow during the work on the Eglinton Street 'slow lines' tunnel I had been in

Slab Track in Eglinton Street No 2 tunnel: typical cross section.

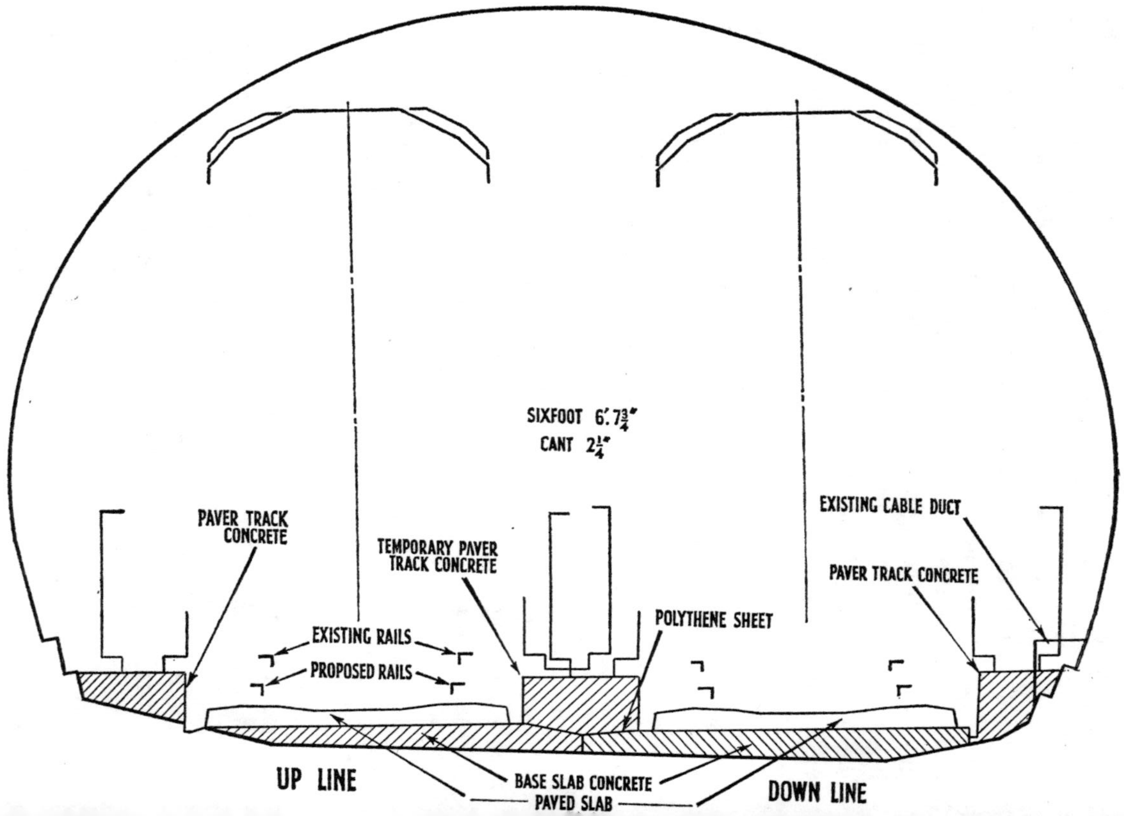

Japan and travelled over parts of the Shinkansen line, at 130mph, on sections of track laid with slab track, in tunnels and on viaducts.

And so, on emerging from the Eglinton Street tunnels, one comes almost to the end of the latest section of main line electrification in Great Britain. The remodelling of the Central station itself took place in readiness for the electrification of the Clyde Coast lines, and of the Cathcart Circle in 1960, when the oldest section of the bridge over the River Clyde was dismantled, and the tracks remodelled so that the entire traffic could be handled over the seven tracks of the newer part of the bridge. Since then, consequent upon the closing of St Enoch station the traffic from the former G&SW lines has been added. There have been some notable changes in signalling to assist in operating facilities at 'Central' to cope with this extra work load, which includes a few trains from the north that are routed into 'Central' rather than Queen Street in order to provide convenient connections to trains for the south.

Glasgow Central may be a terminus station, but one can hardly imagine, or hope that it may be the termination of electric traction developments on the Anglo-Scottish routes. Already there is discussion on possibilities of electrifying the East Coast Route from Kings Cross to Edinburgh; and then surely it will be a natural corollary to electrify also the connecting link between Glasgow and Edinburgh and the line from Edinburgh to Carstairs. In the meantime, engineering-wise, there has been much development in providing for implementation of the present scheme, and it is now time to look at the new equipment in detail.

6: *OVERHEAD LINES AND POWER SUPPLY*

The electrical engineers who have the task of designing and installing that part of the new railway that is covered by the title heading of this chapter have at the same time the most unglamorous and unspectacular part of the whole project. They are assailed by the conservationists for 'disfiguring' the countryside with the supports and overhead wires necessary for the traction supply, while enthusiasts who will log in meticulous detail the running of the electric trains, even to noting the minimal decreases in speed when a neutral section is passed, will probably not give much thought, even if any, to the highly sophisticated business of providing power on the line. In comparing the past interests of steam locomotives' performance particularly on such a route as the West Coast main line north of Carnforth, it is sometimes inferred that electric trains always have an unlimited supply of power at their disposal, through being able to take power *ad lib* 'from the grid', as one commentator has expressed it. It is only when one learns, for example, that acceleration of service on certain electrified main lines in France is held up until further electric supply feeding stations have been installed, that there is realisation of more to electric traction than connecting a locomotive pantograph to the overhead line, and so *ipso facto* it was assumed, to the grid.

In the case of the Weaver Junction–Glasgow project the electrical design engineers had a particularly difficult task. They had to design for the greatest economy, using techniques developed from experience with the earlier stages of 25kV electrification in Great Britain. This applied not only to the actual 'hardware', the overhead line supports and suspension, the switchgear, and the lineside housings, but also in the disposition of the feeder stations and track sectioning cabins along the line. In my earlier book, *Britain's New Railway* I dealt at some length with the general principles of feeding the overhead lines, so that no detailed reference to it is necessary here; but on the Weaver Junction–Glasgow project the need for economy in first cost was so great that consummate skill was needed in designing the system as a whole in order to use the minimum of equipment. In this of course the requirements of power could be determined only by close reference to the demands of the timetable.

This situation, at the very outset, poses an almost fundamental difficulty, in that the operating department, equally with the engineers under pressure to exercise the greatest economy, were required to draft their timetable at the time the system of electrical supply was being designed – that is some four years before one could hope to bring the service into operation. The pattern of railway traffic flows can change very quickly, and what might have seemed entirely adequate four or five years ago might not meet the demands of today. I have mentioned earlier in this book how part of the economic justification for the electrification project was based on the prospect of closing a major part of the Settle and Carlisle line altogether and singling the entire G&SW line in Scotland, between Gretna and Kilmarnock. I have told also how, happily, the traffic situations has already developed in such a way as to postpone both these proposals indefinitely. Nevertheless the design of an electrification system, using the word system in this case to refer to the overall layout of the entire plant for feeding power on to the overhead lines, is based fundamentally upon an accurate assessment of train performance and the energy likely to be consumed in meeting the demands of the timetable. Then the available supplies of power 'from the grid' need to be studied, and consideration given to the best arrangements for locating feeder stations to the line.

On a route like the West Coast main line, and particularly that section of it north of Carnforth the incidence of heavy gradients is an important factor. On the other hand where the ascending road is making heavy demands for power trains in the opposite direction will be coasting. Furthermore there is a considerable variation in the type of train expected to be hauled over this route, ranging from a top-class day Anglo-Scottish express of some 440 trailing tons, to a 'nominated' express freight of some 900 tons; and while the working timetable would undoubtedly space these services out in suitable intervals the modern colour light signalling is designed to afford minimum headway working. Because of unusual circumstances elsewhere on the line one could conceive a situation in which a succession of heavy trains were following each other 'block and block' from Carnforth up to Shap Summit. One could, therefore, have a considerable number of trains making heavy demands on the power supply simultaneously. Strange as it might seem to the person who imagines that unlimited power is available from the mere fact of the pantograph of a locomotive making contact with the overhead wires I have myself experienced a case, not in Great Britain, wherein a very famous express train was brought to a dead stand because of temporary lack of power on the line.

In February 1972 a very interesting paper was presented to the Institution of Electrical Engineers by Messrs E. Claxton and B. Sandham, of the British Railways Board entitled: "System design for 50Hz a.c. electrification", in which two diagrams were shown illustrating the simulated loading of the overhead lines between Garstang and Penrith arising from a normal flow of traffic. There are feeder stations at Catteral, near Garstang, at Natland, between Milnthorpe and Oxenholme and at Penrith, with Intermediate track sectioning cabins at Bay Horse, Hest Bank, Burton and Holme, Grayrigg, Tebay and Harrison's Siding. The traffic assumed to be flowing was as follows:

DOWN LINE

Train ref	*Location*	*Class of train*	*Load tons*	*Speed mph**	*Con-troller notch*
A	Bay Horse	Motorail	600	70	28
B	Hest Bank	Passenger	600	70	coasting
C	Hincaster Jc Site	Nominated freight	850	70	36
D	Hay Fell	Motorail	600	70	36
E	Just over Shap Summit	Passenger	600	70	coasting
F	Bessec Ghyll	Parcels	445	70	coasting
G	Eamont Jc	Passenger	445	70	coasting

* under normal feeding conditions

UP LINE

Train ref	*Location*	*Class of train*	*Load tons*	*Speed mph**	*Controller notch*
H	Clifton	Passenger	600	69	36
J	Approaching Shap Summit	Motorail	600	67½	38
K	Tebay	Passenger	445	70	coasting
L	Near Oxenholme	Motorail	600	70	coasting
M	Near Milnthorpe	Passenger	600	70	coasting
N	Just south of Lancaster	Passenger	600	63	38

The running conditions set out in this simulated example refer to the night service. In the day time express passenger trains have to run at or near the line maximum speeds to keep time. But the interesting part of this particular exercise is that diagrams showed the currents in the line in two different conditions of feeding at the particular moment when the trains referred to in the foregoing tables were at the locations specified. The first diagram shows the currents being taken by the locomotives under normal feeding conditions, and the corresponding currents in the line, while the second shows what could be expected if, in exceptional circumstances the Natland feeding station was not operating, and emergency feeding was in action from Catteral and Penrith only. The anticipated effect on the uphill speeds of the trains is interesting. The two down trains climbing the Grayrigg bank would have their speeds reduced from 70mph to 62½mph. The up sleeper car taken near Clifton would be doing 65mph instead of 69 and the motorail nearing Shap Summit 62 instead of 67½mph. The 600-ton sleeper climbing the 1 in 98 gradient to Lancaster 'Old Junction' site would be making just 60mph instead of 62½ mph. In view of all the factors involved one can readily agree with the authors of this particular paper that the placing of feeder stations and

* under normal feeding conditions

of the track sectioning cabins, can be as much an art as a science. So far as loading on the lines is concerned one may also reflect upon the fact that of the thirteen trains in the foregoing 'instant' example, only six were taking power from the line. One could envisage times when the demand for power would be much heavier.

Many factors are involved in making the choice for the feeder station sites. Other things being equal there is an advantage in locating feeder stations at major junctions, but nowadays this is not an overriding consideration. The situation has become less critical in one important respect since the construction of the original 25kV electrification south of Manchester and Liverpool. In Great Britain the construction of the 'supergrid' at 275kV and 400kV has led to what might be termed the 'degrading' of 132kV lines. The supply authorities are now less restrictive in allowing connections to be made to such lines, while at Elvanfoot feeder station, north of Beattock Summit, for the first time in Great Britain 25kV traction supplies are derived from the 275kV line. The availability of suitable supply points for railway electrification has noticeably increased. Because of this it has been possible over the last ten years to reduce on an average, the distance between the supply point and the railway feeder station, and to be able to locate the latter more advantageously, so far as the railway is concerned. The fact that much of the newly electrified line runs through sparsely populated mountain country has not been a disadvantage, because the grid lines follow approximately the same route.

A very important development in connection with the apparatus design for the trackside switching stations has taken place since the earlier scheme of electrification was complete. The original type of brick-built trackside building was becoming an expensive luxury, and a new type of completely weatherproof steel cabinet was developed, and first used on the Glasgow–Gourock–Wemyss Bay line. But far more important even than the type of housing is the new form of circuit breaker installed in the trackside switching stations of the West Coast main line. For some time prior to the authorisation of the Weaver Junction–Glasgow electrification scheme British Railways had been interested in the application of the vacuum interrupter to circuit breaker operation, and in 1968 a prototype version was installed at a location known to be subject to frequent high intensity faults. As a precaution it was connected in series with one of the existing circuit breakers of the oil insulated type, but with the protection so timed as to give the prototype vacuum interrupter first opportunity to clear the faults. It proved extremely successful, and as it offered the advantage of considerable economy in first cost it was adopted as standard for the new electrification scheme.

The process of opening the circuit under a high degree of vacuum enables a much shorter stroke to be used than with the conventional oil immersed circuit breaker, and this in turn has permitted of a considerable simplification of the actuating mechanism. This, together with the elimination of oil has greatly reduced maintenance. The accompanying drawing shows the general layout. Two vacuum interrupters mounted vertically, and shown on the right of the drawing are connected in series, with the live drive linkage between them. Push-pull motion is

Vacuum Interrupter—general layout.

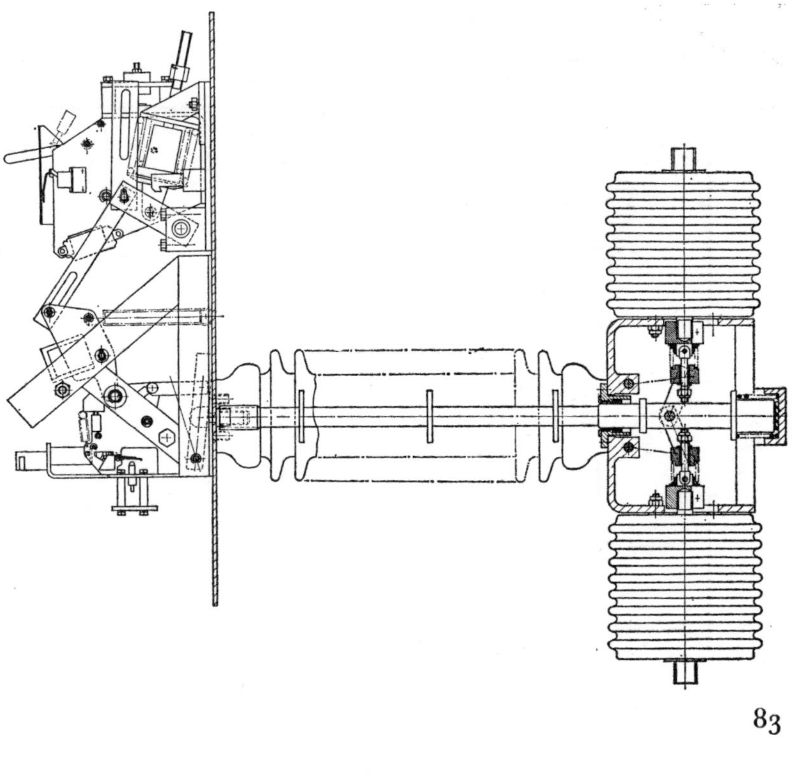

transmitted from a spring closing mechanism by a glass-fibre rod, actuated by a motor operated mechanism of well proved design. There is a hand closing lever to be used for maintenance purposes. A second cross-sectional drawing shows the arrangement of the circuit breaker in the lineside hut, and this demonstrates some further interesting features. The structure has through roof bushings leading to bare overhead connections to the track catenaries. This in itself resulted in a considerable saving in first cost, by eliminating the use of insulated cables.

The use of vacuum interrupters instead of oil immersed circuit breakers made possible another economy in design. With the latter it was normal practice to install isolaters on either side; but with vacuum interrupters these could be omitted. Taking the design all-in-all, with steel housing instead of brick, and with the various advantages and savings in equipment from the use of vacuum interrupters, these self-contained switching stations cost no more, in pounds sterling, than the original brick-housed

Circuit breaker in lineside hut.

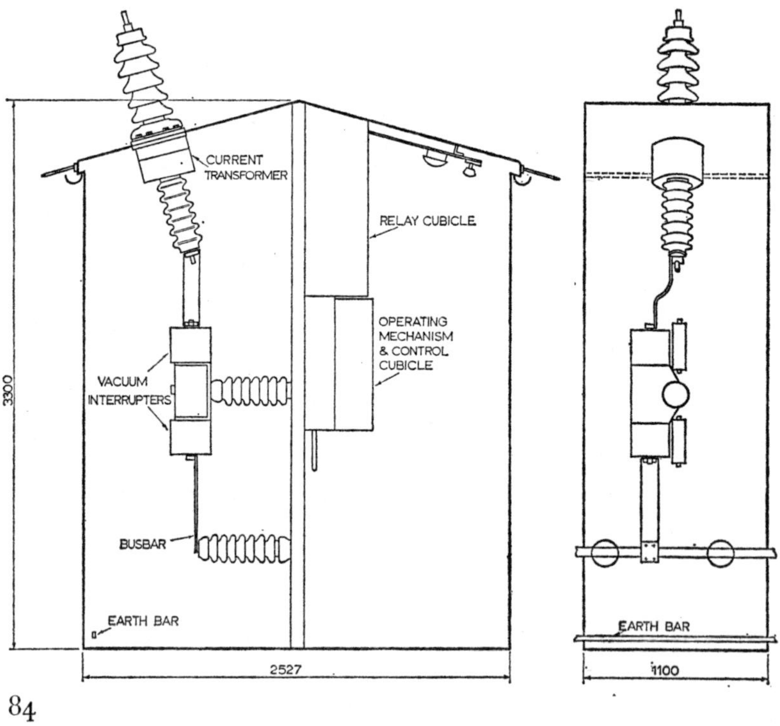

units on the Euston–Liverpool–Manchester scheme, despite the steeply escalating basic costs that have taken place in the intervening eight or ten years. This constitutes a highly praiseworthy example of advanced engineering techniques being used to keep down the actual cost of railway electrification work.

So far as the actual huts are concerned they are built as sectional units, each containing one circuit breaker assembly, and designed so that any number can be bolted together on site. The metal enclosures, as shown in cross-sectional drawing includes a busbar chamber, switchgear and the transformers. A sheet steel wall from roof apex to floor divides the live high voltage busbar and switchgear housing from the operating corridor. Each unit is equipped with a relay panel above the circuit breaker operating mechanism. To sum up, each of the twenty-six self-contained switching stations on the Weaver Junction–Glasgow electrification contains:

1. The high voltage feeder equipments, which are sectionalised where necessary.
2. Local and remote change-over controls.
3. Fault protection equipment of the latest high-speed type with high accuracy of measurement.

In addition to the above there is the supervisory remote control equipment, which requires special mention.

Responsibility for the control of power supply will be shared by the existing electric power control rooms at Crewe and Cathcart, by the installation of electronic remote control equipment of the latest type. The new installation covers the 220 miles of line between Acton Grange (where the line crosses the Manchester Ship Canal) and Law Junction. The point of division between the areas of responsibility of the two control rooms is at Tebay. The entire power supply situation on the line is continuously monitored, by an electronic 'scanning' system. To reduce the time between successive scans of any one outstation it is arranged that the control centre will only transmit the required outstations 'address' (each outstation having a unique address code). The outstation on successfully decoding its own address will reply to the control centre with its own address. On receiving this message the control centre then automatically moves to the next address. However, if the plant has changed state in any outstation since it was last addressed, the outstation instead of just sending its address back will give a full reply giving the state of all plant in the outstation. To back up this it is arranged that after every cycle of the outstations the control will pick the first two outstations and demand the full reply. After the second cycle the control will pick the third and fourth outstations and so on. This will pick up any change of state that may have been missed on normal routine scanning. This information is duly registered on the large scale mosaic diagram that takes up a whole wall in the Control Room.

The entire situation on the line is under the constant scrutiny of the controllers at Crewe and Cathcart. Power supply voltages at any feeder station are constantly monitored and corrective action can be taken by the power supply authorities. Constant liaison is maintained with the grid control staff of the Central Electricity Generating Board, and the South of Scotland Electricity Board.

In my earlier book the development of the design of the contact equipment and its support was described to the time of the opening of the line into Euston in 1966. This used the Mark I compound catenary, as shown in the accompanying drawing. This form was used for all lines with a maximum permitted speed of 100mph brought into service before 1966. But although a high degree of success has been attained with this design the practice of current collection from an overhead line admits of no finality, and development continued. In my earlier book I described the experiments made to secure good current collection where the line passed under low bridges, and subsequent high speed tests showed the effects of varying heights of contact wire between supports. It was shown that a wire that was higher in mid span than at the supporters – 'hogged' as it is termed – gave bad current collection even at quite moderate speeds. On the other hand a sagged contact wire gave improved performance. A study, with a scale model, of the effects of varying dropper spacing, wire tension, and contact-wire sag led to the

Compound-catenary equipment Mark I.

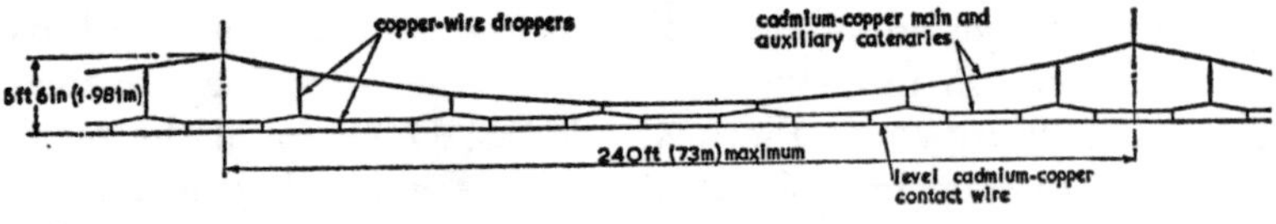

design of a sagged simple catenary equipment that gave promise of good collection at speeds well in excess of 100mph. A prototype installation was built and tests showed clearly that the promise held out by the studies with the model were amply fulfilled.

The sagged simple-catenary equipment was adopted for the Glasgow suburban electrification stage II, that was Glasgow Central–Gourock–Wemyss Bay. This is shown in the accompanying drawing. Comparing this with the Mark I compound arrangement used on the Euston–Liverpool–Manchester scheme, the greater simplicity of design will be immediately noted. The catenary and the contact wire were in hard-drawn copper, with bronze strand droppers. But by the time the West Coast main line scheme was under consideration, and costs were very much to the fore, the high and increasing cost of copper prompted investigation towards the use of aluminium, steel reinforced as an alternative to copper for the catenary. The contact wire would of necessity have to remain in copper. The investigation went into the experience gained with aluminium conductor steel reinforced (a.c.s.r.) conductors in transmission lines, and on other railways, and as a result experimental intallations were made on the Milngavie Branch near Glasgow and at Winsford, some eight miles north of Crewe. Subject to modification of certain details, that resulted in what is known as the Mark IIIA equipment, this form of catenary, with sagged contact wire was adopted for the Weaver Junction–Glasgow scheme. The substitution of a.c.s.r. conductors in the catenary has shown a saving of about £200 a mile over hard drawn copper, and the use of stainless steel droppers gave a further reduction of £110 per single track mile. Furthermore the sagged contact wire has shown considerable improvement in current collection at high speed.

Sagged simple-catenary equipment Mark II.

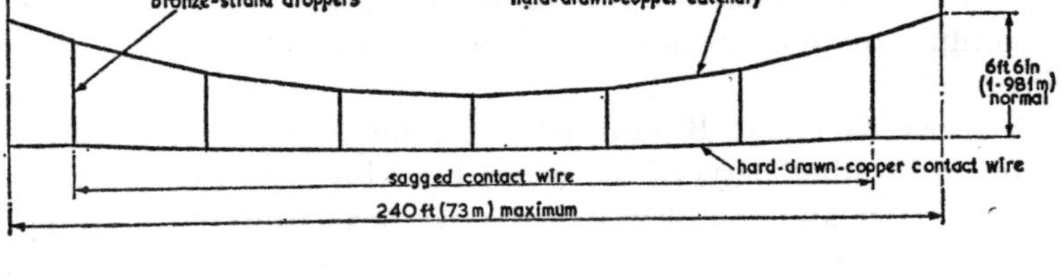

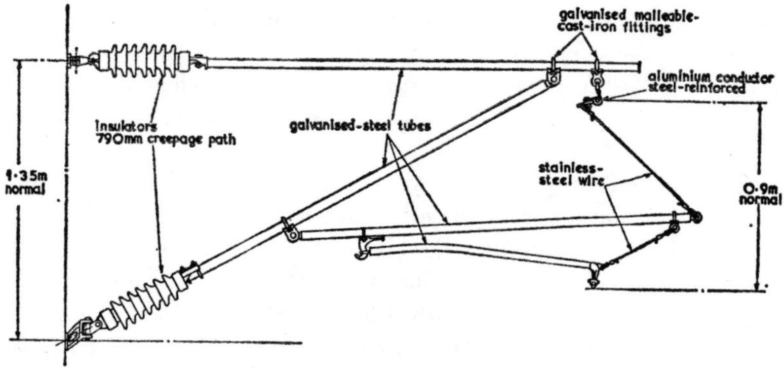

Single-track cantilever Mark IIIA.

There has also been some important development in the methods of support and registration. The single track cantilever support used on the Euston–Liverpool–Manchester lines provided for the compound catenary arrangement shown in the drawing on page 86, but the sagged simple-catenary equipment Mark IIIA has a reduced separation between the catenary and the contact wire, and has a much simpler design of support, as shown in the accompanying drawing, and with a reduction in the height of the supporting masts. The new design makes the overhead system as a whole much less conspicuous in country districts. One of the major criticisms made about the original electrification schemes in the neighbourhood of large stations was the appearance of the railway, with a large number of supporting structures spanning the track. For the original scheme, where multi-track construction was involved massive portal structures were used. Away from junction areas there is a possible advantage, of providing mechanical independence between the equipments on each track. The occasional mishap when a pantograph out of adjustment brings down some of the overhead wires may only affect the particular track itself. It is nevertheless an expensive arrangement. At the time of erection it requires possession on two or more tracks, and at times of repainting of the galvanised steel booms it needs electrical shut down.

Visitors to Great Britain who are familiar with electrified railways in other parts of the world have invariably commented upon the size and complexity of the overhead supports on multi-

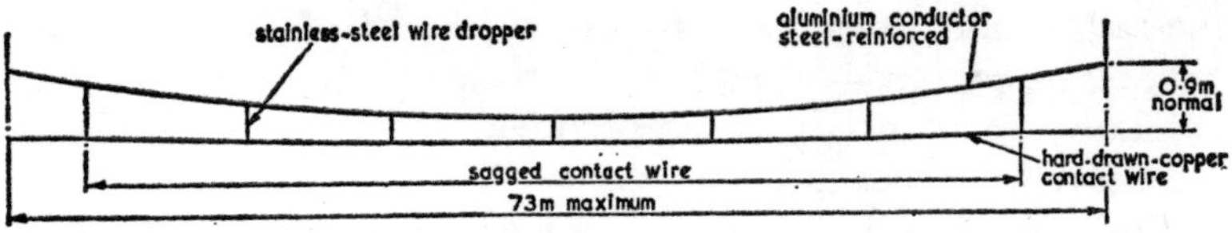

Sagged simple-catenary equipment Mark IIIA.

track sections. From various viewpoints, it was decided to adopt the 'head span' type of construction, and the arrangement of this as applied to a four-track is shown herewith. It will be appreciated that this is a much simpler arrangement than those employed south of Liverpool and Manchester; and that the once-cherished principle of having independent mechanical support for each contact wire has been given up. The only steel 'sections' are those used for the two masts; but even with the great reduction of ironmongery 'in the sky' the head span arrangement has not pleased all conservationists. Bitter complaints from one municipality were received when the standards were first erected. It recalled in my mind the outraged feelings of the citizens of Wilmslow when the new power signal box was erected at an early stage in the Manchester–Crewe scheme. Conservationists apart, the 'new look', north of Preston in particular, is really quite unobtrusive.

There have been some interesting developments so far as construction of the overhead line is concerned. Coupled with the need to exercise every possible economy in carrying out the work with the increasingly high cost of labour in Great Britain; there was consequently the need to mechanise as much of the installation work as possible. One of the operations most suitable for mechanisation has been found to be the constructing and installing of the concrete foundations for the supporting structures. In the work farther south power driven auger borers were extensively used; but so far as the North Country was concerned they had several disadvantages, in that they are not very effective either in very hard, or very soft ground, and that they can produce only circular holes. On the West Coast main line some types of foundation needed to be large and rectangular, and generally speaking the use of hydraulically operated grabs has proved very successful. The photographs on page 29 of the illustrations provides a vivid impression of one of these machines in action. A particular advantage of the rail-mounted type of grab in use is that the hydraulic system has been adapted to propel the wagon, thus avoiding the constant attendance of a locomotive to position it for each successive hole to be dug.

The procedure for concrete mixing was also changed on the sections south of the Border. This was to use a train of wagons each carrying a standard diesel driven drum mixer. Because cement must be kept dry until it is mixed, separate containers are carried on a separate wagon, which is permanently coupled to the one carrying the mixer. These separate containers are raised hydraulically as shown on page 30 of the illustrations to discharge the cement into the mixing drum when the train arrives on site. Sand and aggregate are loaded into the mixers, in accurately weighed quantities, in the depot before the train starts away. This operation is illustrated on page 29 of the illustrations. This procedure has proved very successful, and is more flexible than that used in earlier electrification work, which had only one rather sophisticated mixing plant to a train. If anything went wrong the whole outfit was temporarily inoperative. With the new system, not only are the standard mixers relatively cheap, but with six or more of them in a work train it is not unduly serious if one should break down. One of our pictures on page 30 of the illustrations, shows a concreting train in operation at Shap Summit.

Another novelty concerns the coring of holes in foundations, to receive the masts subsequently planted in. Previously core formers were made of sheet steel, and had to be of considerable depth to reach the bottom of the foundation block. They were expensive; they sometimes collapsed under the pressure of the surrounding concrete when it was poured; and it does not need much to imagine what an inconvenience such a mishap would cause. Furthermore they provided an open hole, and if the mast were not erected soon after this was liable to become filled with water, rubbish and such like. They had to be emptied before the masts were put in. Modern practice is to use solid blocks of expanded polystyrene of the correct shape and length. Being solid they do not collapse under pressure, and completely fill the hole until such time as it is needed for insertion of the mast. Then all that is necessary, in dry conditions is to dissolve the polystyrene with petrol, but in wet conditions a special solvent is necessary.

There is, however, one vital operation for which no method of mechanisation has yet been devised – nor is one likely to be found – and that is the actual erection of the overhead wire. While the running out of the conductors from the cable drums is a mechanical operation, erection of the wires on the overhead support is a highly skilled manual task requiring much painstaking individual adjustment. A wiring train needs absolute possession of the line concerned, and in the previous chapter I have told how Scottish Region speeded up the job south of Carstairs by re-routing the daytime traffic over the G&SW line to allow the wiring trains to have this part of the West Coast main line to themselves. This was not possible south of Carlisle, or north of Carstairs, and it is remarkable that the wiring work has been done on weekdays with so little interruption to the normal flow of traffic. The granting of weekday possessions has been facilitated by the laying in of a number of emergency facing crossover roads, ultimately required for operation of the line, that have enabled single line working to be introduced, where required, without the time-consuming operation of setting back long trains over trailing crossovers.

This is not to say that there have been no appreciable delays. Some travelling experiences in the period of changeover are described in a later chapter, where it will be seen that reaction from a late running southbound express entering upon the intensively used line south of Crewe can extend considerably beyond the running of the train itself. This, however, is the price one has to pay by way of investment for the future when a new railway is being built over the tracks of the old one, and normal traffic is kept running all the time. The incidence of delay was infinitely more severe when the original electrification, south of Crewe, was in course of construction. In the present case the line possessions have been nearly all for the wiring trains. Most of the civil engineering work that has permitted such notable raising of the speed limits had been done previously.

7: ELECTRIC LOCOMOTIVE DEVELOPMENT

Reviewing the experience of the seven years since the Euston–Liverpool–Manchester electrification was brought into full operation there is little doubt that its principal work-horse the Class '86' electric locomotive has proved a remarkable success. The reliability of the service has become something that is nowadays taken almost for granted, and although, somewhat naturally, troubles have developed with the increasing age and very high utilisation of these locomotives, they were, in 1972 averaging more than 25,000 miles per casualty. At the same time in a service operated at such speed and intensity constant study of all aspects of performance is necessary, and as a result of this the design has been subject to some very interesting development. To appreciate the significance of the changes that have been made it is necessary to review something of the past history of the Class '86' locomotives.

It will be recalled that prior to the installation of the original electrification, proposals for high speed 25kV locomotives were called for from a number of manufacturers, who were allowed freedom of design within the general parameters of wheel arrangement, weight, and tractive power. The demand for an 'all-adhesion' locomotive running on two four-wheeled bogies aroused considerable interest and some criticism at the time because in spite of the developments then taking place on the continent of Europe it was generally considered that for a high speed locomotive a pair of leading non-powered wheels was desirable. Although the 'all-adhesion' express locomotive of the Bo+Bo type had originated, in its modern form, with the celebrated Alsthom design for the Bern-Lötschberg-Simplon Railway in Switzerland, on which maximum speeds were necessarily low the type was most successfully developed on the French National Railways both for the 1,500V dc lines, and also for the later 25kV lines. On both groups of lines speeds up a maximum of 90mph were required to be sustained for long distances.

In all, 100 locomotives of varying detailed electrical and mechanical design were put into service on the London Midland Region, and from the most successful features in each of the earlier units the engineers of the LMR developed the standard 'AL6' as it was originally known, and 100 of these locomotives were introduced, with electrical equipment to British Railways requirements built by a number of different manufacturers. The major features of the new standard design were:

1 Axle hung traction motors, without weak field.
2 Alsthom bogies.
3 Silicon rectifiers.
4 High tension tap changing.
5 Rheostatic brake, controlled from the driver's brake valve.
6 Four separate secondary windings, one for each traction motor.

The feature of design that caused some surprise, and some criticism was the use of a traction motor that was axle hung. While this resulted in much simplification mechanically in that there was no need for a flexible drive from the motors to the axles the design involved a considerable amount of unsprung weight. Nevertheless, tests carried out in 1960–1, at speeds up to 100mph indicated that the design should be satisfactory from both the civil and the locomotive engineer's point of view, and so work went ahead with bulk production of the 100 locomotives required for the full Euston–Liverpool–Manchester scheme. In high speed service, in the course of many runs in the locomotive cab I found that there was a fairly consistent bouncing action, to a similar though perhaps more marked extent than I had experienced on the French 25kV Bo+Bo locomotives working between Paris and Amiens. My own personal experience was characteristic of the Class '86' locomotives, which became stigmatised as having bogies that gave 'a poor vertical ride'.

While locomotive enginemen are always ready enough to put up with a degree of rough riding on a machine that is master of its work, as the Class '86' units quickly proved themselves to be, a locomotive with a poor vertical ride is not a good thing to have in continuous high speed service, and this is one of the features of design that was given much re-consideration. Mechanically also, the abandonment of the flexible drive, and the subjecting of the traction motors to all the unsprung effects of direct mounting on the axles, led to poor commutation performance. This was probably accentuated in that so much of the braking was done rheostatically, by electrical interaction, rather than through the simple action of brake blocks on the wheels. From whatever cause the Class '86' locomotives had a shorter life between commutator attention, and thus increased maintenance cost. While the rheostatic braking was a fundamental requirement that was subsequently developed for use in later locomotives the experience of the vertical 'bouncing' has led to a different design of bogie suspension and motor mounting. In the summer of 1969 one of the standard Class '86' locomotives, E 3173, was fitted experimentally with a flexicoil secondary suspension, and tested at speeds up to 125mph. The excellent riding qualities displayed in these tests has shown no signs of deterioration, after nearly 200,000 miles of running.

The desirability of rheostatic braking is mentioned. Renewal of brake blocks was always a major point in the servicing of steam locomotives with either air or vacuum brake, and with the high speed and heavy duty in electric service it was found that locomotives had to return to depot every seven to fourteen days for renewal of brake blocks. With rheostatic braking locomotives could be away from depot for at least fourteen days, thus contributing to their availability in traffic. On the Class '86' locomotives the control of the rheostatic brake was combined with the driver's automatic brake valve. Although there is, on first application, a very brief period when the air brake is in use prior to the rheostatic braking becoming effective, this application on the Class '86' locomotives, was, so far as is known, the first instance anywhere of a rheostatic brake forming the normal service brake of a locomotive. The resultant braking effort is greater than can be obtained from the air brake, except at low speeds, and has proved popular with the men who have to use it.

In actual service the Class '86' locomotives have been exhilarating to those logging the running of express trains in detail. In the early summer of 1973 I had a characteristic run on the 10.05 from Euston – the 'Royal Scot' – on which, not needing the recovery time built into the schedule we passed Colwich 5½min early. The 10.00 train to Manchester must have been running equally well, for throughout the 127 miles from Euston we never sighted any signals except greens! The average speed over the 121·6 miles from Willesden to Colwich was 92mph with only one very brief occasion when the stipulated line maximum speed of 100mph was slightly exceeded. It will be seen from a study of the log that sectional times were closely observed, save from Weedon to Rugby where the availability of 4½min of recovery time enabled us to draw ahead of booked time. The speedometer in the locomotive cab was reading accurately, and frequent checks on the speed by stop watch failed to note any greater excess over the line maximum that 101mph just north of Lichfield.

The speedometer needs a particular mention, because in travelling on, and behind the Class '86' locomotives instances have been noted when the instrument has not been accurate. A recent journey included a case when it was reading 5mph high at 100mph. This meant that the maximum speed on a journey when maximum recovery was needed, on account of checks from engineering slacks on the line, did not exceed 95mph. In consequence we lost about one minute of recovery time every 20 miles, and were not keeping our normal booked point-to-point times. Occasionally, also, there are examples of the other kind, and this probably accounts for certain occasions when accurate observers from the train have noted speeds somewhat in excess of the line maximum. I must add at once that these have been recorded on straight and favourable sections of line, and that the definite speed restrictions such as Leighton Buzzard, Rugby, Atherstone and Stafford have been meticulously observed. The figures about to be quoted are done so in respect of locomotive capacity, in view of the constant references now being made to higher maximum, or indeed of 'cruising' speeds. They are not quoted as examples of everyday running between Euston and Crewe.

LM Region : 10.05 Euston—Crewe
Load: 12 coaches, 402 tons tare, 420 tons full
Locomotive: Class '86' No 3137

Dist miles		*Sch min*	*Actual m s*	*Speed mph*
0·0	Euston	0	0 00	—
2·4	South Hampstead		4 43	—
5·4	Willesden Junction		7 06	—
8·1	Wembley		8 51	96

11·4	Harrow		11 51	100
13·3	Hatch End		12 02	95
17·5	WATFORD JUNCTION	14½	14 40	97
21·0	Kings Langley		16 47	100
24·5	Boxmoor		18 53	100
28·0	Berkhamsted		21 05	90 *
31·7	Tring	23	23 28	95
36·1	Cheddington		26 07	100
40·2	Leighton Buzzard		28 41	79 *
46·7	BLETCHLEY	33½	32 58	100
52·4	Wolverton		36 35	80 *
59·9	*Roade (site)*		41 40	93
62·8	*Blisworth (site)*		43 30	98
69·7	*Weedon*	49	47 53	78 *
75·3	*Welton*		51 44	94
80·3	*Hillmorton*	(4½R)	54 49	100
—			sigs slight	
82·6	RUGBY	62½	57 05	50
88·1	BRINKLOW		61 38	91
91·3	*Shilton*		63 41	100
97·1	NUNEATON	72½	67 12	100
102·4	Atherstone		70 42	69 *
106·5	Polesworth		73 35	98
110·0	TAMWORTH	81	75 45	97/100
116·3	Lichfield		79 41	96/101
124·3	Rugeley		84 35	98
127·1	Colwich	92	86 31	84
—		(3R)	sigs	—
133·6	STAFFORD	100½	**93 00**	—
—			93 10	—
138·9	Norton Bridge	104½	99 08	90
—			pw slack	46 *
147·6	Whitmore		106 46	72
153·1	Betley Road	(4½R)	110 38	92
—			sig stop	(2min)
158·1	CREWE	123½	121 05	

* Speed restrictions

On basis of running to Colwich, Crewe could have been reached in 111min, average speed – 85mph

ARLISLE IN TRANSITION

ove: The south end in July 1967: t to right Class '47' No D 1874 on lasgow–Liverpool express; sleeping r; Class '37' diesel No D 6737; ritannia' class 4.6.2 No 70051 on lasgow–Morecambe express / *Derek oss*

Below: The 'Midland Scot' arriving (April 1971) hauled by two Class '50s', Nos D 400 and D 448 / *Derek Cross*

18

CARSTAIRS—STRAWFRANK JUNCTION

Above: Before route improvement, with a permanent way train shunting in foreground (Clayton diesel No D 8574, and Perth–Euston express approaching, hauled by two Class '50s', D 443 and D 411 / *Derek Cross*

Below: On a Sunday diversion in July, a 'Deltic' hauled Edinburgh–Kings Cross express is entering upon the West Coast main line over the ne track layout / *Derek Cross*

ELTICS ON THE WEST COAST

bove: In November 1970, Aberdeen–
ings Cross express hauled by
o D 9019 passes Beattock Summit /
erek Cross

Below: A Sunday diversion of June 1972, with a Kings Cross—Edinburgh express climbing Beattock Bank: Locomotive No 9020 / *Derek Cross*

1M61
D409

SCENES AT CARSTAIRS
Far left, Top: Before modernisation: Aberdeen–Perth–Euston express approaching (August 1970) hauled by a Class '50' No D 409. / *British Rlys*

Far left, Bottom: The station rebuilt, and 'under the wires'—view looking south / *British Rlys*

RECONSTRUCTION IN SCOTLAND
Above: Bailey bridge (right) used during the rebuilding of Merry Street bridge, Motherwell / *British Rlys*

Left: Lowering the track formation level at Cambuslang / *British Rlys*

ɜft: Work underway on lowering the ackbed on 1,000 yards of railway ɜtween Cambuslang and Newton ations. On the left: 60 feet panels of ack stacked near Cambuslang Station. ı the distance: tractor shovels scrape vay the old track foundations/ *ritish Rlys*

DIESELS AT GLASGOW CENTRAL

Above: A Class '40' No D 364 / *British Rlys*

Below: A Class '47' No D 1623 prior to departure with the up Royal Scot / *British Rlys*

24

ERECTION WORK ON THE WIRING

Above: Girder support being raised: note the prepared foundation in the foreground / *British Rlys*

Below: Winwick Junction, looking north, showing wiring train on up main line / *British Rlys*

IRING ON THE SHAP INCLINE

ove: Wiring train on Birkbeck aduct (north of Tebay) / *British Rlys*

Below: The concreting train at Shap Summit / *British Rlys*

TRACKSIDE SWITCHING STATIONS

Left: Motor operated spring closing mechanism for vacuum circuit breaker. Hand-closing lever in use for maintenance purposes / *GEC Switchgear Ltd*

Below, Left: 300 MVA vacuum circuit breaker, with front wall plate removed for access in maintenance / *GEC Switchgear Ltd*

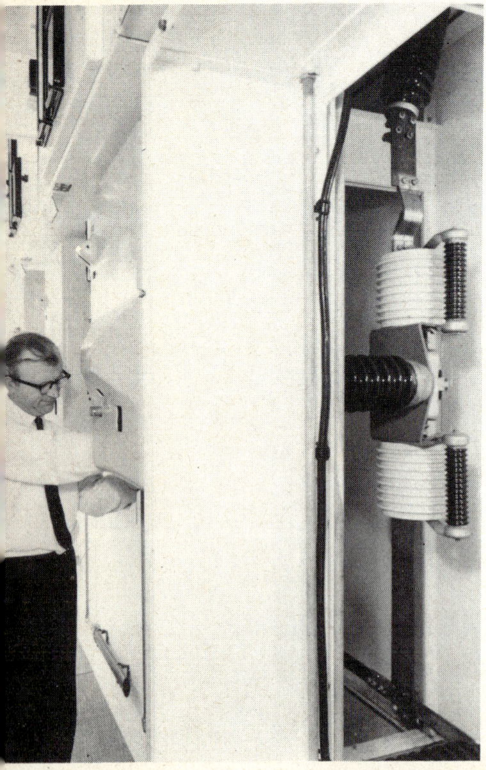

ADJUSTMENT OF OVERHEAD WIRES

Above Right: At Winwick Junction, with rear of express on down line / *British Rlys*

Right: On the Shap Incline, north of Tebay / *British Rlys*

ELECTRIFICATION
EUSTON TO GLASGOW
60

OVERHEAD WIRES IN THE NORTH COUNTRY

Left: Adjustment by ladder-access north of Shap. / *British Rlys*

Below: Mounting of an overhead support in the Lune Valley near Tebay: M6 motorway viaduct in background / *British Rlys*

PREPARING FOR WIRE SUPPORTS

Right: The vertical digger in action / *British Rlys*

Below Right: Concrete pouring at foundation / *British Rlys*

Poclain
KEEP CLEAR
KEEP CLEAR

30 **THE 'CONCRETE' TRAIN**

Above: Hopper in the raised position / *British Rlys*

Below: Preparing to pour at Sha
Summit / *British Rlys*

HE INTRICATE WORK OF
IRING

bove: Adjustments from flat roof of iring train / *British Rlys*

Below: Pre-fabricating jigs for the overhead supports / *British Rlys*

32 **THE CLASS '86' LOCOMOTIVES AT WORK**

Above: No E 3182, leaving Euston with the down 'Royal Scot' / *British Rlys*

Below: No E 3133, at Euston, waiting to depart with the 21.25 for Inverness. / *Anthony A. Vickers*

Some little time ago, one of the Class '86' locomotives hauling an ordinary service train attained maximum speeds of 105mph between Stafford and Rugby, and followed this with two instances of speed slightly in excess of 110mph between Rugby and Watford. What was perhaps more noteworthy was that speed was worked up to 102mph on the rising 1 in 335 gradient between Cheddington and Tring, with a gross trailing load of 325 tons. So far as capacity to run uphill is concerned, the example in the log of my own recent journey on the Royal Scot is perhaps even finer with an acceleration up the 1 in 335 gradient from Wembley to exactly 100mph at Harrow, with a gross trailing load of 420 tons. Nevertheless, the ability of these locomotives to run at speeds considerably above the prescribed line maximum of the present makes all the more essential the modification to the bogie suspension that were successfully tested on locomotive No E 3173.

When the Weaver Junction–Glasgow electrification was first projected it was estimated that no more than thirty additional locomotives would be needed, but this has been increased as explained later, to thirty-six. Of course, with the longer runs that would be electrically hauled an even better utilisation was anticipated. It was originally expected that the new locomotives would be of Class '86', but the problems with the traction motors and the bogies previously mentioned had become severe enough to necessitate re-design of those parts of the locomotives. The experience with the flexicoil suspension was good enough to justify the incorporation as a standard feature of a re-designed bogie. More important still perhaps was the mounting of the motor on the bogie frame, and use of a cardan-shaft drive, through the armature shaft on to an axle-hung gearbox.

Primary suspension of the bogies consists of Alsthom type links guiding independently sprung roller bearings axleboxes. Vertical movements are damped by hydraulic dampers fitted between axleboxes and bogie frame. Bogie traction and braking forces are transmitted to the locomotive body via resilient units bearing upon a king pin attached to the body at the bogie centre position. Secondary suspension, body to bogie, is of the flexicoil type, ie four groups of three springs each symetrically positioned on the transverse bogie centre-line. Vertical, lateral and rotational movements between body and bogie are damped by means of hydraulic dampers. To achieve maximum saving of weight of unsprung items, hollow axles and monobloc road wheels have been used.

The second feature of re-design has been to make less onerous the conditions of motor commutation. Instead of the compromise characteristic of the Class '86' controls, with a large air gap to avoid the introduction of field weakening, the new locomotives are being fitted with two stages of field weakening. The continuous power rating of the locomotives at the wheel tread has been increased from 4,000 to 4,500 horsepower. The electric power circuits in the new locomotives have been kept the same as in Class '86'. The reliability in service in this respect has been remarkable, particularly of the silicon rectifiers, used for providing the direct current for the traction motors. These latter devices have been reported as 100 per cent reliable – a remarkable record – and fully justifying the change from the mercury-arc type of rectifiers incorporated in the earliest electric locomotives of classes 81–84. The new locomotives, Class '87', have been fitted with the simple high-tension tap changing system of motor control as used on the Class '86' locomotives with thirty-eight 'notches' on the driver's controller.

At the present time electric railways in many parts of the world are experimenting, or even standardising thyristor control, instead of the time-honoured system of tap-changing. It is recognised, of course, that this 'solid-state' switching gives smoother notching, and that with further sophistication can be made to include regenerative braking. It is however more expensive, and the advantages are so far not considered enough to justify it financially. Furthermore the reliability of the thirty-eight-notch tap changing arrangement fitted to the Class '86' locomotives is of the order of 100,000hr between failures; and the thyristor system would be required to surpass that before it could be considered justified. A further claim made in respect of thyristor control is that it provides a 25 per cent increase in haulage capacity, and by one form of simple arithmetic this could suggest that a given tonnage of traffic could be handled by fewer locomotives. Construction of a thirty-sixth, Class '87' locomotive has been authorised, and this, for experimental purposes, will have thyristor control. But with a service having the characteristics of the West Coast main line, added to those of the Euston–Birmingham–Liverpool–Manchester services it is not quite so simple as that.

Applying no greater wisdom than that of arithmetic one could convey the same tonnage of traffic by running heavier trains and fewer of them; but this would cut diametrically across the entire philosophy of modern West Coast operating, which is to provide a frequent, regular interval service of trains between all major centres. The night 'sleepers' and the nominated 'company' trains are run to slightly slower scheduled paths than the day express passenger trains, and although conveying heavier loads are at present foreseen to be within the haulage capacity of a single electric locomotive. The possibility that a thyristor controlled locomotive could haul a heavier load is therefore of no more than academic interest on the West Coast main line. Even so, it is interesting to find that the new Class '87' locomotives have been equipped for working multiple, unlike all previous electric locomotives on the London Midland Region, because in climbing Shap and Beattock double-heading will be needed with the heaviest trains.

This does not mean that British Railways are shutting the door against a development in control that is being pursued with vigour and enthusiasm by some overseas railway administrations and manufacturers with lengthy experience of electric traction. Thyristor control is also being experimented with on two multiple unit trains, and the numerous claims of advantage for this form of control, including that of increased haulage capacity, investigated in view of the definite possibility that service speeds of 125 rather than 100mph may be required before very long. It is perhaps not without significance that countries that are adopting thyristor control include some that experience winter weather of a severity rarely known in Great Britain, combined with exceptionally severe gradients. The smoothness of 'notching' with thyristor control could be a factor in reducing the tendency to slip in bad rail conditions. In this connection it is interesting to find that particular attention has been paid to the arrangements for sanding on the new Class '87' locomotives. The sand boxes are integral with the locomotive underframe and the filling points are located in the cab side plate. Ejectors are fitted at the hopper and at the outlet of the delivery pipes to ensure an efficient supply of abrasive fines to the locomotives leading wheels. The locomotives are fitted with an electronic device developed by BR for controlling wheelslip. This compares traction motor currents, and contains a unique feature which provides automatic sensitivity adjustment to take account of varying machine tolerances. The speedometer and traction motor overspeed protection equipment are controlled by means of magnetic probes measuring gearwheel velocity.

There are several other features of the new locomotives that are of interest. Unlike the earlier classes, '81–85', which were vacuum only, and Class '86' which is dual braked, they are equipped only with the air brake. The Euston–Manchester–Liverpool electrification was introduced when there was a large percentage of vacuum fitted stock still in service, but all these earlier classes of locomotive have since been dual fitted. The Class '87' locomotives will be used only on air braked trains, this applying equally to the nominated 'company' freight trains, to 'motorails' and sleeping car services, as to the daytime high speed passenger trains. To ensure a clean environment for the control devices of the inter-coupled air and rheostatic brake, and also that adequate maintenance facilities are available, two 'brake' cubicles have been built into the superstructure of the locomotive. The total weight of the Class '87' locomotive remains the same as that of Class '86', namely 80 tons, and in outward appearance there is not a great deal to distinguish the two classes, except the running numbers. The new locomotives are 87001 to 87035, plus the thyristor controlled 87036, while the older ones are being renumbered to make their classes readily identifiable. The Class '87' locomotives have only two driver's windows, and do not carry the Train Code Indicator.

This question of identification is now important. Originally it was intended, and carried out in daily practice that any electric locomotive was capable of any job on the line. But now a subdivision of Class '86' has been made; 86–1, consisting of locomotives 86,001–048, is in future to be allocated to services not exceeding a speed of 80mph, while 86–2, including those fitted with Class '87' prototype bogies, and re-geared will be used with the new Class '87' on the fastest express passenger services. The situation as regards the electric locomotive fleet generally may now be considered. On various occasions three Class '81' and two Class '82' locomotives had been damaged beyond repair, and at the beginning of the year 1972 the respective strengths of the six original classes was as follows, quoting their original and re-allocated numbers:

ORIGINAL		NEW		
Type	*Numbers*	*Class*	*Numbers*	*Total*
AL1	E 3001–23*	81	81,001–022	22
	E 3096–7			
AL2	E 3046–55†	82	82,001–008	8
AL3	E 3024–35	83	83,001–015	15
	E 3098–3100			
AL4	E 3036–45	84	84,001–010	10
AL5	E 3056–95	85	85,001–040	40

* Three of original locos scrapped. † Two of original locos scrapped.

Additional to the above there are the 100 locomotives of the original Class 'AL6', numbered E 3101 to E 3200, thus making a total of 200 for the complete Euston–Birmingham–Liverpool–Manchester service. Of the originals, Classes '83' and '84' were perhaps the least reliable, and when experience in operating the service showed that it could be worked with less than the 200 locomotives provided these two classes were withdrawn in 1968–9, and put into store pending a decision as to their future. It was perhaps natural that the operating department, without prior experience with this form of motive power, planned for lower levels of availability and utilisation than were actually attained, and thus had something of a surplus of locomotives. It was in the light of this experience, that despite the additional services to the public added in the 1972 summer timetable, only thirty additional locomotives were estimated to be required for the extension of electric service to Glasgow. However construction of a further five was subsequently authorised to replace the three Class '81', and the two Class '82', scrapped as a result of earlier mishaps, plus the thyristor controlled Class '87'.

The seventy locomotives of Classes '81', '82' and '85' have given reasonably good service though the conversion equipment on all three has now been changed to silicon rectifiers. The fifteen locomotives of Class '83', and the ten of Class '84', have been refurbished, and fitted with silicon rectifiers in place of the mercury arc rectifiers and they are being returned to traffic. On completion of the thirty-six new locomotives of Class '87' the West Coast services will have a fleet of 231 electric locomotives available.

Reverting to Class '87', the driving cabs of the locomotives are similar to previous layouts but some changes have been made as a result of engineering and scientific developments. Maximum protection for the crew is afforded by the fitting of Triplex 'High Impact' electrically heated windscreens. These incorporate the new 'Hyviz' clear resistance film for demisting, de-icing and maintenance of the interlayer material temperature for peak impact resistance. Forced ventilation has also been introduced to the cab design and the system automatically controls the cab temperature whilst ensuring changes of fresh air. Added driver comfort results from the provision of *punkah* louvres fitted in the desk console. Trico-Folberth BPM pneumatic windscreen wipers are fitted at the bottom of both windscreens in order to meet modern requirements the motor has two speeds, automatic parking and a travelling water jet for washing purposes. A desk combined control valve operates the complete cleaning system.

The Class '87' locomotives are the first batch to include a new safety feature developed by British Railways. It is a drivers vigilance system comprising a two-position foot pedal, incorporating an electric switch, audible signal device and relay unit. With the master controller in the driving position the pedal must be kept depressed. After 60sec a continuous audible signal commences, and if the pedal is not released and depressed to reset the system an emergency brake application will occur after a further period of 5 to 7sec. The system can be reset at any time during the cycle that is convenient to the driver, and to assist with operation of the driving controls an alternative desk-mounted hand switch is provided. Resetting the standard Automatic Warning System equipment in response to a cautionary signal aspect also resets the time cycle.

Another new feature in the cab is the introduction of a push button operated electro-hydraulic parking brake. This employs an electric motor to drive the hydraulic pump unit located in the body of the locomotive to generate oil pressure in the 'application' pipe line which feeds the hydraulic brake actuators on the bogie. This applies the brakes which are then automatically locked 'on'. To release the parking brake the hydraulic actuators are pressurised via the 'release' pipeline. The hydraulic pump unit is also fitted with a hand operated pump to permit manual operation of the parking brake.

8: RESIGNALLING: WEAVER JUNCTION TO KIRKPATRICK

There is yet no sign of finality in modern British signalling practice. I use the word 'practice' in the sense of how the job is done, rather than of the indications displayed to the driver. For in this latter respect the truly momentous changes of the mid-1920s, when multi-aspect colour light signalling was first installed in the London suburban area of the Southern Railway and in the resignalling of Manchester Victoria and Exchange stations on the LMSR have stood the test of time, and continue to provide a thoroughly adequate system of signalling for the 100mph railways of today. It stands by its very simplicity, and in the down-to-earth logic of the sequence of indications. But the way in which multi-aspect colour light signalling is being used as an indispensable tool of the operating department, and the ever-increasing sophistication of its controls is one of the railway wonders of this present age.

Riding through from Euston to Glasgow in the locomotive cab one would see no difference in signalling principles from start to finish, yet the techniques incorporated in the signal boxes north of Weaver Junction are such as to make great installations of ten years ago, like Manchester (Piccadilly), Euston, and Birmingham (New Street) already look obsolete. In this chapter I am concerned with the new work done in the London Midland Region, and the basic scheme of the signalling between Weaver Junction and Gretna is arresting in itself. When the earliest of the large panel boxes were being installed in Great Britain some thirty-five to forty years ago it was often said that with the machines then in course of development there were no technical obstacles to the infinite enlargement of the control area. The major developments were then on the East Coast Route, and it was said there would then have been no difficulty in operating Waverley station in Edinburgh from a panel at King's Cross. There were then many incidental, economic and psychological reasons why such a feat was not likely to be attempted; but today, if not yet attempting anything quite so spectacular, we are certainly on the threshold.

In the 135 miles between Weaver Junction and the point of demarcation north of Gretna there are only three signal boxes, and each of these controls not only a lengthy mileage on the electrified main line but a plethora of connecting lines leading into the major traffic centres of Warrington, Preston and Carlisle. Before going into any details of the 'how and why' of these new power boxes the operating philosophy of their control areas is worthy of close study. No main line of railway, unless it be an entirely separate line like the New Tokaido Line in Japan, can be considered by itself. However important, however high the priority of its through trains there must be connections, not only carrying local business but providing additional traffic to the main lines. One has only to glance at a signalling plan of the first area on the LM section of the West Coast main line to be commissioned, and note that prior to resignalling there were no fewer than twenty manually worked signal boxes concerned with the through main line traffic in the 25 miles between the northern extremity of the Weaver Junction signal box control area and the southern extremity of Preston.

Some of these signalboxes that have now been replaced were little more than intermediate block posts, with one or more siding connections to the main line, but Acton Grange Junction, Walton, Winwick, Golborne, Springs Branch and Wigan all involved connections to subsidiary main lines at times carrying quite a heavy traffic. In the era of manual block signalling, with signalmen at key junctions such as Acton Grange and Golborne, aware of little more of the traffic situation at any particular moment than what was indicated by the occupancy of their own block instruments, the man on the spot could not be expected to act – so far as priority at junctions were concerned – with regard to the traffic situation as a whole. He would certainly ring adjacent boxes to ascertain the whereabouts of important trains before deciding to make a crossover movement; but at the very best his actions could be based on information collected in an unwieldly manner, and almost certainly not representing the 'up to the minute' situation.

The shortcomings of earlier techniques were realised well enough when it came to installing some of the earlier examples of power signalling particularly with panel boxes, and arrangements were made to advise the signalmen in such boxes of the approach of traffic impinging upon the main line, and thus provide details in the general situation that would lead to more effective regulation. The extent of the signalling controls applied to these 'fringe' connections has tended to grow, as signalling techniques have advanced, but the extent of the 'East and West' appendages of the main line signalling has never previously been greater than those incorporated in the Warrington, Preston and Carlisle panel boxes, South of Warrington there are connections towards Chester and Stockport, while from the Winwick and Golborne Junctions not only are the immediate connecting lines controlled but a 14-mile length of the original Liverpool and Manchester Railway from Rainhill in the west to Astley, on the edge of the notorious Chat Moss. The entire length of the branch line from St Helens (Shaw St) to Springs Branch Junction is included, and from Wigan a section of the former L&YR main line to Manchester as far east as Crow Nest Junction.

Of course the advantages derived from the inclusion of these connecting lines in the new main line panel box schemes are not confined to the possibility of improved regulation, important though this is. In the Warrington scheme alone a total of nineteen mechanical signal boxes on the connecting lines alone have been closed, this resulting in very considerable economies in operating costs. It is these closures, coupled with the twenty mechanical boxes on the main line now dispensed with, that have provided much of the justification of the resignalling scheme as a whole. It will be appreciated also that the whole strategy of connecting line co-ordination determined the locations of the new signal boxes along the main line. Earlier chapters of this book have emphasised the importance of Preston as a traffic catchment centre for the new electrified railway; but it is now in a surely unique position so far as signalling controls are concerned. The immediate connections from the main line at Euxton and Farington Curve Junctions follow the same pattern, with colour light signals to Midge Hall on the former L&YR to Ormskirk and Liverpool, and for 8 miles from Euxton Junction on the main line through Chorley towards Bolton. But it is the ramifications east of Preston that are so comprehensive.

The concentration of signalling control into a single box for the entire west-east route of the former L&YR would have been an outstanding piece of work on its own, including, en route, such populous centres as Blackburn, Accrington and Burnley; and it has been extended eastwards to Todmorden, and then both ways along the historic Manchester and Leeds Railway – southwards through Summit Tunnel to Littleborough and Smithy Bridge and eastwards through the Calder Valley to Hebden Bridge, thus incorporating almost 11 miles of this trunk route. This is not all. Extensions from this subsidiary main line network controlled from Preston include 10 miles of the line southwards from Blackburn to within 3 miles of Bolton, and two short fringe connections in the immediate environs of Burnley. So the new Preston power box has to control some 65 miles of subsidiary main line extending eastwards and southwards from Bamber Bridge in addition to its prime function of the electrified West Coast line between Euxton Junction and a point between Carnforth and Oxenholme.

As a piece of signalling design it is probably without parallel the world over, not only in the total track and route mileage covered but in the density and diversity of the traffic flowing. Of course the section eastwards from Bamber Bridge has no more than a slight connection with the electrified West Coast main line, except, as at Warrington, that in the number of mechanical signal boxes it has been possible to close it provided a large financial saving in operating expense. North of Preston, control from the new power box extends to Salwick, 7 miles on the main line to Blackpool; the lines intersecting with the West Coast main line at Lancaster and Carnforth lie somewhat outside the present scheme. Nevertheless, in view of what has been accomplished east of Bamber Bridge there would be no technical difficulty in bringing the entire Furness line on to the Preston panel. The route from Carnforth to Barrow is considerably less complicated from a track and traffic point of view than that through Blackburn, Accrington and Burnley; and were it so desired the centralised signalling control from Preston could readily be extended to Whitehaven. Such suggestions are no longer pipe dreams. Anything is possible after the Bamber Bridge–Hebden Bridge installation, not that there were any technical difficulties there.

The last of the power boxes on the LM section of the new electrified line is Carlisle, controlling 61 miles of the former

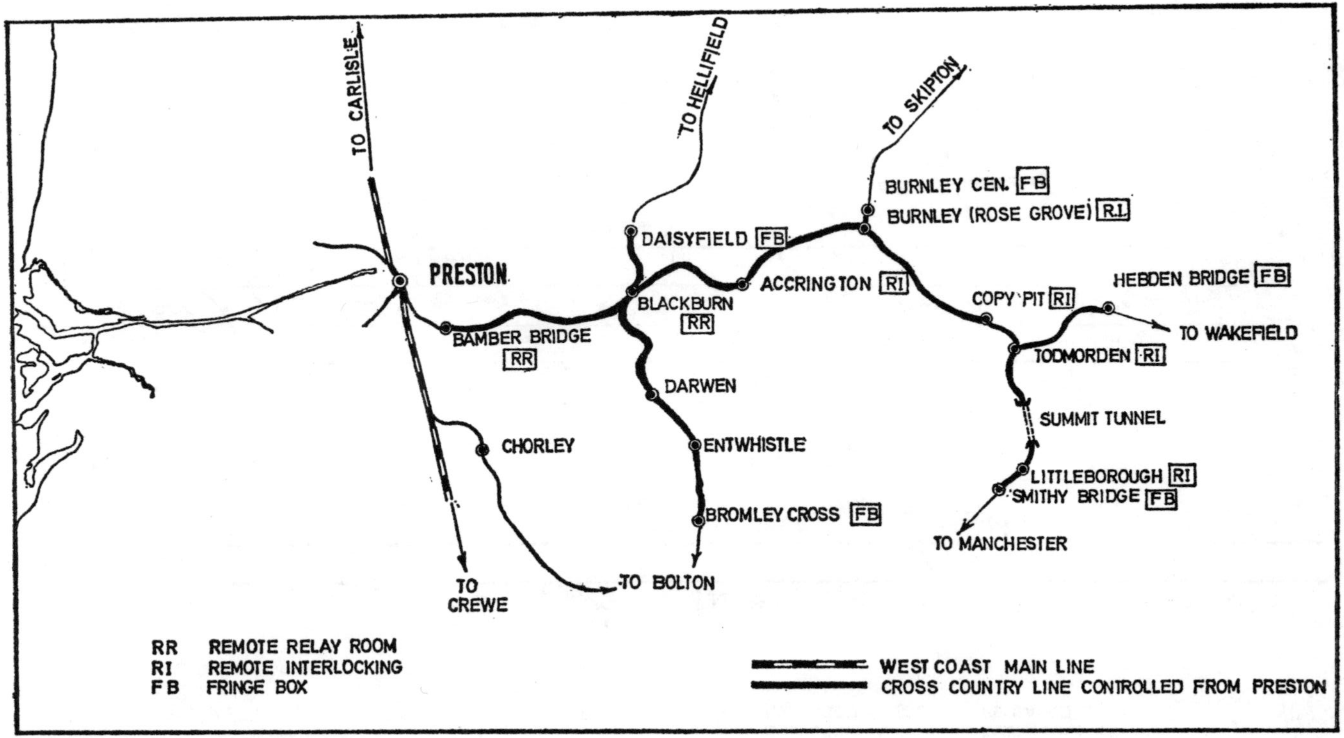

Cross-country line: Preston–Todmorden.

West Coast Main Line: Farington Curve Junction southwards.

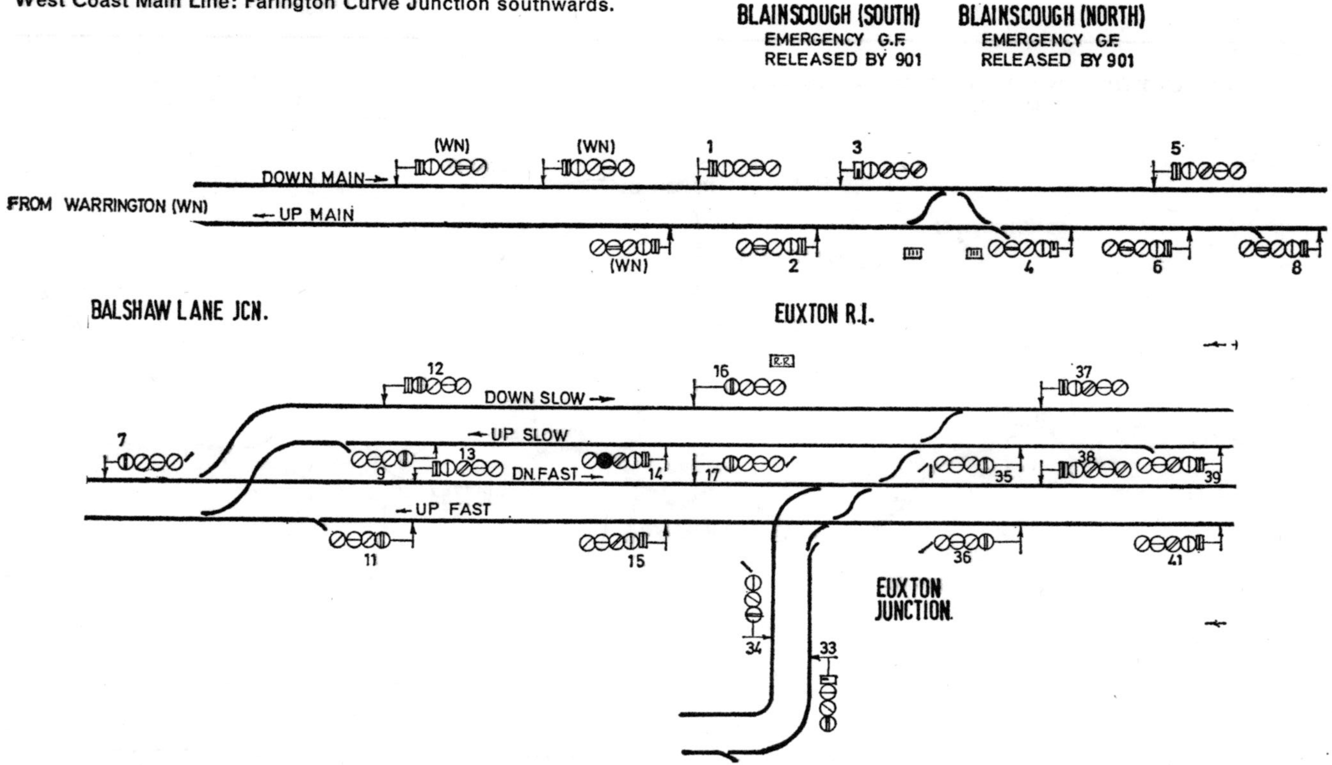

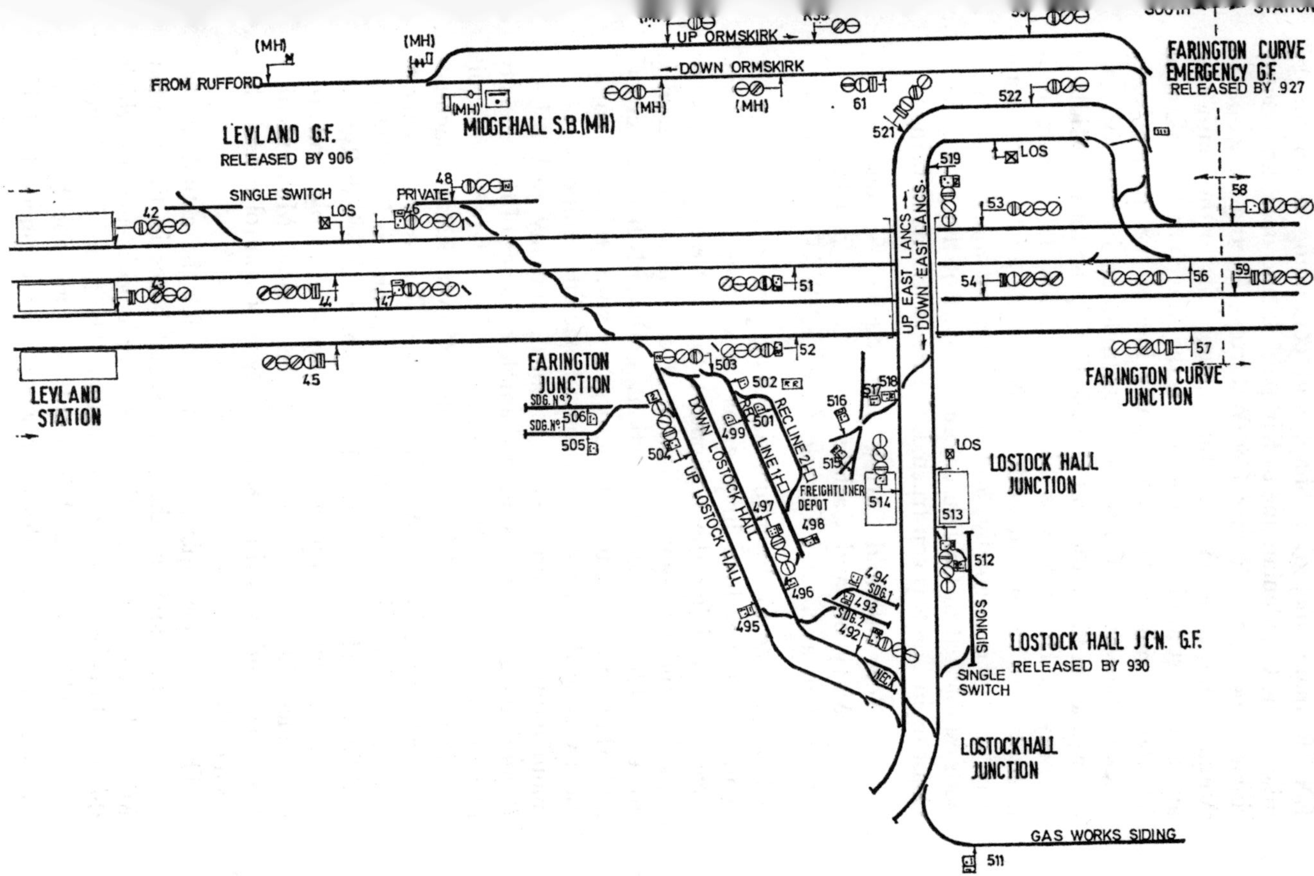
FROM RUFFORD
(MH)
UP ORMSKIRK
DOWN ORMSKIRK
MIDGEHALL S.B.(MH)
LEYLAND G.F.
RELEASED BY 906
SINGLE SWITCH
LOS
PRIVATE
42
43
44
45
46
47
48
51
52
53
54
56
57
58
59
61
521
522
519
LEYLAND STATION
FARINGTON JUNCTION
SDG. No.2
SDG. No.1
505
506
503
502
501
499
504
REC LINE 2
LINE 1
DOWN LOSTOCK HALL
UP LOSTOCK HALL
FREIGHTLINER DEPOT
497
498
496
495
494
493
492
SDG.1
SDG.2
516
515
517
518
514
513
512
511
UP EAST LANCS.
DOWN EAST LANCS.
FARINGTON CURVE EMERGENCY G.F.
RELEASED BY 927
FARINGTON CURVE JUNCTION
LOSTOCK HALL JUNCTION
LOSTOCK HALL JCN. G.F.
RELEASED BY 930
SIDINGS
SINGLE SWITCH
LOSTOCK HALL JUNCTION
GAS WORKS SIDING

LNWR main line, over Shap, and continuing north for 13 miles of the Caledonian line to Kirkpatrick, and over the recently singled line of the former G&SWR from Gretna Junction to Annan, 9 miles. Some interesting connections to the south-west and south-east are included. There is the Maryport line, as far as Wigton, 12 miles; the cross-country line of the former North Eastern Railway, to Corby Gates $4\frac{1}{2}$ miles on its way to Newcastle, and on the Settle and Carlisle line of the former Midland Railway to Howe & Cos Sidings, 5 miles. In passing it is interesting to recall that both the Newcastle and Carlisle Railway, as it was originally, and the Maryport and Carlisle were both established in Carlisle before any part of the present West Coast main line was constructed, the respective dates being:

Newcastle and Carlisle (later NER)	1836
Maryport and Carlisle	1843
Lancaster and Carlisle (later LNWR)	1846

Coming now to the actual signalling techniques used in the control of these three huge areas, in visiting the new signal boxes and studying the equipment the interesting process of evolution and near-standardisation of control console design is apparent. On the electrified sections southwards from Liverpool and Manchester, because of the urgency with which the equipment was needed the standard control machine equipment of the manufacturers concerned was accepted, and my earlier book *Britain's New Railway* contained ample evidence of the diversity of designs that were installed, including the adaptation to suit ac electric traction of the miniature lever frame machines installed during World War II at Crewe. The very diversity of this power signal box equipment, not only on the LMR electrified lines but elsewhere enabled the engineers of British Railways to make a general appraisal of equipment available, and from experience since the launching of the original Modernisation Plan the standard British Railways type of control console has been evolved.

The mosaic principle has been used for the actual display on the panel, and for the three signal boxes in the London Midland Region the Westinghouse M3 type is used in which the individual mosaics are rectangular. The main panel is near-vertical, while below and in front of it are ancillary panels catering for the train describer set-up and telephone facilities.

After wide experience with the different forms of route-setting procedure, the 'entrance–exit' principle was decided upon, in preference to the 'one-control-switch' used in many of the earlier interlockings on the LMR electrified lines. The 'one-control-switch' (OCS) system, while requiring only a single movement on the part of the signalman to set up a route requires a separate thumb switch for each route, and these were grouped on a sloping keyboard below the main panel. The 'entrance-exit' system enables all the push-pull circuit controllers for route setting to be mounted in their true geographical position on the track diagram, and facilitates the production of a very compact panel layout. This is a very important feature with installations of such wide extent as those at Warrington, Preston and Carlisle.

On the track diagram two different coloured indications are provided in rectangular apertures at $\frac{3}{4}$in centres: white indicates that a route has been set along that track; red indicates that the particular track circuit is occupied by a train. The interlocking is entirely through electrical circuits. To set up a route the signalman presses a button adjacent, on the diagram, to the signal at its entrance. This may read over several alternative routes, and to select the required route the button at the exit is pressed. The route through the interlocked area is set from one signal to the next. If a signalman should inadvertently attempt to set up a route that is already occupied, or one that would conflict with a route already set no response would follow the pressing of the buttons. The route setting procedure operates and locks all points in the route, and also locks conflicting routes. Not until all points have thrown and been detected in position, the tracks proved clear, and all other necessary conditions met with will the signal at the entrance to the route clear.

The dark rectangles seen in the photograph of the panels contain the train description indications to which reference is made later. Considerable ingenuity in layout design has been shown in arranging the complicated geographical areas covered by the signalling controls within the confines of the panels. The guiding principle in layout has been to group areas of co-ordinated activity together for operation by one signalman, so that each man on duty at the panel has the minimum of walking about to do, and can see all the various track indications, train descriptions and other visual aids from his normal stance. In areas of such complexity, of course, trains will frequently be

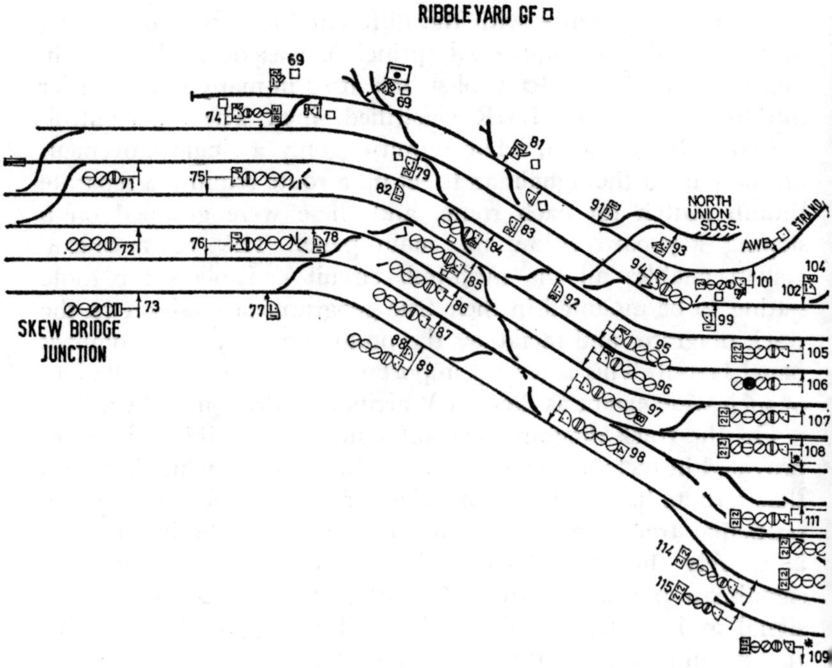

Preston station and immediate environs: resignalling arrangements.

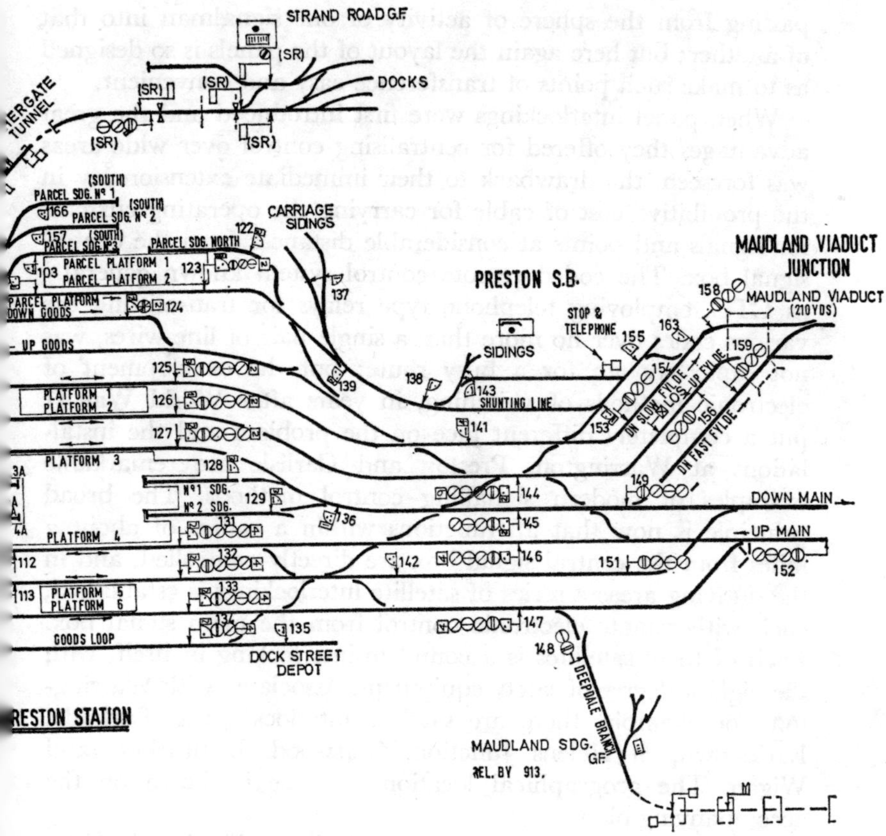
STRAND ROAD G.F.
DOCKS
(SR)
ERGATE TUNNEL
PARCEL SDG. Nº 1 (SOUTH)
PARCEL SDG. Nº 2 (SOUTH)
PARCEL SDG. Nº 3 (SOUTH)
PARCEL SDG. NORTH
CARRIAGE SIDINGS
PARCEL PLATFORM 1
PARCEL PLATFORM 2
PARCEL PLATFORM
DOWN GOODS
UP GOODS
PLATFORM 1
PLATFORM 2
PLATFORM 3
Nº 1 SDG.
Nº 2 SDG.
PLATFORM 4
PLATFORM 5
PLATFORM 6
GOODS LOOP
DOCK STREET DEPOT
PRESTON S.B.
SIDINGS
SHUNTING LINE
STOP & TELEPHONE
MAUDLAND VIADUCT JUNCTION
MAUDLAND VIADUCT (210YDS)
ON SLOW FYLDE
UP SLOW FYLDE
UP FYLDE
ON FAST FYLDE
DOWN MAIN
UP MAIN
DEEPDALE BRANCH
MAUDLAND SDG. G.F.
REL. BY 913.
RESTON STATION

passing from the sphere of activity of one signalman into that of another; but here again the layout of the panels is so designed as to make such points of transference easy and convenient.

When panel interlockings were first introduced and the great advantages they offered for centralising control over wide areas was foreseen, the drawback to their immediate extension lay in the prohibitive cost of cable for carrying the operating currents for signals and points at considerable distances from the central signal box. The coded remote control system known generally as CTC, employing telephone type relays for transmitting the various codes over no more than a single pair of line wires, was not rapid enough for a busy route; but the development of electronic methods of switching, in years after World War II put a completely different face on the problem and the installations at Warrington, Preston and Carlisle are remarkable examples of modern signalling control methods. The broad principle is now that all functions within a radius of about 2 miles from the central signal box are directly controlled, and in the outlying areas a series of satellite interlockings is established, each with remote electronic control from the main signal box. Each of these satellites is a complete interlocking in itself, with the highest degree of safety equipment. Associated with Warrington, for example, there are satellite interlockings at Parkside, Earlestown, St Helens Junction, Garswood, Bamfurlong and Wigan. The geographical location of these is shown on the accompanying plan.

At the central interlockings and at all the satellite interlockings what is termed 'geographical circuity' is employed. For each type of function to be operated there is a standard type of packaged control unit, pre-assembled in the manufacturer's works, wired complete, and tested. This system saves an immense amount of time in wiring and testing on site. There the only wiring to be done is that of interconnecting the various 'geographical' units, and adding the relatively few additional relays, and so on, that cannot be incorporated in the geographical layout.

Although the signalling equipment now in standard use on British Railways has reached a very high degree of reliability one cannot neglect to make provision against the occasional failure – not, I hasten to add of any kind that could set up a dangerous condition, but a failure on the safety side, which

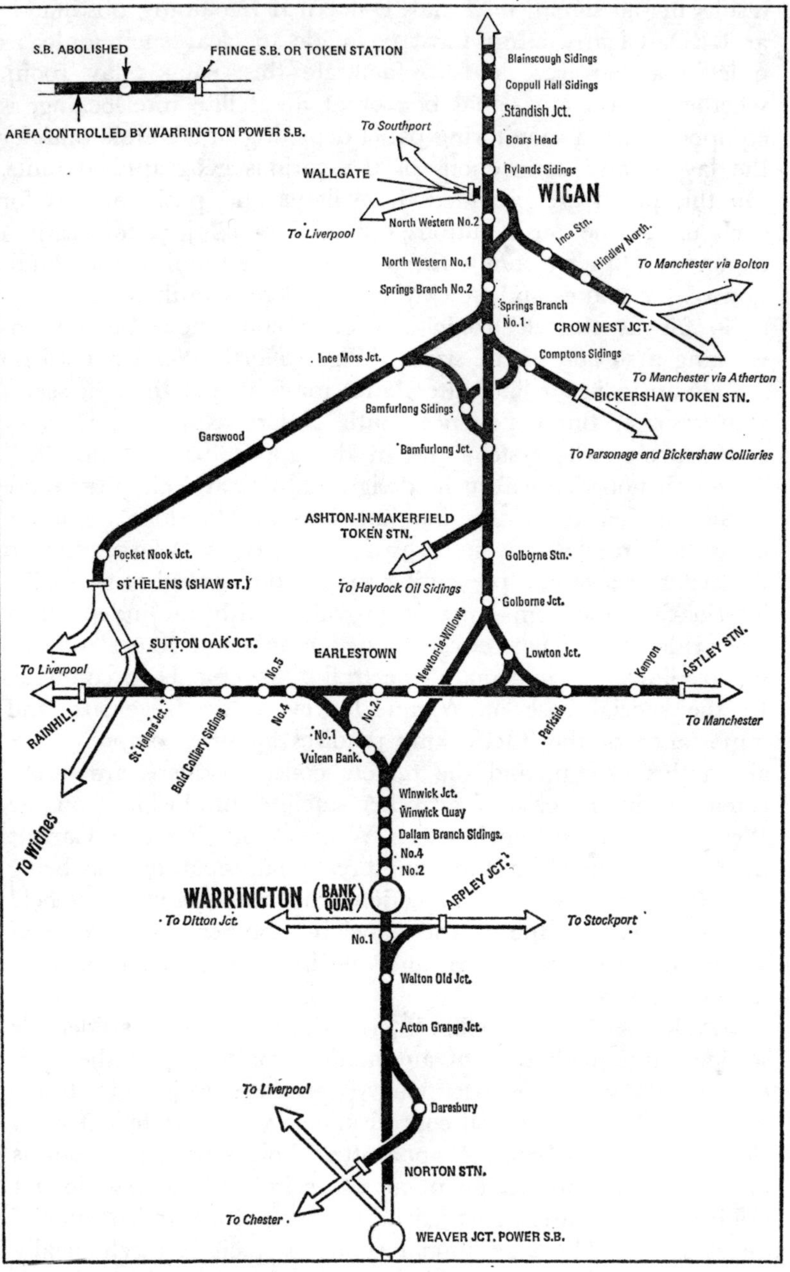

Diagram of Warrington resignalled area.

results in the signal, or signals concerned remaining obstinately at RED. Clearly effort must be made to clear such faults as quickly as possible, and to facilitate this, each relay room, whether in a main signal box or at a satellite interlocking, is equipped with a monitoring panel depicting in a simple manner the layout and connections of the various geographical units. On this panel are provided 'free' lights and push buttons for each unit. The push buttons operated in conjunction with a common voltmeter enable the technicians to monitor the condition of the route, and quickly trace where a fault lies.

So far as the electronic control is concerned the idea of working a station of the size of Wigan North Western with no signalman in immediate attendance may, at first thought seems venturesome. But experience south of Crewe has given every confidence in the system and in the apparatus now installed. Although not identical in its design features and circuitry there is the case of the main line junctions at Hanslope, remotely controlled from Rugby some 26 miles away. At Warrington, in the event of a failure preventing the remote control of a satellite interlocking the signalman is provided with an independent 'over-ride' circuit whereby a limited number of routes may be set to allow principal main line traffic movements to continue. In the special case of Wigan, however, the large size and importance of the interlocking requires a more comprehensive alternative system, and the remote control systems are duplicated. As in the case of all other satellite interlockings on the West Coast main line between Weaver Junction and Carlisle the remote control links are uni-directional, separate links being used for controls – in one direction – and indications, from field functions back to the central panel by another. In the case of Wigan there is one control and one indication system on continuous standby.

In addition to the satellite interlockings there are considerable sections, intermediately, of automatic signalling, and the indications of track circuit occupancy from these sections are transmitted back to the central control panel by a separate system of electronic remote control apparatus. This separate system is also used for transmission of all other indications that do not originate in the areas covered by the remote controlled satellite interlockings. These additional functions include mechanically operated ground frames, which are electrically released when it

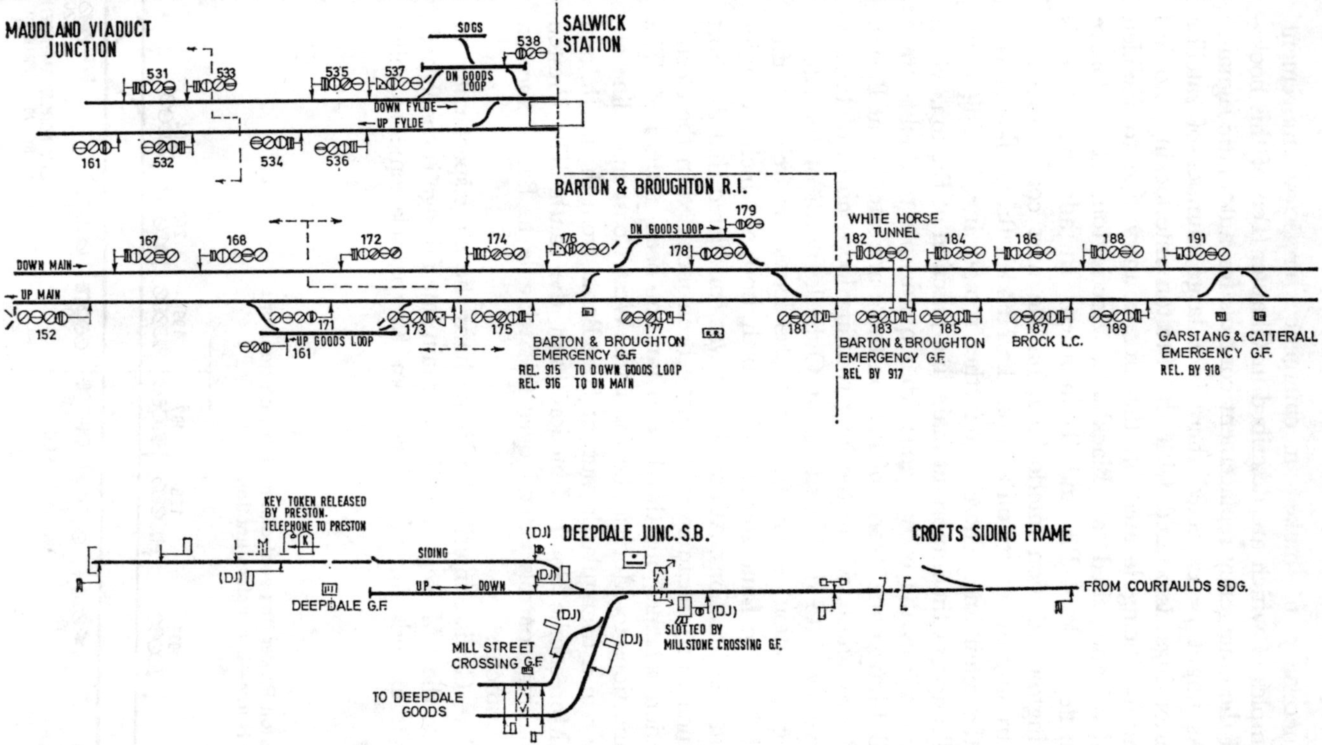

Preston Power Box controls: northward extension:
Preston yard—Bay Horse.

is necessary to make an emergency crossover movement-examples of which are described in Chapter Ten of this book – and the emergency replacement controls for automatic signals.

As might be expected there is a large number of satellite interlockings associated with the Preston interlocking, no less than five being located on the cross-country line to Hebden Bridge, and sited at Blackburn, Accrington, Rose Grove (Burnley), Copy Pit and Todmorden. In addition there is Farington Junction interlocking, on the west coast main line, controlling the routes on and off the Hebden Bridge line as well as the main line. There is a further remote interlocking south of Preston at the important main line junction of Euxton, which also controls the convergence from quadruple to double track at Balshaw Lane. North of Preston there are satellites at Barton and Broughton, where the long running loops north of Preston converged into double track; at Oubeck, north of the site of Galgate station, where there are also loops for freight traffic, and finally at Lancaster and Carnforth, both of which are major main line junctions. At one time it was considered that the short branch to Morecambe might have been included in the electrification scheme, but this has so far not been authorised. The connections to Morecambe from the West Coast main line are made in a triangular layout, at Hest Bank, from the north, and at Morecambe South Junction from the south. The Preston signalling controls extend over this triangle to Bare Lane, on the branch.

The Carlisle interlocking is perhaps the most spectacular of all on the LM Region, so far as main line mileage is concerned, for it extends for 74 miles – from Kirkpatrick some 13 miles

Preston Power Box controls: northward extension: Bay Horse—Lancaster Junction.

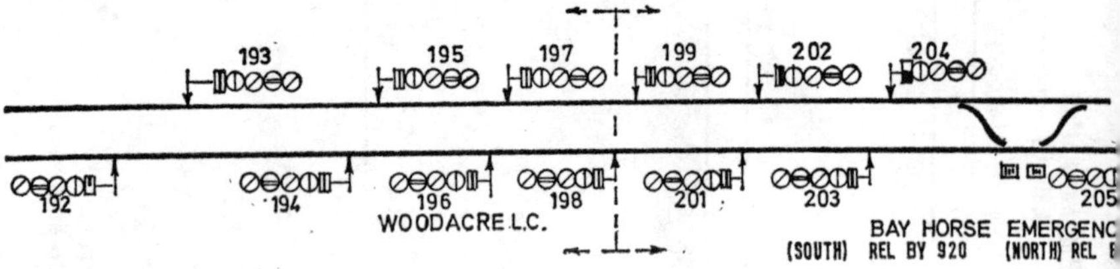

to the north, to a point between Oxenholme and Carnforth, where it links up with the Preston interlocking. On the former LNWR line there are no fewer than eight satellite interlockings sited, at Plumpton, Penrith, Eden Valley, Harrison's Sidings, Shap Summit, Tebay, Grayrigg and Oxenholme. Penrith and Oxenholme are the only remaining passenger stations; the latter provides the junction with the Windermere branch, which has now been singled and is operated under the 'one train working' regulations. Carlisle panel box controls the movements on and off the branch at Oxenholme, where the driver obtains the single line token from a release instrument on the station platform. Of the others, Harrison's Sidings and Shap Summit are both concerned with the traffic in granite, and limestone, while Plumpton, Eden Valley, Tebay and Grayrigg have running goods loops. In the Carlisle central area all the junctions from the Midland, North Eastern and Maryport lines are directly controlled from the central panel, and the first satellite to the north is at Etterby Junction, which controls access to the Kingmoor Diesel Depot.

Three-quarters of a mile north of Etterby is Kingmoor. This is a satellite interlocking, with a difference. It is an unmanned satellite, controlled from Carlisle in similar fashion to the other satellites, but as Kingmoor power signal box had been commissioned as recently as 1963, as part of the fully mechanised marshalling yard scheme, it was decided to retain the 'non-geographical' type of interlocking there, together with the interlocking at Etterby which was controlled by direct wire from Kingmoor, and transfer control to Carlisle signal box. The console in Kingmoor signal box has been removed, and normal

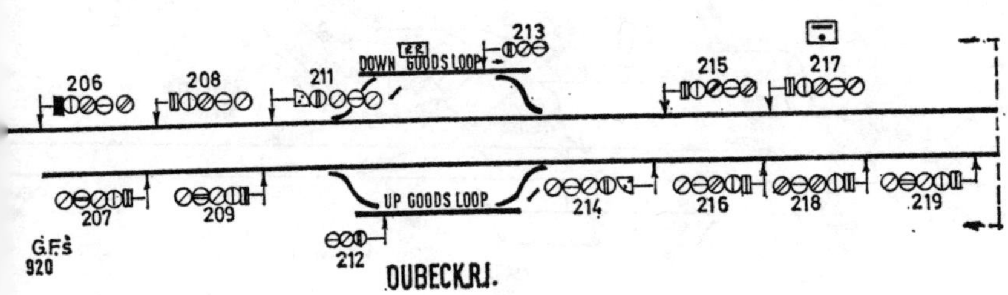

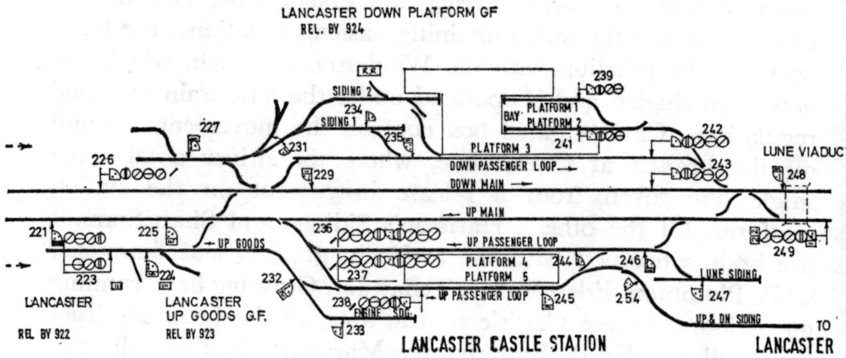

Preston Power Box controls: northward extension: Lancaster Remote Interlocking.

Preston Power Box controls: northward extension: Carnforth Remote Interlocking.

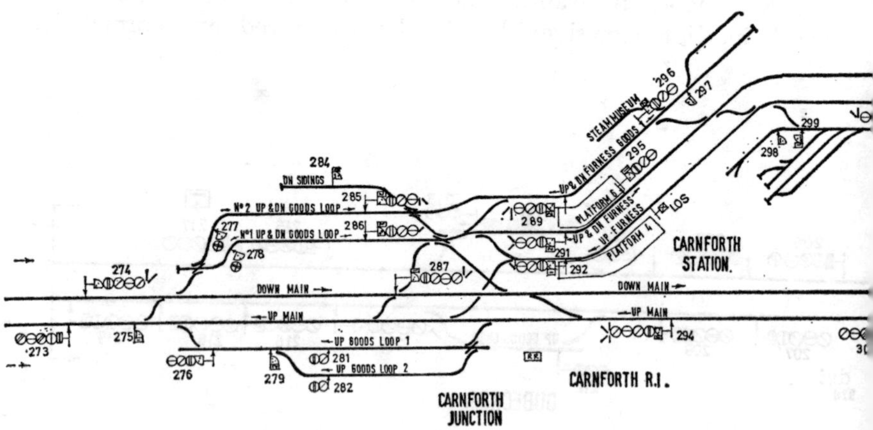

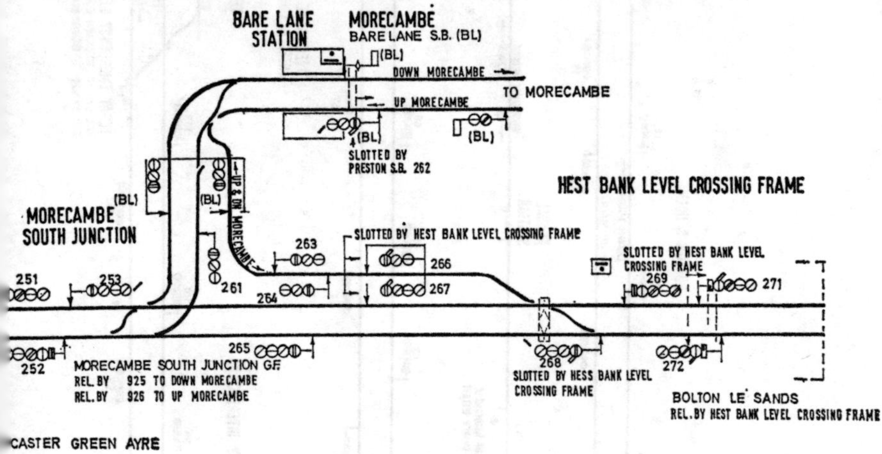
BARE LANE STATION
MORECAMBE
BARE LANE S.B. (BL)
(BL)
DOWN MORECAMBE
TO MORECAMBE
UP MORECAMBE
4 (BL)
(BL)
SLOTTED BY PRESTON S.B. 262
HEST BANK LEVEL CROSSING FRAME
MORECAMBE SOUTH JUNCTION
(BL)
(BL)
UP & DN MORECAMBE
SLOTTED BY HEST BANK LEVEL CROSSING FRAME
SLOTTED BY HEST BANK LEVEL CROSSING FRAME
251
253
263
266
269
271
261
264
267
265
252
268
272
MORECAMBE SOUTH JUNCTION G.F.
REL. BY 925 TO DOWN MORECAMBE
REL. BY 926 TO UP MORECAMBE
SLOTTED BY HESS BANK LEVEL CROSSING FRAME
BOLTON LE SANDS
REL. BY HEST BANK LEVEL CROSSING FRAME
CASTER GREEN AYRE

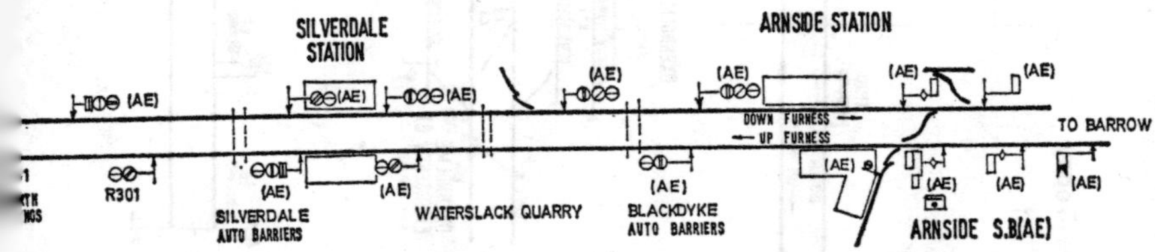
SILVERDALE STATION
ARNSIDE STATION
(AE)
(AE)
(AE)
(AE)
(AE)
(AE)
(AE)
DOWN FURNESS
UP FURNESS
TO BARROW
R301
(AE)
(AE)
(AE)
(AE)
(AE)
(AE)
(AE)
(AE)
SILVERDALE AUTO BARRIERS
WATERSLACK QUARRY
BLACKDYKE AUTO BARRIERS
ARNSIDE S.B(AE)

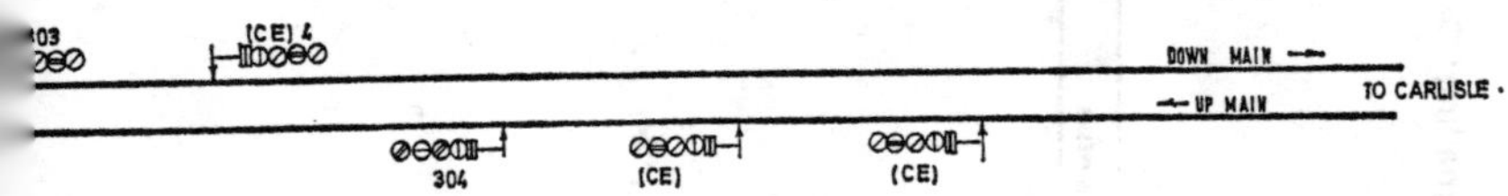
03
(CE) 4
DOWN MAIN
TO CARLISLE
UP MAIN
304
(CE)
(CE)

Resignalling: Oxenholme–Tebay

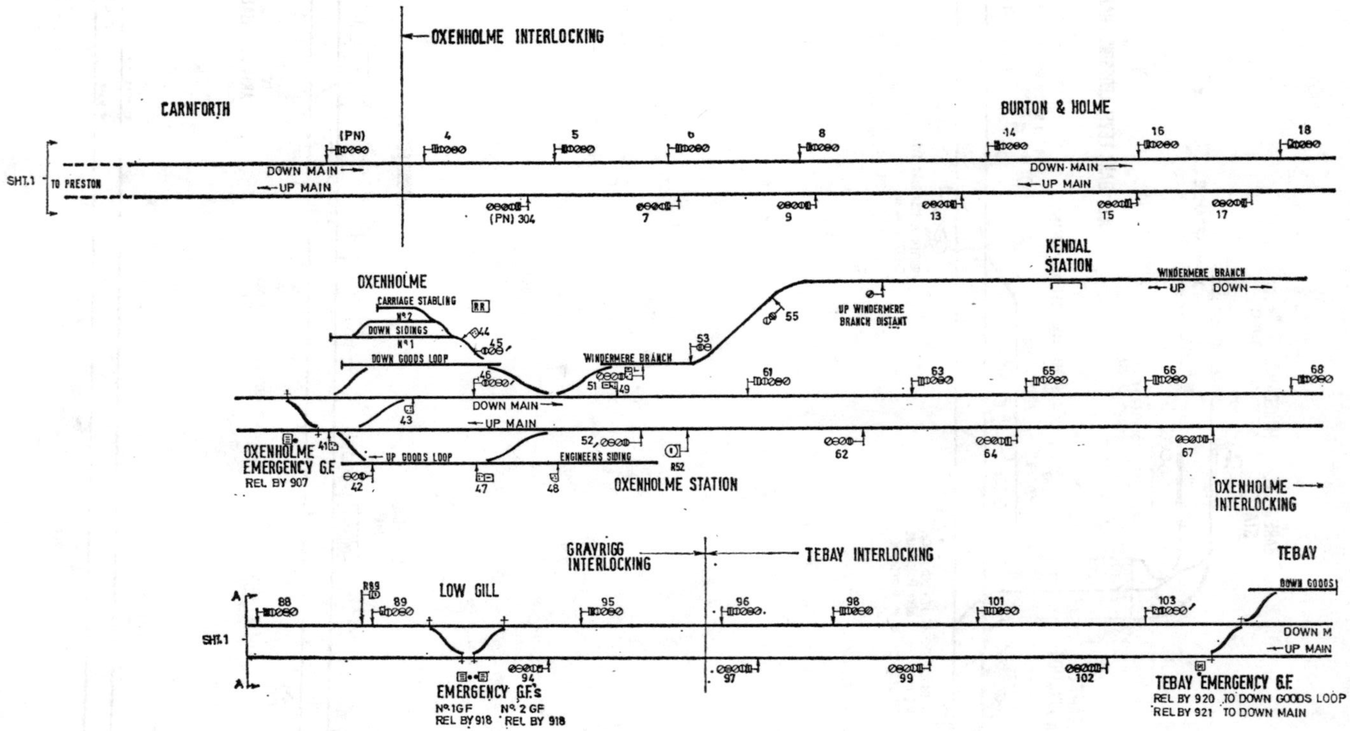

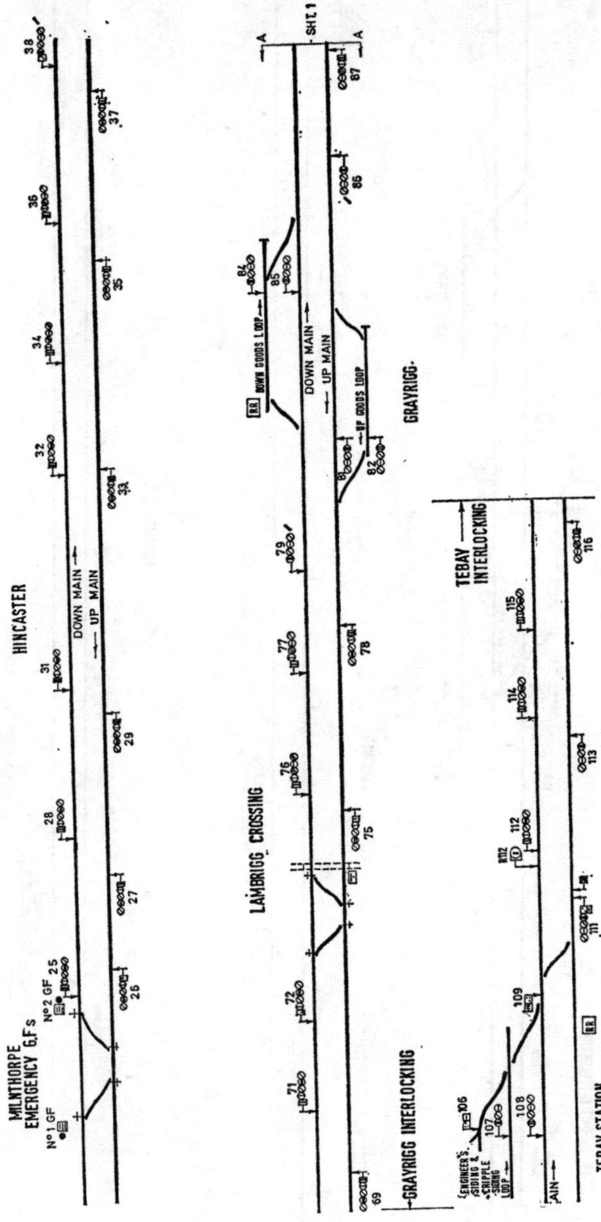
HINCASTER
MILNTHORPE EMERGENCY G.F's
N° 1 GF
N° 2 GF
DOWN MAIN
UP MAIN
LAMBRIGG CROSSING
GRAYRIGG INTERLOCKING
DOWN GOODS LOOP
UP GOODS LOOP
GRAYRIGG
SHT. 1
TEBAY INTERLOCKING
ENGINEER'S SIDING & CRIPPLE SIDING LOOP
TEBAY STATION (CLOSED)

Resignalling: Shap Summit–Wreay.

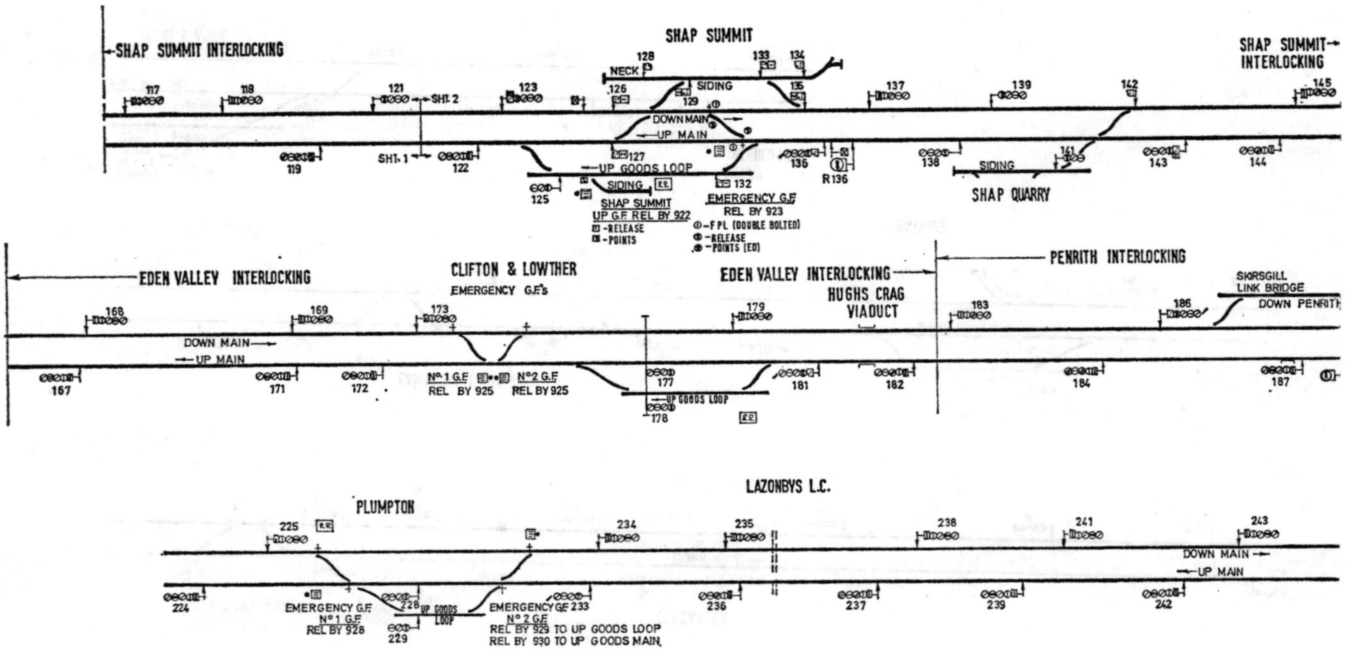

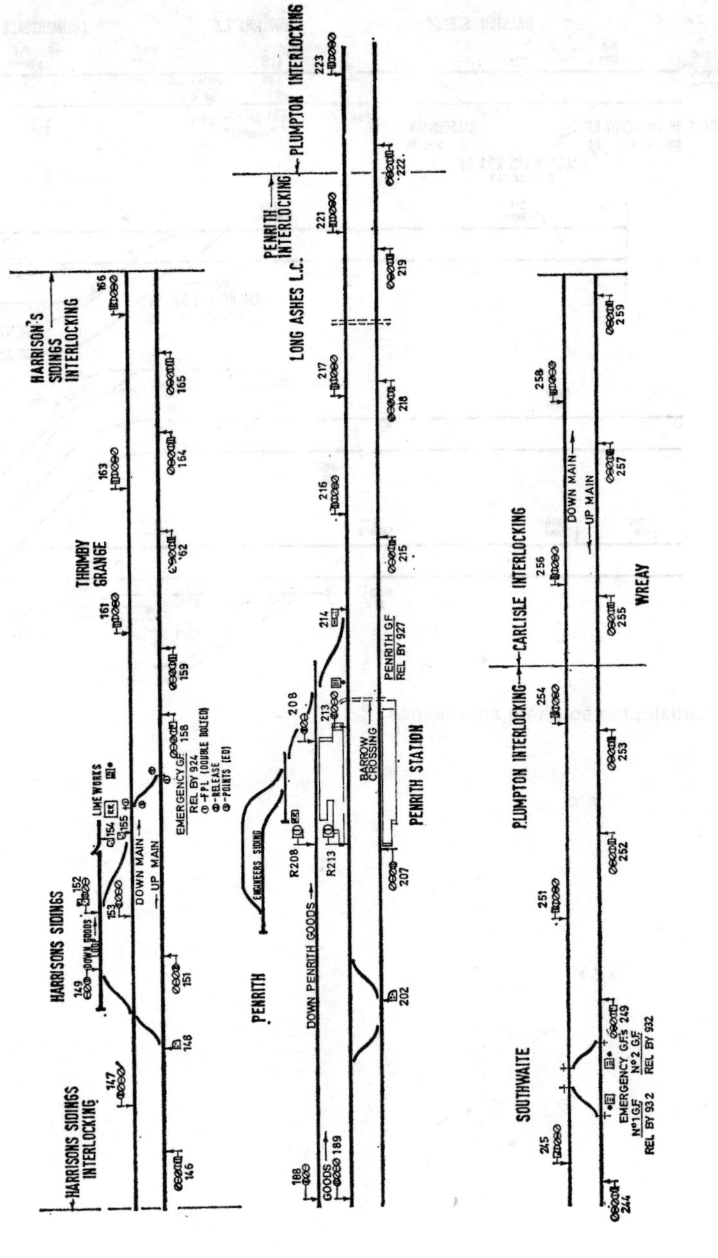
HARRISONS SIDINGS INTERLOCKING
HARRISONS SIDINGS
DOWN GOODS LOOP
LIME WORKS
DOWN MAIN
UP MAIN
EMERGENCY G.F. 158
REL BY 924
FPL (DOUBLE BOLTED)
RELEASE
POINTS (ED)
THRIMBY GRANGE
HARRISON'S SIDINGS INTERLOCKING
PENRITH
DOWN PENRITH GOODS
GOODS
ENGINEERS SIDING
BARROW CROSSING
PENRITH STATION
PENRITH G.F.
REL BY 927
LONG ASHES L.C.
PENRITH INTERLOCKING
PLUMPTON INTERLOCKING
SOUTHWAITE
EMERGENCY G.F.s 249
No1 G.F.
REL BY 932
No2 G.F.
REL BY 932
PLUMPTON INTERLOCKING
CARLISLE INTERLOCKING
WREAY
DOWN MAIN
UP MAIN

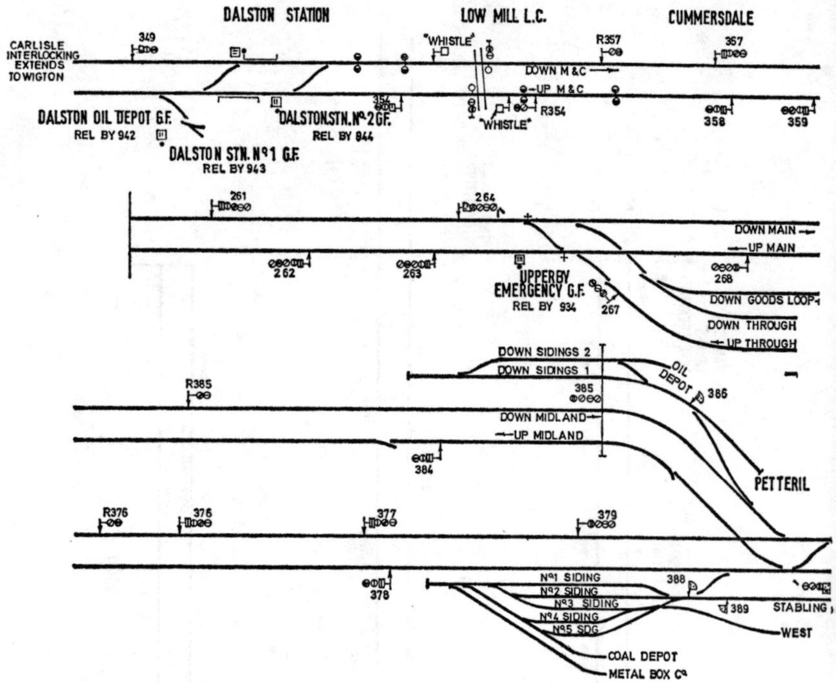

Carlisle: the southern approaches.

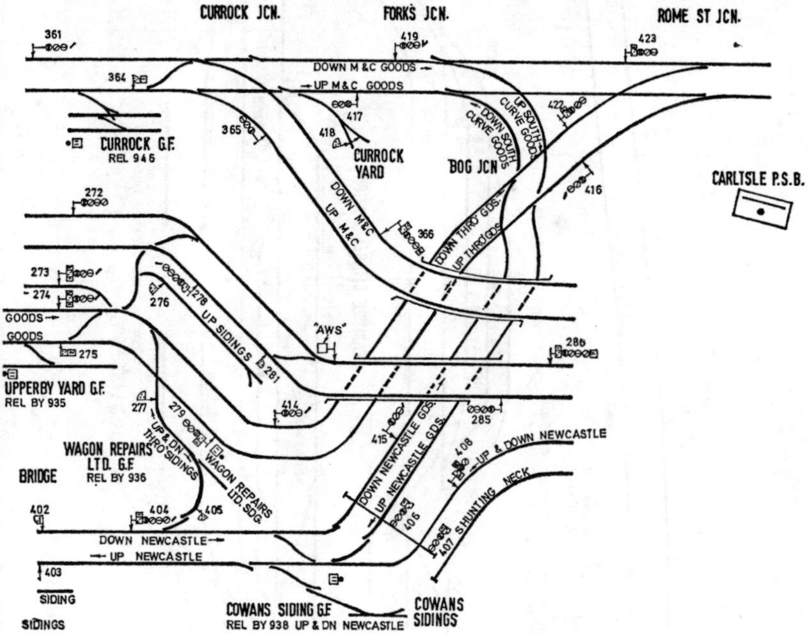
CURROCK JCN.
FORKS JCN.
ROME ST JCN.
361
419
423
DOWN M & C GOODS
UP M & C GOODS
364
417
418
365
CURROCK G.F.
REL 946
CURROCK YARD
BOG JCN
UP SOUTH CURVE GOODS
DOWN SOUTH CURVE GOODS
422
416
CARLISLE P.S.B.
272
DOWN M&C
UP M&C
366
DOWN THRO' GDS
UP THRO' GDS
273
274
276
278
UP SIDINGS
GOODS
GOODS
275
"AWS"
281
286
UPPERBY YARD G.F.
REL BY 935
277
279
414
285
UP & DN THRO' SIDINGS
WAGON REPAIRS LTD. SDG.
WAGON REPAIRS LTD. G.F.
REL BY 936
BRIDGE
415
DOWN NEWCASTLE GDS.
UP NEWCASTLE GDS.
408
UP & DOWN NEWCASTLE
SHUNTING NECK
406
407
402
404
405
DOWN NEWCASTLE
UP NEWCASTLE
403
SIDING
SIDINGS
COWANS SIDING G.F.
REL BY 938 UP & DN NEWCASTLE
COWANS SIDINGS

Carlisle: the Citadel station area.

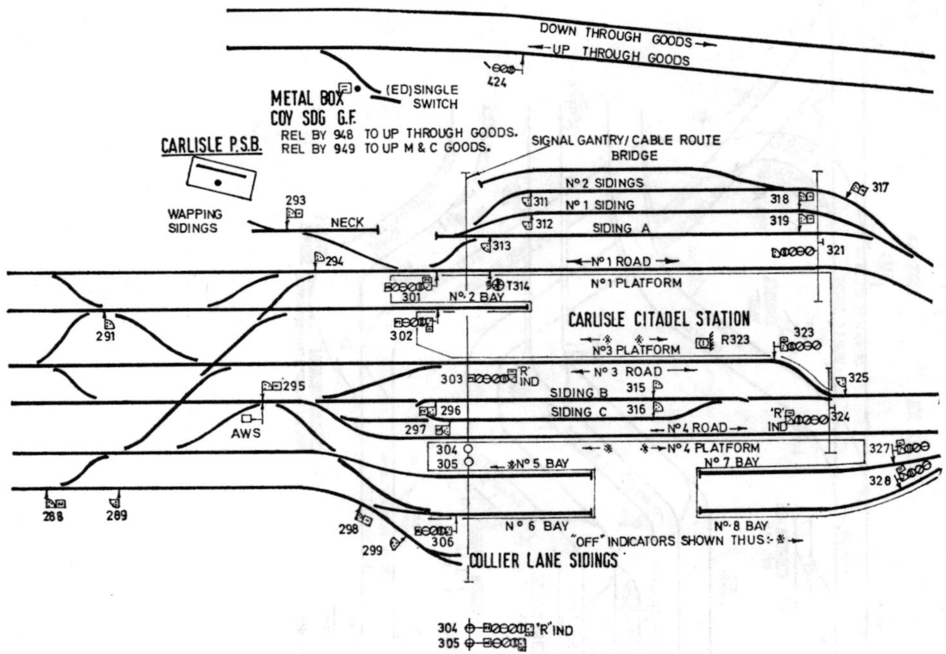

CARLISLE INTERLOCKING

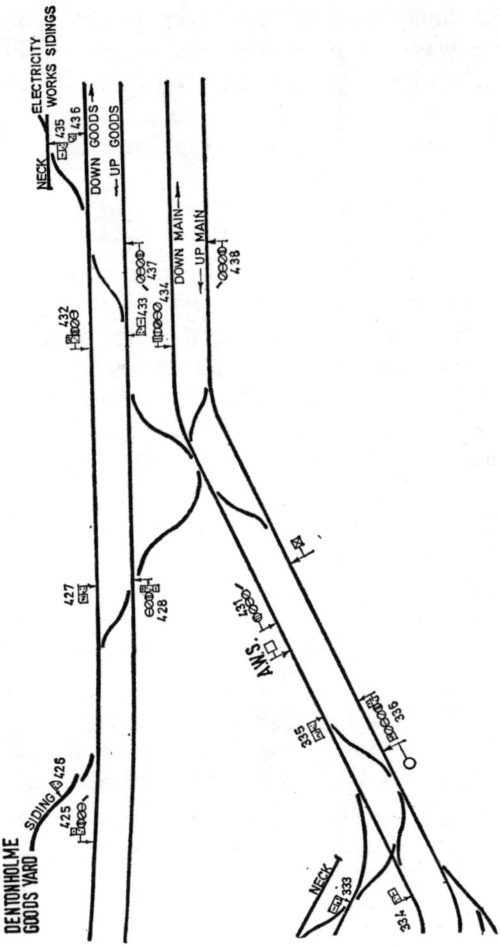

physical over-ride circuits provided to cover remote control system failure. There was also a similar type of remote interlocking at Floriston, which signalled the northern access to Carlisle Up Yard; the control of this has been transferred from Gretna Junction signal box to the new Gretna Junction satellite interlocking.

The closing of all except three signal boxes in the entire LMR area, on the West Coast main line north of Weaver Junction, and the consequent abolition of the former box-to-box reporting of the progress of trains renders of the greatest importance the practice of train description, to advise the signalmen on the central panels of the class and destination of trains running through their control area. Trains entering the areas are described from the appropriate 'fringe' signal boxes, marking the places where the control from the new power boxes end. This applies where there is a changeover, at the 'fringe' to manual block, or signalling other than with one of the new panel boxes. The signalman at the fringe box uses a set-up code and this code is transmitted to a computer, in Warrington, Preston or Carlisle power box as the case may be. In the case of through trains on the electrified main line, descriptions are transmitted between Warrington, Preston and Carlisle boxes automatically at the appropriate time.

The computers in the power boxes, receiving the train descriptions as they are received from the fringe boxes, 'process' them, as the term now goes, which means that the 'code' of the train concerned is displayed by cathode ray tubes in the panel track diagram, adjacent to the signal immediately concerned. The background for display of the code is the dark rectangular screen that can be observed in the photographs of the complete panels. Each of the four figures in the display of the code is derived from a 5 x 7 matrix of 'bright-up' dots activated by the electronic beam. In passing one must comment upon the vast improvement in display of train description indications that has been effected since the original installations made south of Liverpool and Manchester. The new apparatus installed through the West Coast main line north of Weaver Junction displays an exceptionally clear and distinct indication, that can be clearly read not only by the signalman, but by those seated at the regulating desks some little distance in rear, as can be seen in the photographs.

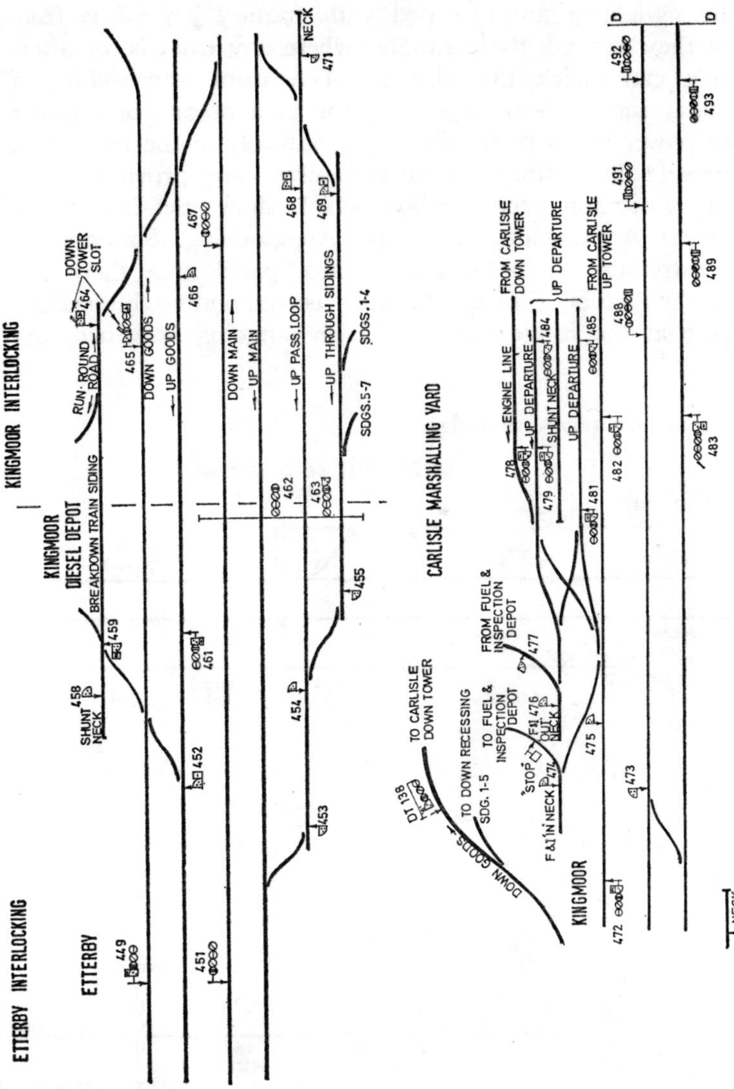

Etterby and Kingmoor resignalling.

The signalmen are provided with enquiry keyboards from which they can ask the computer where any train is, or alternatively can check the identity of a train approaching a particular signal. A train leaving the area of one or another of the power boxes is described automatically to the fringe-box concerned. The fringe boxes themselves are provided with optical projection type displays which show 'Set-Up'; 'Last Sent'; 1st Approaching, and 2nd Approaching. Similarly at each extremity of the central control panel area there are cathode ray tube displays showing corresponding indications to those at the fringe boxes, on both outgoing and incoming

LM Region: the northern extremities.

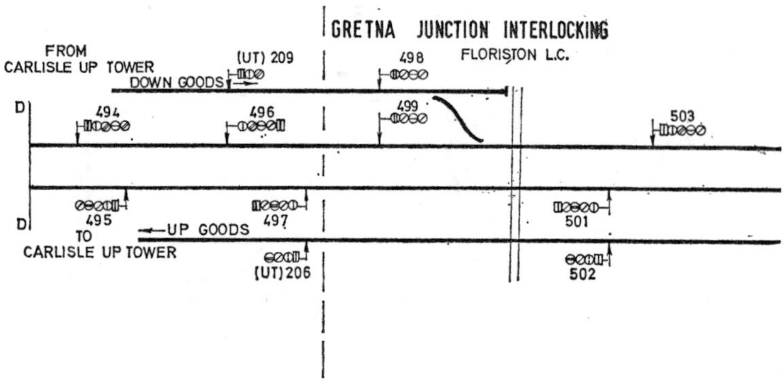

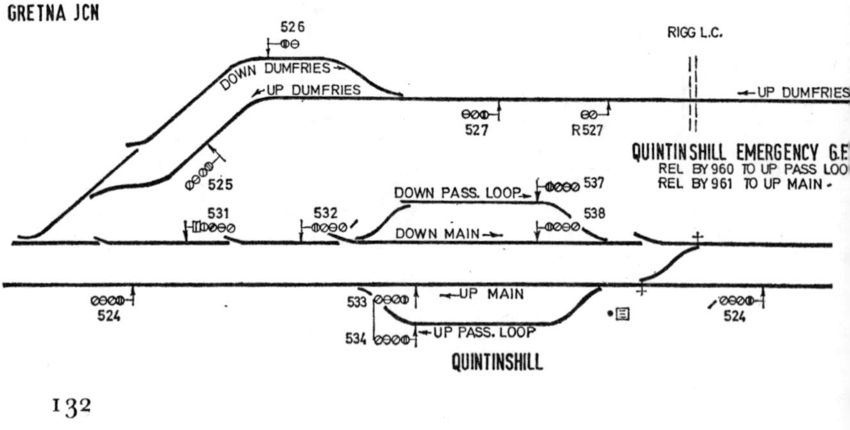

lines. Should a train enter the control area from a fringe box, or from a ground frame connection without being described an alarm bell sounds and the appropriate display screen shows an asterisk. The 'not described' alarm also sounds if a train proceeds from one signal to another within the control area, without a description. It will be appreciated that on some of the connecting lines, particularly those concerned with special freight workings there are movements apart from the through running of trains. Certain lines on which trains may run in both directions are provided with bi-directional description screens. There are also some goods lines where permissive working is in force, which is

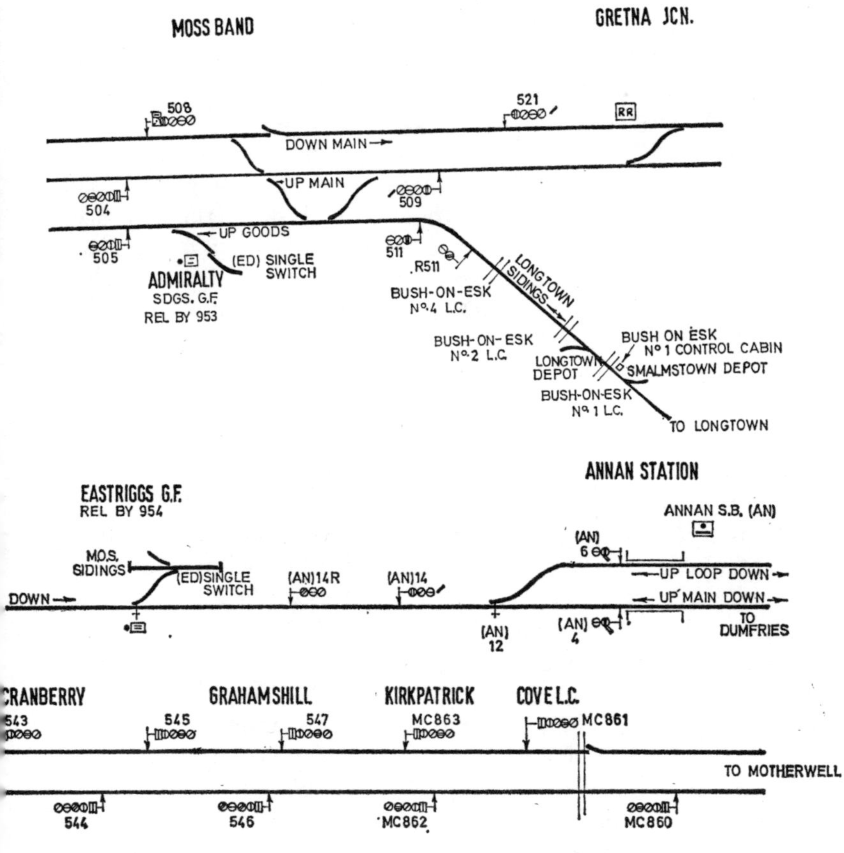

provided for by special arrangements within the train description system, while on certain sections heavy diesel-hauled freight trains require rear-end banking assistance.

An important operating factor arising from the kind of centralised signalling control represented by this modern work on the West Coast main line is the need for the train crews to be able to keep in touch with the power boxes, even though they might be scores of miles away in open country. The new power boxes are centres of a comprehensive telecommunications network, which for operational and administrative purposes, embraces all stations, offices and remote relay rooms, and by means of direct lines and automatic systems. Telephone systems are also provided for emergency single line working, for communicating with the electric traction control rooms and for communication from the lineside to anywhere on the railway trunk dialling network, using portable telephones plugged in to the cable termination units provided every 540 yards along the track, this latter facility being for use in emergencies. Comprehensive alarm and monitoring systems are also provided to indicate the condition of telecommunications equipment at unmanned locations. Staff 'paging' systems, using loudspeakers every half-mile along the track, enable the signalmen to call maintenance staff of the three engineering departments to the nearest telephone wherever they are working, by broadcasting in selected areas the call sign unique to the department concerned. The telecommunication problems created by distance have been overcome by using multi-channel carrier systems, and those of interference from the traction system by using lineside cables screened by a corrugated aluminium sheath, which is earthed at regular intervals.

The regulation of traffic over the entire electrified main line from Weaver Junction to Gretna from no more than three control rooms is made much more efficient, with each regulator having the broad overall picture of the traffic position that the large illuminated panel diagrams provide; but on this newly electrified railway advantage has been taken of modern electronic technique in connection with the train description system to provide a novel instant-information service to the various Divisional Controls and to the central train control office of the entire London Midland Region, at Crewe. For very many years the traffic control system of the former LMS

Railway, which was adopted in principle for the LMR, provided for the routine reporting of train movements passing a number of selected timing points on the line, points corresponding to those at which passing times for each train were specified in the working timetable. These reports were originally made by telephone, and later by teleprinter. This process, satisfactory as it has generally proved over the years, necessarily involves a certain time-lag, in which signal box staff have to set up the necessary transmission; and now, additionally, a system of automatic train reporting has been inaugurated. This is activated by the train description apparatus, which transmits, instantaneously, the time at which trains enter the berth track circuit of each signal. A tape record is produced of all train movements within the area of each power signal box. This records, literally up to the minute, the time of transmission, the signal number from which it was made, and the timetable reporting number of the train. The reporting number is also displayed on the panel diagram in the main signal box concerned. When all is flowing smoothly the receipt of this information at Crewe is a matter of routine; but it does not need a great stretch of the imagination to appreciate how invaluable it is at times of unusual circumstance on the line.

Another important factor arising from the virtual disappearance of all lineside signal boxes, and the closing of practically all intermediate stations is that the observance of train running from the lineside has practically ceased. At one time, between Preston and Carlisle for example, there were intermediate signal boxes every 2 or 3 miles, and any irregularity in the running of trains, particularly of the freights would be noticed by signalmen and the train quickly stopped for examination.

As part of the automatic train reporting system, the operators at each of the three power signal boxes have the facility of being able to check the speeds of trains passing six pre-selected points in their control areas. After setting up the appropriate code on their teleprinter keyboards, they receive a printed report of the speed (in mph) of each train as it passes the checking point they have selected. This is deduced by the computer from the time-lag between the occupation of successive track circuits, the exact lengths of the speed measuring track circuits having been included in the computer program. This

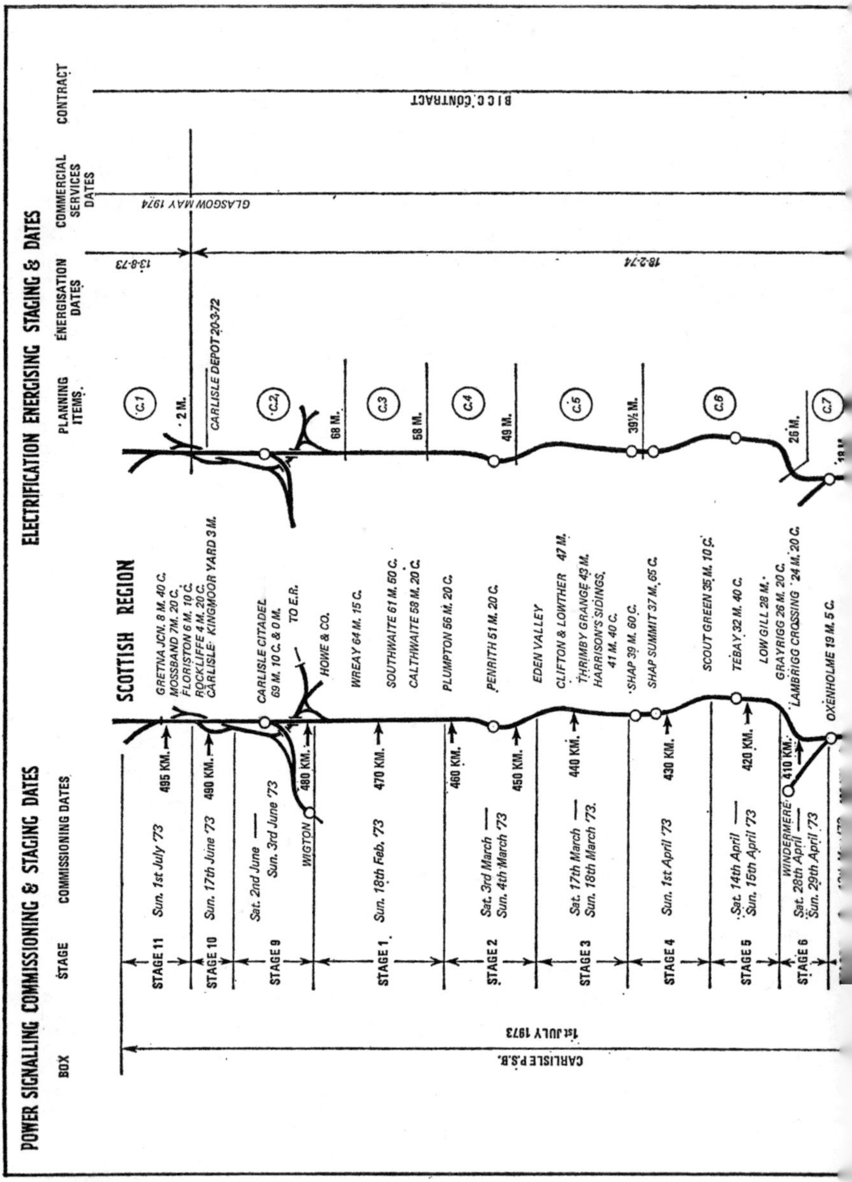

Weaver Junction–Gretna Junction; staging dates for signalling and overhead line energisation.

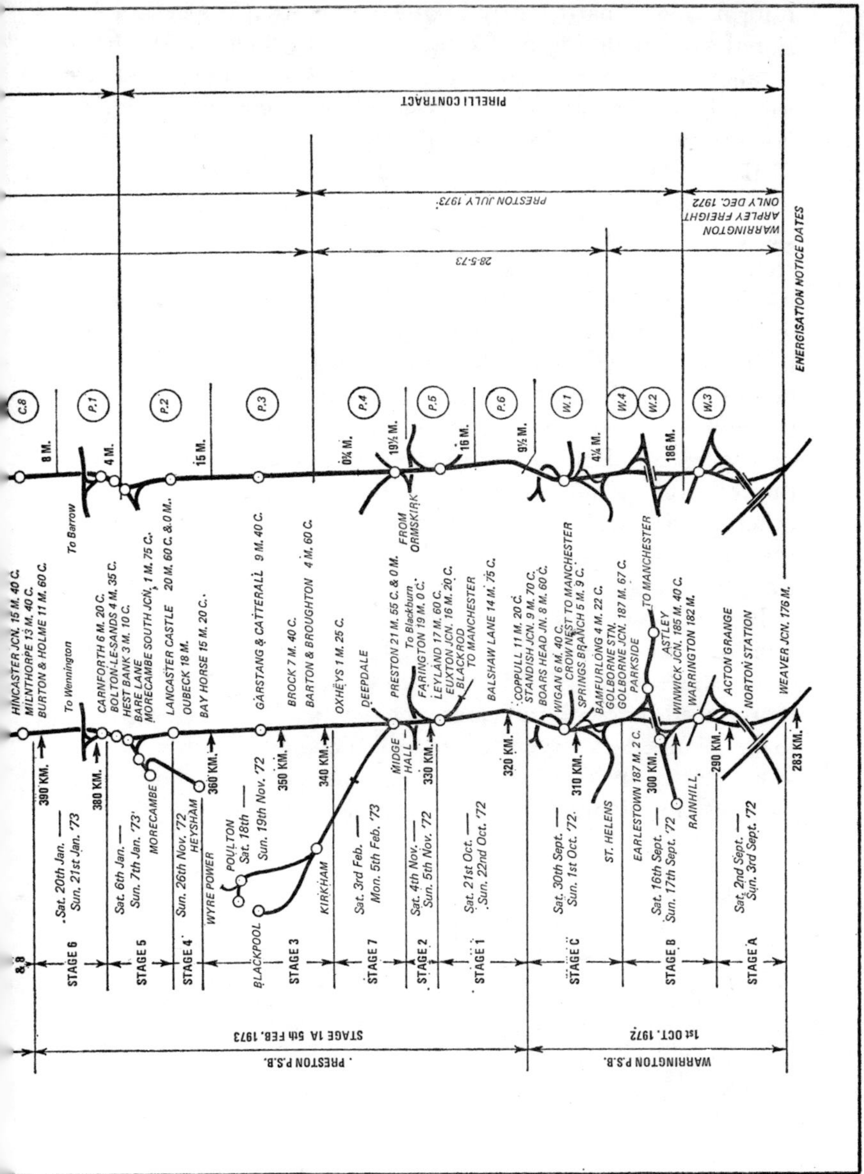
PIRELLI CONTRACT
PRESTON JULY 1973
28-5-73
WARRINGTON ARPLEY FREIGHT ONLY DEC. 1972
ENERGISATION NOTICE DATES
C.8
P.1
P.2
P.3
P.4
P.5
P.6
W.1
W.4
W.2
W.3
8 M.
4 M.
15 M.
0¼ M.
19½ M.
16 M.
9½ M.
4¼ M.
186 M.
To Barrow
FROM ORMSKIRK
TO MANCHESTER
HINCASTER JCN. 15 M. 40 C.
MILNTHORPE 13 M. 40 C.
BURTON & HOLME 11 M. 60 C.
To Wennington
CARNFORTH 6 M. 20 C.
BOLTON-LE-SANDS 4 M. 35 C.
HEST BANK 3 M. 10 C.
BARE LANE
MORECAMBE SOUTH JCN. 1 M. 75 C.
LANCASTER CASTLE 20 M. 60 C. & 0 M.
OUBECK 18 M.
BAY HORSE 15 M. 20 C.
GARSTANG & CATTERALL 9 M. 40 C.
BROCK 7 M. 40 C.
BARTON & BROUGHTON 4 M. 60 C.
OXHEYS 1 M. 25 C.
DEEPDALE
PRESTON 21 M. 55 C. & 0 M.
To Blackburn
FARINGTON 19 M. 0 C.
LEYLAND 17 M. 60 C.
EUXTON JCN. 16 M. 20 C.
BLACKROD
TO MANCHESTER
BALSHAW LANE 14 M. 75 C.
COPPULL 11 M. 20 C.
STANDISH JCN. 9 M. 70 C.
BOARS HEAD JN. 8 M. 60 C.
WIGAN 6 M. 40 C.
CROW NEST TO MANCHESTER
SPRINGS BRANCH 5 M. 9 C.
BAMFURLONG 4 M. 22 C.
GOLBORNE STN.
GOLBORNE JCN. 187 M. 67 C.
PARKSIDE
ASTLEY
WINWICK JCN. 185 M. 40 C.
WARRINGTON 182 M.
ACTON GRANGE
NORTON STATION
WEAVER JCN. 176 M.
390 KM.
380 KM.
360 KM.
350 KM.
340 KM.
330 KM.
320 KM.
310 KM.
300 KM.
290 KM.
283 KM.
MORECAMBE
HEYSHAM
WYRE POWER
POULTON
BLACKPOOL
KIRKHAM
MIDGE HALL
ST. HELENS
EARLESTOWN 187 M. 2 C.
RAINHILL
Sat. 20th Jan. — Sun. 21st Jan. '73
Sat. 6th Jan. — Sun. 7th Jan. '73
Sun. 26th Nov. '72
Sat. 18th — Sun. 19th Nov. '72
Sat. 3rd Feb. — Mon. 5th Feb. '73
Sat. 4th Nov. — Sun. 5th Nov. '72
Sat. 21st Oct. — Sun. 22nd Oct. '72
Sat. 30th Sept. — Sun. 1st Oct. '72
Sat. 16th Sept. — Sun. 17th Sept. '72
Sat. 2nd Sept. — Sun. 3rd Sept. '72
& 8
STAGE 6
STAGE 5
STAGE 4
STAGE 3
STAGE 7
STAGE 2
STAGE 1
STAGE C
STAGE B
STAGE A
STAGE 1A 5th FEB. 1973
1st OCT. 1972
PRESTON P.S.B.
WARRINGTON P.S.B.

information is particularly useful to the Area Supervisor in the signal box in deciding whether or not to 'loop' a freight train to allow an express to overtake. If the speed report shows that the freight is keeping up a good speed, he may well decide to let it continue to run in front of the express.

The hot box detector assesses the level of infra-red radiation from each axlebox, as it passes, and the alarm circuit operates if there is a significant difference between the levels of radiation from a pair of boxes on the same axle, as well as if there is a particularly high level from any individual box. Because of its great sensitivity, the hot box detector is able to pick out an incipient hot axle box before too much damage is done to the bearing, and this is one of its great virtues. The geographical positioning of the hot axlebox detectors, is carefully planned so that when an alarm has been received, the signalman can divert the train off the main line before stopping it, to avoid disrupting other traffic, and a special siding is provided at this point so that the faulty wagons can be detached and allow the rest of the train to proceed.

Before leaving the new signalling works between Weaver Junction and Gretna it is interesting to put on record details of the stage work by which the work was installed. The diagram reproduced herewith indicates most vividly how the progress had to be planned in order to keep traffic moving with minimum interference during the intervening period. The diagram also includes the planned stages for energising the overhead line.

9: RESIGNALLING: KIRKPATRICK TO GLASGOW

On the Scottish section of the West Coast main line electrification the running conditions differ considerably on the southern and northern parts of the line. From Gretna Junction where Scottish Region begins, for a distance of 65 miles, the route is virtually 'plain line'. There are no intermediate junctions; only one intermediate station, at Lockerbie, and the only track configurations requiring diversion of trains from the simple two track line occur at places where there are running loops, for the temporary berthing of freight and other slower traffic to give priority to faster trains. These loops are at Quintinshill – within the sphere of LMR signalling control – Lockerbie, Beattock, Beattock Summit and Abington, until the more complicated part of the route commences at Carstairs. There are also emergency crossovers at Kirtlebridge, Lockerbie, Wamphray, Summit, Abington, and Symington. The track layout as rationalised is shown in the accompanying diagram. The whole of this southern part of the line, from the link up with the LMR is under the control of the new power box at Motherwell 86 route miles in all. It would be as straightforward a stretch of multiple-aspect colour light signalling as could be imagined, but for the incidence of the very severe gradients leading to Beattock Summit.

The actual gradients are little steeper than the steepest part of the ascent to Shap Summit from the south, though the Beattock Bank is roughly twice as long; and with express passenger, and priority freight trains no particular difficulty, or appreciable diminution in speed is expected. There is however a difference in the traffic pattern. Over the electrified LMR line south of Carlisle it is intended that none save fully fitted trains will be operated, and all run-away catch points on the steep gradients have been removed. North of Carlisle the pattern is expected to be different. Some of the fully fitted trains working over the Shap route will take the G&SW line from Gretna, while some

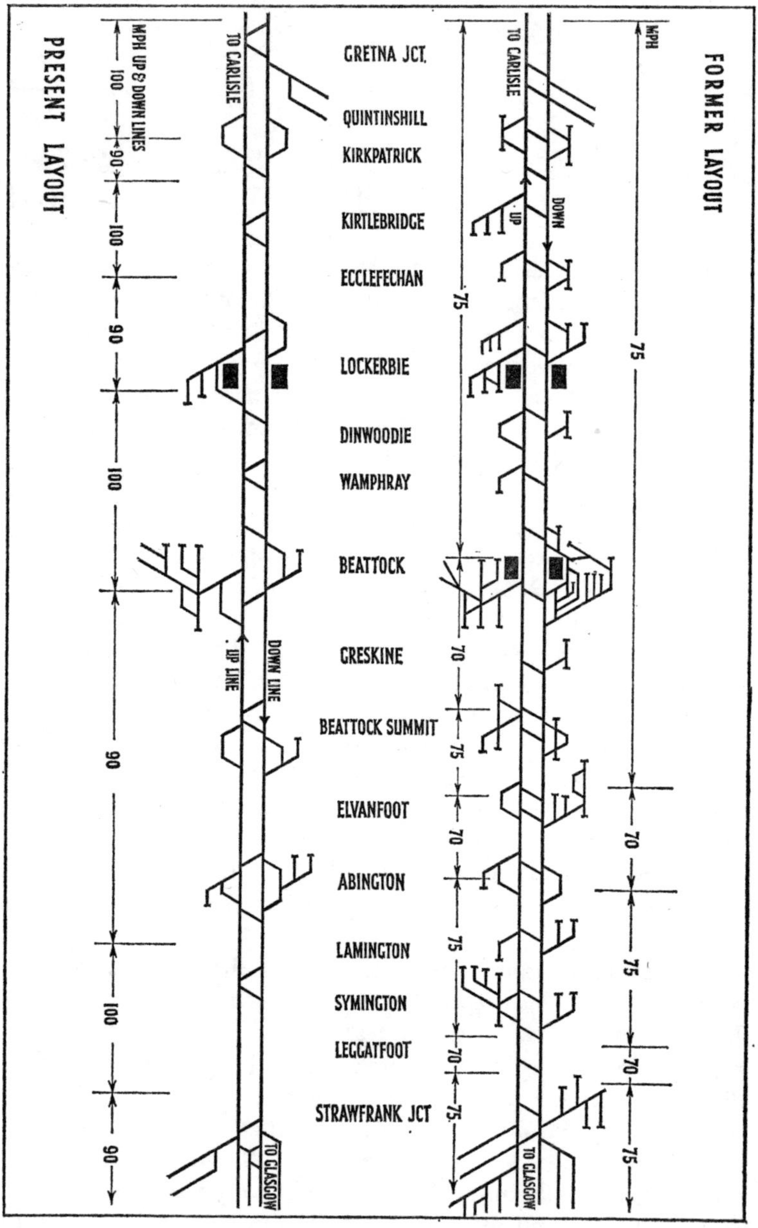

Gretna–Carstairs track rationalisation; original and present arrangements.

partially fitted trains using the Settle and Carlisle line, to or from the south, will run over the electrified line north of Gretna. For this reason it has not been possible to dispense with run-away catch points on the steeper gradients, and such sections that might otherwise have been simple automatic signalling have had to receive special attention. The total number of them has however been greatly reduced.

In the 10 miles of the Beattock Bank going north, on gradients of about 1 in 75 throughout, there are, for example, several sets of catch points on the down, or ascending road. The colour light signals immediately preceding these catch points are controlled, and when an unfitted, or partially fitted train is ascending – unless it should have a bank engine in rear – this controlled signal may not be cleared again until the train has cleared the next set of catch points higher up the bank. Of course with express passenger and fully fitted trains the signal leading to a pair of catch points can be set as soon as the preceeding train has cleared the next automatic signal ahead. During the early months after the first commissioning of the new signalling on this section of the line the signalmen were a little unused to the operation of these controlled signals protecting catch points. The following two incidents may be mentioned, not in any spirit of criticism but in appreciation of the unfamiliarity of the men with the new arrangements. Both of these incidents I saw personally from the locomotive cab.

On the first occasion I was riding north from Carlisle on one of the London expresses, and the locomotive inspector who joined me at Carlisle said that we might not get a very good road, because one of the Liverpool trains had experienced engine trouble and had left only just ahead. We did quite well however until we got on to the Beattock Bank, and then began to receive restrictive aspects. Once however a 'red' to which we were crawling changed immediately to 'double yellow', and a second 'red' changed without any intermediate clearing straight to 'green', showing in both cases that the signalman on the Motherwell panel was not clearing those controlled signals as quickly as he was entitled to do. The second incident was at Elvanfoot going south. The controlled signal at the foot of the final rise up to Beattock summit was 'on', and we had to stop and 'phone the box. In this case the signalman was obviously preoccupied with certain other movements on his section, and

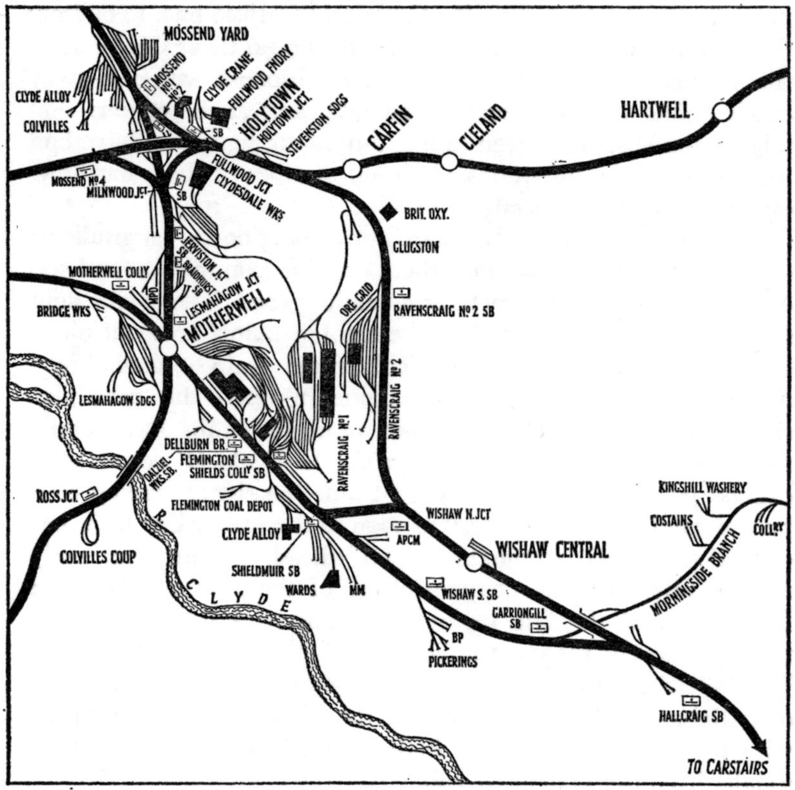

Motherwell area: the track complex.

had not noted our position. On his attention being drawn he pulled straight from 'red' to 'green' and we went on at high speed to find not another train anywhere on the line until nearing Carlisle.

The new panel-box at Motherwell, in its equipment, follows the standard practice of British Railways, as exemplified on the West Coast main line farther south. It is notable however in controlling the longest stretch of colour light signalling anywhere in Great Britain under the surveillance of one signal box. Its area extends from Kirkpatrick in Dumfriesshire to Cambuslang, a total of 80 miles. In addition, to the principal main line, as indicated in my references to the physical features of the electrified route, in Chapter 6, there are the many ramifications in the Motherwell area. Traffic working in this complex network is bound to benefit from the concentration of control in one centre As with the installations farther south, control of the outlying areas is effected through a series of satellite interlockings, and these are located at Abington, Beattock, Summit, Carmyle, Carstairs, Holytown, Hamilton, Law, Lanark, Lockerbie, Mossend, Newton, Uddingston, Whifflet and Wishaw. It now represents the largest geographical area in Great Britain controlled from one centre. It is of additional interest in that the single line branch to Lanark is arranged for automatic working at its terminus. The total of the control from Motherwell are as follows:

Track Circuits including separate cut-sections	881
Signals, running and ground, irrespective of the number of signal units at each	545
Number of signalled routes	741
Number of point machines	329

As a signalling contractor who has been associated with work in the Glasgow area since the year 1930 I have been exceptionally interested in developments in readiness for electrification. One of the interim stages, commissioned as part of the earliest phases of the Modernisation Plan, was the resignalling of Newton station, now a part of the Motherwell centralised interlocking. Track remodelling at Newton demanded new signalling, and a relay interlocking of the standard 'OCS' type was installed, with multiple aspect colour light signals. It was then no more than an isolated piece of modernisation, sandwiched between the manual block signalling on either side. In the present modernisation it remained the last part of the Motherwell control area to remain 'independent', as it were; but it has now been linked to the Motherwell interlocking as a 'satellite' not normally manned. The Newton installation forms the last section to be controlled from Motherwell, and beyond Cambuslang one passes into the area of control of Glasgow Central signal box. It may be remarked that in the 227 miles of electrified main line from Weaver Junction to Glasgow there are now only five manned signalboxes.

The area controlled by the modernised Glasgow Central signal

Glasgow, the eastern approaches.

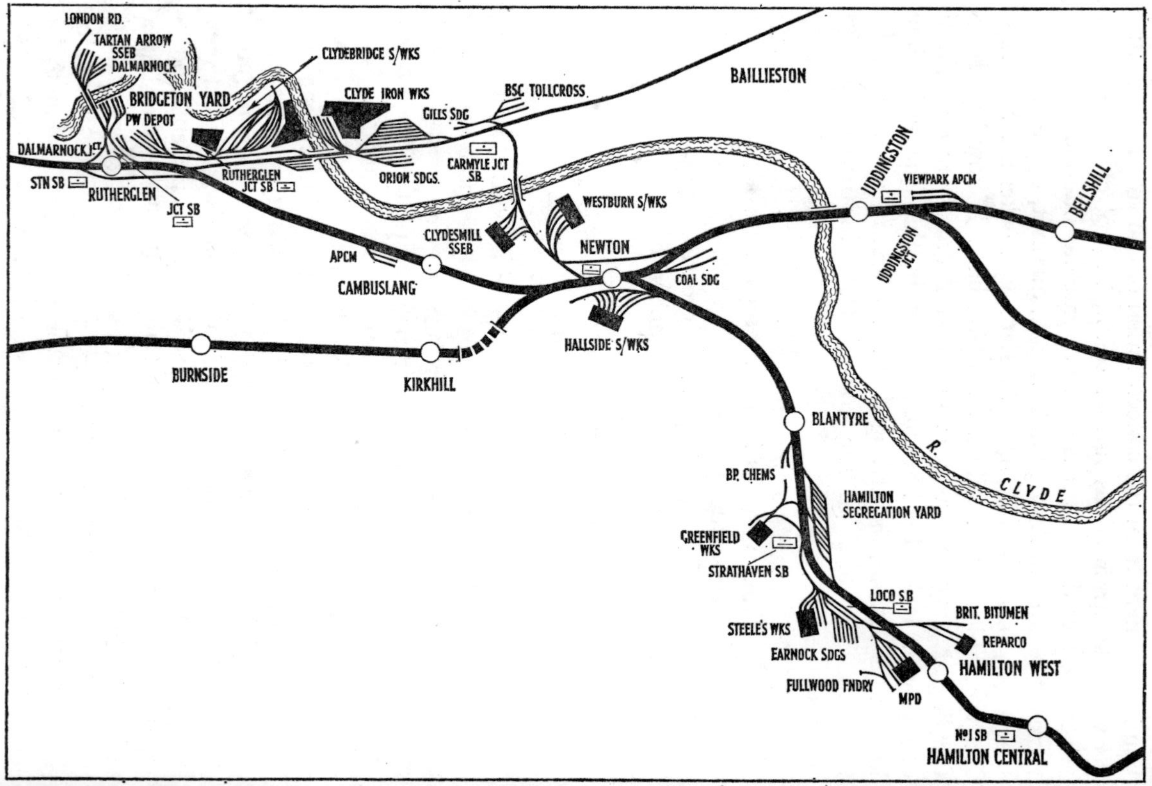

HE 5000 HORSEPOWER CLASS '87'

ove: The BP 9 bogie fitted to the lass '87' weighs 18·1 tons, the ısprung weight of each axle is 6 tons. Primary suspension consists Alsthom type links guiding dependently sprung roller bearing :leboxes. Secondary suspension is of e 'flexicoil' type using the three coil rings on each bogie that give the locomotive distinctive appearance. / *British Rlys*

Below: Roof mounted equipment on the Class '87' locomotive includes air blast circuit breaker, earthing switch and rheostatic brake exhaust louvres. Power for the locomotive is taken from the 25kV 50 Hz overhead supply by a 'cross arm' pantograph /*British Rlys*

WARRINGTON RESIGNALLING

Below: Exterior of the New Panel Box / *British Rlys*
Bottom: View in the operating room / *British Rlys*

MODERN SIGNALLING TECHNIQUES

Right: Time-division multiplex equipment for control and indication of remote interlockings / *British Rlys*
Below Right: Monitoring panel to facilitate easy and quick fault-finding *British Rlys*

36

PRESTON PANEL BOX
Above: A striking impression of the huge control console / *British Rlys*
Below: A close-up, showing the layout at Farrington Junction / *British Rlys*

WARRINGTON CONTROL CONSOLE
Right: A close-up, showing layout of tracks on the diagram at the passeng station, with the dark rectangles on which train descriptions are displaye
British Rlys

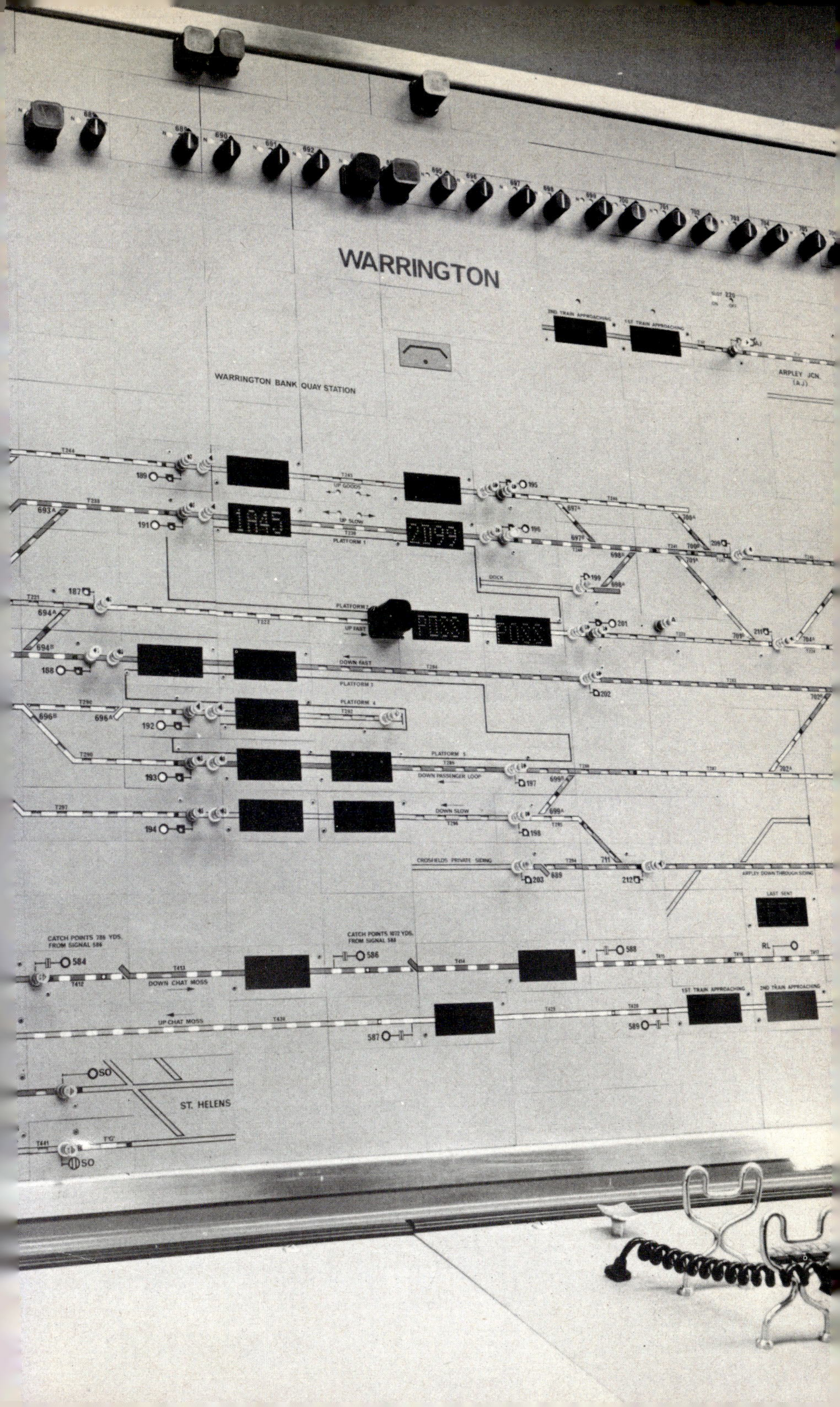
WARRINGTON
WARRINGTON BANK QUAY STATION
ARPLEY JCN. (A.J.)
1A45
2D99
DOWN FAST
DOWN CHAT MOSS
UP CHAT MOSS
ST. HELENS

38

Above: The constructional depot, for overhead wiring installation, at Carlisle / *British Rlys*

Below: Hot box detector display panels in Preston panel box / *British*

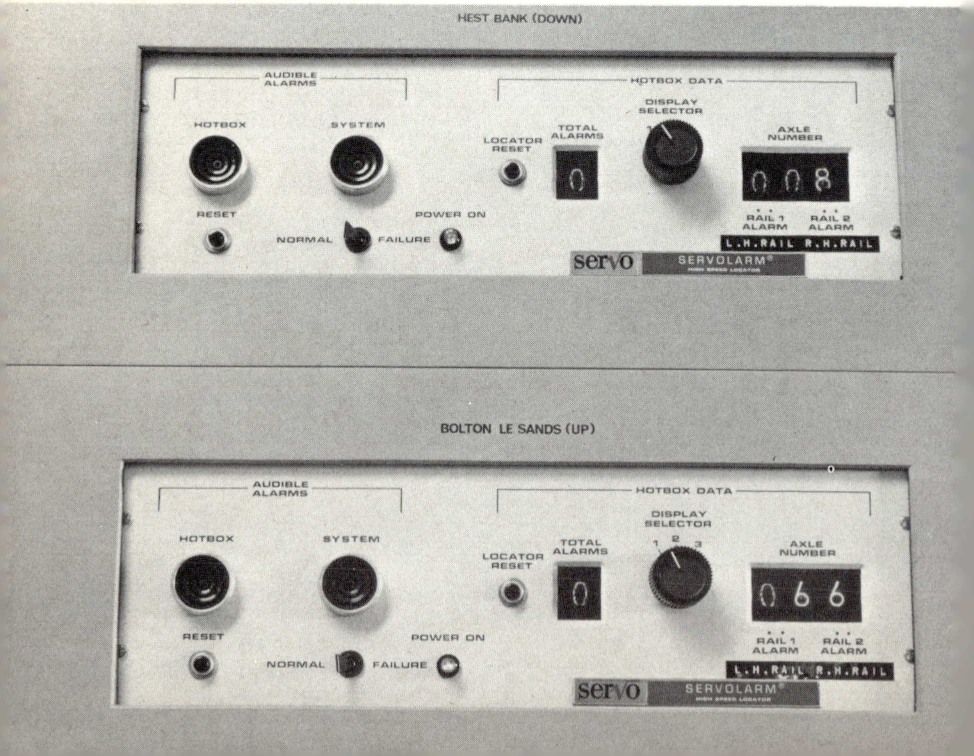

GNAL STRUCTURES

ove: At the north end of Preston rd, with the line to Blackpool rving away to the left. / *British Rlys*

Below: The new Shields (Glasgow) electric traction depot as background to a colour light signal gantry / *British Rlys*

40

TRAIN DESCRIPTION
Part of the computerised installation at Warrington showing:—
Left: The continuous train log and record sheet / *British Rlys*

Below: Close up of keyboard and sheet, on which is recorded times of passage of trains, reporting numbers, and speeds / *British Rlys*

DIVERSION TO THE G&SW LINE
Right: Glasgow–Euston express (locos D 445 and D 410) leaving Kilmarnock—May 1971 / *Derek Cross*

Below Right: Glasgow–Euston express in the beautiful scenery of the Drumlanrig Gorge: Class '50' locomotives D 440 and D 423 (August 1970) / *Derek Cross*

1M30
445

1M18

42

STILL WIDER G&SW DIVERSIONS

Above: Sunday Glasgow–Euston express east of Falkland Junction, Ayr, because of permanent way work at Kilmarnock, November 1971. Class '50' locomotives D 424 and D 423 / *Derek Cross*

Below: In May 1969: Euston–Glasgow sleeping car express at Lochgreen Junction, Troon, because of permanent way work at Kilmarnock. Class '50' locomotive No 441 / *Derek Cross*

DIVERSIONS IN 1972

Above: Liverpool–Glasgow express approaching Kilmarnock: Class '50' locomotive No D 417 / *Derek Cross*

Below: Glasgow–Birmingham express in the Drumlanrig Gorge. Locomotive No D 423 / *J. H. Cooper-Smith*

THE TWO ROUTES TO GLASGOW

44 *Above:* Glasgow–Euston express near Sanquhar in September 1971—hauled by Class '50' locomotive No D 419 / *Derek Cross*

Below: Liverpool–Glasgow express just after crossing the Clyde at Lamington, with two Class '50' locomotives, D 409 and D 423 / *J. H Cooper-Smith*

Right: Constructional days north of Oxenholme: the down 'Royal Scot' running 'wrong line' on the Grayrigg Bank, during occupation of the down main line. Class '50' locomotives 416 and 441 / *J. H. Cooper-Smith*

1S57

| THE ELECTRIC LOCOMOTIVE ABS

ft: Driving instruction on a Class '86' Scotland / *British Rlys*

low: *Left*, The cab of a Class '87': iver's cab of the first locomotive to completed. Features include forced ntilation with automatic temperature ntrol, high impact resistance ctrically heated windscreen, two-eed window wipers with travelling ater jet and push button operated ctro-hydraulic parking brake. The ass '87s' are the first production build of locomotives to include a new design of Drivers Vigilance System which ensures even greater safety of operation / *British Rlys*

ELECTRIC LOCOMOTIVES IN SCOTLAND

Bottom: Class '86/2' No 86202 with test car No 4 at Beattock / *Derek Cross*

Below: Test train on the Beattock Bank near Auchencastle, with No 86202 at the head end, and Class '85', No E 3085 in rear / *Derek Cross*

ELECTRIC TESTS ON BEATTOCK BANK—MAY 1973

Above: Test train ready to leave site of Beattock station, with No 86202 and E 3085 at the rear / *Derek Cross*

Below: Test train at Hartrope Viaduct / *Derek Cross*

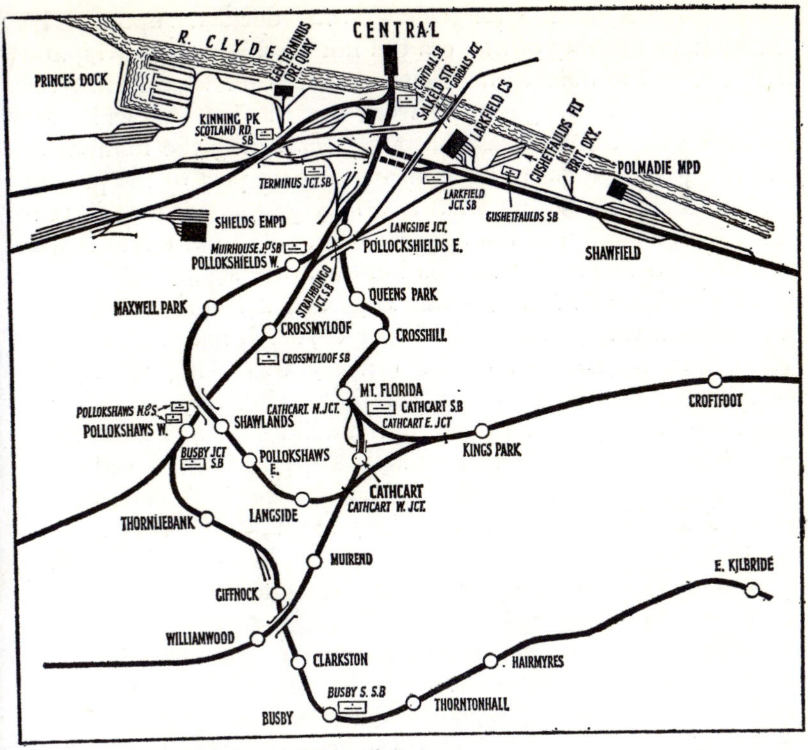

Glasgow: Central station and its outlets.

box is one of the most complex and most diversely used anywhere in Great Britain. One is mindful of other large interlocking areas, not least those in the London suburban area served by the Southern Region; but as the accompanying diagram shows, Glasgow Central is far from exclusively concerned with traffic into and out of a very large passenger terminal. The area has always been one receiving particular attention from the signalling point of view, and the process of evolution from the time when power signalling was first installed, in 1908, to the present fine plant forms in many ways an epitome of British main line signalling practice. In less than twenty years before the turn of the century the passenger traffic at the Central station, both in number of trains and passengers conveyed had roughly trebled, and it was when the number of passengers using the station annually topped the sixteen million mark that enlargement was decided upon. The Caledonian Railway of that era did not do things by halves, and they decided to *double* the accommodation for trains. How the very difficult civil engineering work was carried out, while the operating department was constantly *increasing* the number of trains run—upheaval or no upheaval—is no part of the present story and retrospect; but what is strictly germane is that a complete reorganisation of the approach lines took place and it was this that led to the first installation of power signalling.

The station of the 1890s was approached from the south by a four-track viaduct across the River Clyde. It had been built in 1879, and by the end of the century was being worked to saturation point. Some enlargement in keeping with the enlargement of the platform and passenger facilities of the station itself would have been a logical enough step; but the Caledonian management, with a wisdom for which British Railways have many times had ample reason to be grateful, decided not merely to double their capacity across the Clyde, but to *treble* it. The new viaduct, downstream from the older one was built to carry no fewer than nine tracks abreast. It was then that the decision was taken to operate the entire station from one signal box. The electro-pneumatic system of power signalling was chosen, and the grand total of 258 signals and 79 pairs of points operated from one interlocking frame. It proved to be the largest ever constructed for service in Great Britain, and had a total of 374 levers. But it controlled only the Central Station and its immediate approaches, and communication with adjacent boxes was by block telegraph.

This great installation had become a 'period piece' so far as signalling practice was concerned by the late 1920s, and in the years that followed it was slightly modernised by the addition of track locking on the facing points. But it continued to give effective and reliable service for another twenty years, until the Modernisation Plan of British Railways was launched, and with it plans for electrifying the suburban lines both north and south of the River Clyde. By that time passenger traffic had fallen somewhat below that of the peak years of the Caledonian, before World War I, but it was expected to increase again with the forthcoming electrification of the Cathcart Circle, and to Gourock and Wemyss Bay. But then a complication arose, in that the original four-track viaduct of 1879 was showing such signs of deterioration as to make its complete replacement necessary. It was in meeting this admittedly difficult situation that the first step was taken towards the modernisation scheme that has now been completed. There were a number of operating factors that had to be borne in mind. While electrification of the Clyde Coast and Cathcart Circle services would replace locomotive hauled trains by multiple unit sets, and light engine movements would thereby be lessened two features of the working at Glasgow Central also lessened the chances of relief, from these changes.

The Cathcart Circle trains were operated from the short platforms 6 and 7, both connected by short leads to an engine siding reserved for the tank engines engaged on the service. While each train on arrival had to be re-engined for the next trip it was done by movements virtually independent from the rest of the station working. So that while these small light engine movements would be eliminated with electrification, this would not provide any relief to the volume of traffic, or engine movements over the approach lines across the River Clyde. The Gourock and Wemyss Bay trains were accommodated at the extreme west platforms 12 and 13; but after unloading the empty stock was usually propelled by the incoming train engine to the various carriage sidings on the south side of the river. Trains propelled thus, by a locomotive in rear, right through the interlocking area of the Central Station signalbox, to sidings such as Smithy Lye, were the equivalent of a 'set' train as far as signalling movements were concerned, since no light-engine working was involved in their clearance from the platforms. A multiple-unit electric train would offer no simplification of movement over these smartly run 'empties'. Where a definite reduction would be possible with electrification was in light engine movements to and from Polmadie motive power depot, where the majority of the steam tank engines engaged on the Clyde Coast services were stationed.

Having regard to the great improvements in control rendered possible by signalling practice, as it had developed by the early 1950s, a feasibility study of the first importance was carried out on the train workings across the Clyde into Glasgow Central. In addition to the services immediately scheduled for electrification, the local and semi-fast services on other routes were being changed from steam-hauled coaching stock to diesel and multiple-unit trains, thus still further reducing the number of train and engine movements required in the terminus. A still more cogent factor in this feasability study was the facility afforded, by modern signalling and complete track circuiting, that with electric route locking each running line could be signalled for either direction running, to make the fullest possible use of line capacity. It was determined that by signalling thus every one of the eight running lines then in use across the 'new' bridge of 1904, it could be made to carry the entire traffic of the 1960s, and that the original bridge of 1879 could be dispensed with.

Having reached this conclusion, an operating point arose. Systems of power signalling, with control from panel diagrams instead of interlocking frames, indicated the extent of a route set by a chain of white lights on the appropriate section of the track diagram. How could this be applied to the eight running lines across the River Clyde, all of which were to be signalled for either direction running? Furthermore, the approach to a number of the platform roads in the station could be made by quite a number of alternative routes. This facility was recognised as being of great advantage in providing flexibility of working at times of heavy track occupation; but the signalling arrangements necessary to provide this facility in a way that gave the simplest possible aspects to enginemen, and did not introduce undue complications so far as the actual setting up of the routes was concerned, was a matter of much discussion and careful detailed planning. There were for example, with the re-arranged track layout, five ways of getting from No 57 signal to platform 7 – one of those used for Cathcart Circle trains; and no fewer than nineteen ways of making a special propelling move from No 7 platform to No 4 carriage sidings.

The Scottish Region operating authorities of that period decided upon the 'one-control-switch' system of operation, as this was generally favoured at the same time on the London Midland Region, and it had been successfully installed at Cowlairs, on the northern side of Glasgow. But the alternative route facilities available in the track layout at Glasgow Central posed a problem in route setting. Eventually a system that has proved the only one of its kind ever installed was adopted. As in the normal 'OCS' type of control panel and console, the route setting switches were arranged on a sloping keyboard below the illuminated track diagram, and in connection with the following equipment was mounted on the keyboard:

(*a*) A push button for each of the destinations.
(*b*) A rotary route selection switch.
(*c*) A signal thumb switch.

Taking the example of No 57 signal, this controlled entry to routes leading to eleven out of the thirteen platforms in the station, while from No 58 signal one could proceed to every one of the thirteen platforms. For each of these destinations there was a push button on the sloping keyboard. The rotary selector switches had a special function. Having pressed the button for the destination required the signalman turned the rotary switch till the pointer indicated which of the alternative routes was free. This indication was provided on the illuminated track diagram in the same manner as the 'route set' lights on the ordinary 'OCS' type of panel. But here again, Glasgow had its specialities. If the route was free it was indicated by a chain of magenta coloured lights. The signalman had then to set the route, which he did by turning the signal thumb-switch. It was considered necessary in so complex a layout to give a clear distinction between a route that was set for a train entering and one that was leaving, in view of the fact that all running lines were signalled for either direction running. So the setting of an ingoing movement was indicated on the panel in yellow lights, and for an outgoing movement in white lights. Production of the miniature lamp units, in which three separate colours had to be displayed through a single aperture involved some intricate problems in design.

Whereas the signal box of 1908 was sited at the north end of the Clyde viaduct, between the 'old' lines leading to the original four-track viaduct over the river, and the 'new' lines, the new signal box of 1961 was sited adjacent to the former Bridge Street Junction, in the 'V' formed by the junction of the Clyde Coast lines and the main line to the south. It was a very large one, and the topmost of the four storeys contained the operating room. The control panel, with switch setting for over 1,000 routes was, at the time of its commissioning, believed to be the largest in the world operated from one control desk. This latter originally had four sections, with the illuminated diagram spaced at some little distance to the rear, for satisfactory viewing, while the traffic regulator, and other staff based in the control room had desks on raised dais in a central position in the room. The train description system was of the type then currently in use, indicating the class and destination of trains on a large display panel, above, and almost as long as the illuminated track diagram itself.

Although this installation of 1961 was so large it replaced no more than two signal boxes in addition to the old electro-pneumatic box of 1908. These latter were those at Eglinton Street, and Bridge Street Junction. The controls extended just beyond the 'parting of the ways' between the Clyde Coast and the main lines to the south. It covered only what had formerly been Caledonian territory. In 1961 St Enoch station of the former G&SWR was still in use, and from that station, Clyde Coast, and Anglo-Scottish services were still being operated. But prior to the inauguration of electric services on the former Caledonian route to Gourock and Wemyss Bay, in 1967, an extensive rationalising of routes in the Glasgow area had taken place. The working at 'Central' had settled down to the new conditions sufficiently to be able to absorb certain traffic formerly handled at St Enoch and in 1966 this latter station had been closed altogether. With electrification the Clyde Coast services were re-organised so as to be worked entirely from 'Central', while Anglo-Scottish expresses coming up from the south via the G&SW route took the left hand fork at Strathbungo Junction, and came into 'Central' on the route of the Cathcart Circle trains.

Signalling-wise there were important developments, constituting a further step towards the present concentration at 'Central'. All intermediate signalboxes on the Clyde Coast line between Glasgow and Paisley were closed, and the new colour light signalling, including that for the new double-line junction at Shields connections to the former Canal line was controlled by a new panel interlocking operated from the main control room of the Glasgow Central signal box. Following this modernisation there were only three signal boxes concerned with the coast services south of Clyde – Glasgow Central, Paisley and Gourock. This work provided yet another example of the way in which modern signalling can reduce maintenance and other charges; because with the close headway working possible with multi-aspect signalling it was found possible to dispense with two of the four running lines previously existing between Shields and Paisley. It was perhaps understandable that four tracks should have been found necessary when this part of the route was being used, in pre-grouping days, by the trains of two separate companies, in keen competition with each other.

Such then was the situation in the Glasgow area when plans were being made for the electrification of the West Coast main line northwards from Weaver Junction. The signalling at the Central station had been modernised, according to the practice of the early 1960s, and a high degree of co-ordination effected in the working of the Clyde Coast services, again with modern equipment. But even then the ceaseless onrush of evolution in signalling practice was making work done no more than ten years earlier look obsolete, and in view of the establishment of standard panel designs by British Railways the Glasgow installations, new as they were, had to be seriously reconsidered. It was in any case desired to complete the integration of all signalling control in the central Glasgow area south of the Clyde, bringing in the main line as far east as Cambuslang, linking up with the existing panel box at Cathcart, and incorporating the former G&SW freight lines from Shields, and Langside Junctions respectively to College goods station. So it was decided to replace the 'OCS' type panel, with its unique switching arrangements, and the subsidiary panel controlling the Shields junctions by a new panel of the standard British Railways 'entrance exit' type, which would incorporate all lines in the central Glasgow area on a single instrument of the most up-to-date type.

It was not an easy decision, because the plant in the relatively new Glasgow Central signal box represented a large capital investment. The equipment and circuitry of interlocking was modern, and fully acceptable in itself; it was that the more modern practice of panel operation, and above all the latest form of train description that made possible so much more compact a layout, with the facility of incorporating readily all the desired extensions. The very difficult course was therefore decided upon, to retain all the existing relay interlocking for the Glasgow Central and Shields areas and install a system of 'interface' connections that would allow it to be controlled from an 'entrance exit' type of panel. The earlier train description system would however need to be completely replaced, by the latest computerised type. In this way a large amount of the equipment of 1961 would be utilised, including all the outside gear – signals, point operating mechanisms and so on.

Then however there was the physical task of installing the new type of panel – *in the same control room* – while the older one continued to handle the traffic. There was not much room to spare! Space at the southern end of the room had been taken up by the Shields panel. The fortunate thing was that the new entrance-exit panel was much smaller than the original one. But some highly intricate planning was necessary to carry out the various stages whereby, section by section, the work could be transferred from the old to the new. The first sections of the new panel could not be installed in their final place at first, and temporary mountings had to be arranged, and temporary wiring. But the numerous stages in the changeover were carried out according to plan, and by June 1973 when I had the privilege of visiting the box once again the transformation from the old equipment that I knew so well in the early 1960s was complete. Although supplied by a different manufacturer the panel itself is in much the same style as those newly installed on the London Midland Region, with similar excellent indications on the computerised train description apparatus. The progress in design that has enabled these indications to be so compactly arranged on the panel diagram – a diagram which is in itself much smaller – is perhaps the most impressive feature of the modernised Glasgow Central box, in comparison with the work completed only twelve years earlier.

10: THE TIME OF TRANSITION

One of the great problems of a work of this magnitude involving what has previously been so aptly described as the building of a new railway over the tracks of an old one, and keeping normal traffic running all the time, is to keep faith with one's customers, not subjecting them to undue inconvenience and delay while work essential to the construction of the new railway is in progress. It is never an easy task, and the travelling public with alternative methods of transit, by air, and by private car so accelerated by the completion of the motorway, often seems ready enough to follow a popular pastime and 'knock' the railways, It was certainly so to an alarming extent during the construction of the electrified line south of Crewe, though the end result when the electric trains did begin to run was gratifying almost beyond belief.

At the time the electrification scheme was authorised, in February 1970, traffic on the main line north of Preston was considerably less intense than that south of Crewe, for example; and in planning for the considerable amount of line possession that would be needed by the department of the Chief Mechanical and Electrical Engineer it was considered that much of the work might be done by granting weekday rather than weekend possessions. It was appreciated that these would involve single line working, but it was hoped not to an extent that would cause serious delay or inconvenience to the existing train service. In Scotland, as mentioned earlier in this book the step was taken of closing the Caledonian line during the normal daytime working hours, and routeing traffic over the G&SW line.

During the period of discussion before the electrification scheme was authorised the possibility of attractive acceleration by using two Class '50' diesel electric locomotives was constantly in mind, and in the summer of 1970 a very considerable speed up of services between Crewe and Carlisle was made, cutting the time of the southbound 'Royal Scot' for example from 148½ to 121½min over the 141 miles from Carlisle to Crewe. The time of down expresses calling at Preston was cut to 75½min for the 90 miles northward to Carlisle. On the trains running non-stop between Crewe and Carlisle a total of 8min recovery time was included in the schedule, though this provided for no more than temporary restrictions of speed, for engineering work, without any diversion from the normal track. By that time the process of route improvement had been carried sufficiently far for the fastest trains, hauled by a pair of Class '50' diesels in multiple, to average 75mph between Crewe and Carlisle, or vice versa, when running up to full recovery standard. By that time several stretches of line north of Weaver Junction were already cleared for 100mph running.

It was a most enterprising acceleration, and immediately proved fully practicable in operation. Difficulties did arise however if *two* Class '50' locomotives were not available for the more sharply timed trains. With a complete absence of delays the recovery time in the schedule enabled expert drivers with a single Class '50' locomotive to get very near to exact time; but there was not the slightest margin. When electrification work began it was necessary to ease out these fast schedules to provide recovery time for instances of single line working, resulting from weekday possessions and to minimise delay the 'Rules of the Route' were specified in close detail. Weekday possessions were permitted during definitely specified hours between Preston and Gretna Junction. During 1973–4 some of those permitted may be quoted, first of all those between Preston and Lancaster:

HOURS AUTHORISED

Down Line	*Up Line*
From 04.15 to 11.00	From 04.00 to 11.00

On the down line possessions could begin after passage of Train IM 43, the 01.09 Parcels, Huddersfield to Carlisle Yard; it was required to finish in time to give Train IS 47, the 08.00 Euston to Glasgow a clear run. Similar specific trains were specified for the up line possession.

No weekday possessions were permitted between Carnforth and Shap Summit during 1973–4, but between Summit and Carlisle, possessions lasting up to 13hr, between 05.00 and 18.00 were permitted. To facilitate traffic working however the 13hr period could be divided between two locations. The Rules of the Route laid down however that two instances of single line working could be permitted between Preston and Gretna Junction (excluding the section between Carnforth and Shap Summit) provided that they were on opposite lines, and at least three single-line sections apart. To provide recovery margins in the case of trains meeting cases of single line working, the schedules of non-stop trains between Crewe and Carlisle were eased to 130min.

In general, no weekday possessions were permitted between Weaver Junction and Preston, and the diversion routes in connection with weekend possessions were as follows:

Section	*Diversion*
Weaver Junc–Acton Grange Junc	SLW or via Halton Junc and Frodsham Junc
Acton Grange Junc to Winwick Junc	Fast, or slow lines as available
Winwick Junc to Golborne Junc	Via Earlestown
Golborne Junc to Wigan	Fast or slow lines as available
Wigan–Balshaw Lane	Single line working (SLW)
Balshaw Lane–Preston	Fast or slow lines as available

At certain times however the Earlestown diversion route was used on weekdays, in which case a generous amount of extra time was included in the schedule. At the time of some of the busiest electrification work, in February 1973, two cases of actual running will be of interest. On one weekday occasion the 08.15 Birmingham to Glasgow was taken forward from Crewe by two Class '50' diesels, and a very rapid start was made, covering the first 22 miles from rest in 16½min. Speed had been maintained between the narrow limits of 96 and 100mph throughout from Winsford to Weaver Junction. Then at Winwick Junction the train was turned on to the Grand Junction line, and proceeded, very slowly, through the succession of junctions, along the Liverpool and Manchester line, and finally back to rejoin the West Coast main line at Golborne Junction. As a result of this perambulation the 9·9 miles from Warrington to Bamfurlong took 16¼min. It was nevertheless remarkable that despite this, and because mainly of the very rapid start, the train was able to pass Wigan, $36\frac{3}{4}$ miles by this longer-than-normal route, in 36min from the dead start at Crewe. Further slowings for permanent way work followed but with fast concluding running the 51·8 miles from Crewe to Preston by this route were completed in $52\frac{1}{4}$min, and on the schedule of this train, which then included a good deal of recovery time, the arrival at Preston was slightly ahead of time. By comparison, on a more recent journey when no checks were experienced, and the normal route was followed Preston was passed – on a Crewe–Carlisle non-stop run – in $39\frac{1}{2}$min, for the distance of 51 miles.

On the same day as the diversion run via Earlestown, the 11.15 Glasgow to Euston, again hauled by two Class '50' locomotives, was subject to heavy delay between Coppull and Golborne Junction, taking $17\frac{1}{4}$min for this distance of 11·7 miles. This included a diversion from fast to slow line at Wigan, and a return to fast line at Golborne Junction. This train then had an allowance of 57min for the 51 miles from Preston to Crewe, but with fast running before and after the delayed central part of the journey, a late start of 3min from Preston was easily converted into an arrival 4min early at Crewe – total time for 51 miles being 50min.

It was however not always possible to maintain even the lengthened schedules during the period of the most intense constructional work. In one instance noted, when a slight mishap on an adjoining line had led to the 16.05 Euston to Glasgow leaving Preston 26min late, it had not been possible to provide a second Class '50' for haulage, and with a twelve-coach train a single engine would have had difficulty in keeping time in any event. There was in addition a temporary reduction of speed for engineering work at Bolton-le-Sands, so that the Shap ascent was commenced at only 70mph instead of the permitted 90mph through Carnforth. Booked time for the 31·4 miles up to Shap Summit was $26\frac{1}{2}$min, for *two* locomotives. The single engine, with a gross trailing load of 425 tons did well to complete this adverse stretch in $28\frac{1}{4}$min, but because of the check at Bolton-le-Sands and the overload for one engine the train had lost a further four minutes between Preston and Shap Summit. The locomotive itself was performing well, and on the 1 in 133 gradient of the Grayrigg Bank was sustaining an output of 2,100 drawbar horsepower, at 62mph. Another temporary speed restriction near Penrith caused a further loss of 2min, and on approaching Carlisle the train was so far out of its normal path that it was stopped outside, waiting for a platform to be vacated.

During the early summer of 1973 weekday possessions between Shap Summit and Carlisle were frequent, and these necessarily caused some disruption of train working. The normal time for West Coast express trains, provided with two Class '50' locomotives, was 28min for the 31·4 miles from Carlisle to Shap Summit. With a twelve-coach train there was not much margin, although some recovery time was included in the schedule south of Tebay. Typical runs, on both of which I was in the locomotive cab, gave times of 27½ and 27¾min, with full power used wherever possible. Unfortunately however, as notes on the route in Chapter 4 emphasise, the continuous curvature between Clifton and Shap station, through Bessie Ghyll, necessitates a speed limit of 75mph for some miles; and although the adverse gradient there is 1 in 125, the full power of two Class '50' locomotives would ordinarily enable the gradient to be climbed at between 80 and 85mph.

Although the line is not so intensively used as that south of Preston there are sufficient trains for reaction from weekday possessions to spread extensively at times, particularly in the middle of the day. The 11.40 Glasgow to Euston provided an example of this, a situation that was made worse in that a single Class '47' locomotive was provided for a thirteen-coach train of more than 450 gross trailing tons. Although there was not any single line working at first, checks due to occupation of the line with preceding trains made the initial 17·9 miles from Carlisle to Penrith take 27½min, instead of the scheduled 16min. Then came a lengthy wait at Clifton for two northbound trains running in close succession to clear the section of single line working, and it took 39¼min to climb the 13½ miles from Penrith to Shap Summit – 66¾min from Carlisle. After that we had a completely clear road to Preston, but with one Class '47' locomotive instead of two Class '50' little more than keeping of overall point-to-point times was possible. The 58·5 miles from Shap Summit to the stop at Preston took 45¼min – lengthened, of course, by the inability of the locomotive to reach line maximum speed between Lancaster and Preston.

At the same time delays to express passenger trains from weekday possessions must be viewed in their true perspective. On a single day when I noted a particularly severe case in the working of the down 'Royal Scot', the 'possession' which led to a succession of delays was 'off' relatively early in the afternoon, and from the new panel signal box at Carlisle I noted, on the illuminated diagram, the entirely undelayed running of the 12.05 Glasgow express from Euston, which although having only a single Class '50' locomotive arrived in Carlisle punctually. On the same day I travelled south by the 17.53 train, and we passed Carnforth, 62·8 miles, in 50¾min, again with no delays at all on the mountain section. There would seem to have been an important principle involved in the timing of the periods in which weekday possessions were permitted, in that late afternoon and evening business trains were least likely to be affected; and while there would be a natural desire to get the actual work done during normal working hours its early completion each day it has meant that business travellers, making use of fast evening services have not suffered the frustration of late running at the end of the day, when other people's difficulties are not liable to be looked upon with much toleration!

In view of the frequent references in the projection stage of the electrification scheme to the possibility of fast alternative service using Class '50' locomotives in pains, some details of maximum performances of such combinations during the transition period are worthy of study as indicating what might have been possible had electrification not eventually been authorised. When the accelerated services of 1970 were introduced the booked time from Carnforth to Shap Summit was 24min, requiring an average speed of 78·8mph against an average adverse gradient of 1 in 188. I have full details of five runs on which the distance was covered, respectively, in 22min 18sec; 23min 0sec; 22min 17sec; 22min 0sec and 22min 37sec – very consistent work, involving actual average speeds of 84·5, 81·9, 84·5, 85·7 and 83·3mph. The third and fourth occasions were notable in that one coach more than the normal twelve-coach load was being conveyed. All these journeys were made at the time when the speed limit of 60mph over Shap Summit was still operating, and similarly 75mph over the curves between Grayrigg and the point where the alignment becomes straight in the deep recess of the Lune Valley.

On a journey when I was riding in the cab of the leading Class '50' locomotive very complete details were taken of the ascent from Carnforth with the locomotives working at full power from Bolton-le-Sands to Grayrigg summit. The maximum speed limit was slightly exceeded at Milnthorpe, where 103mph was touched, and then 11 miles, between posts 15 and 26, were covered at an average speed of 83·3mph. On the 1 in 133 section of the incline speed was sustained at 82mph, involving an output of an equivalent drawbar horsepower of about 3,150. This of course, could be handsomely surpassed by a single electric locomotive of Class '86'. On the Shap Incline proper, on the gradient of 1 in 75 the sustained speed was 75mph until power was shut off for the restriction in speed over the summit. The equivalent drawbar horsepower here was at least 4,700 – clearly approaching a maximum effort for two locomotives with a combined engine horsepower of 5,400.

The electric timing from Preston to Carlisle as discussed earlier in this book is to be 68min in the down direction, including some recovery time, while the two-diesel timing of 1970 was 75min. While actual observation has shown that overall times of less than 70min were attainable in favourable weather and traffic conditions there was little, or no margin when running up to these standards. Even allowing that the intended relaxation of certain speed limits would help it is fairly evident that to provide the standard of service now programmed with electrification something more than the power available from two Class '50' diesels would have been necessary. It must be conceded however that the use of these locomotives has been important during the time of transition, and details of a run with a pair of them, working practically up to the limit of the line, provides an interesting commentary upon the improvements in track that have been made between Crewe and Preston. A detailed log is shown on page 165 of a run with the down 'Royal Scot' from which it will be seen that with no delays, other than certain restrictive signal aspects in the immediate approach to Preston, this first 51 miles of the northward journey from Crewe was covered in 39½min, a start to pass average of 77½mph.

It will be seen from the log that continuous running at 100mph was needed to maintain the sharp initial timing of 18½min to Warrington, but after the restriction to 70mph at Winwick Junction it was hardly possible to take advantage of the relaxation to a full 100mph between that point and the 80mph restriction at Golborne Junction. But 94mph was attained before the Wigan restriction, observed to 69mph, and recovery up the steep adverse gradients that followed produced no more than 90mph at Coppull. An electric locomotive would clearly have shown to great advantage here. There was some fast running downhill towards Preston, getting time in hand to offset the likelihood of delays north of Shap Summit. As it transpired, the 109·6 miles from Crewe to this latter point were covered in 86½min, and the train was then 8min early; but a weekday possession was in effect between Harrison's Sidings and Clifton, and the regulator in Carlisle power-box was clearly in some difficulty in arranging the priorities of down and up trains over the section where single-line working was in force. We were brought to a stand first, at a colour light signal adjacent to Milepost 41 (from Lancaster) 112·9 miles from Crewe, having taken 90min 53sec start to stop – 74·5mph average; but such were the subsequent delays that the remaining 28 miles down to Carlisle took nearly 77min.

The delay on this occasion was not entirely due to the section of single line working, where two trains in one direction and three in the other were at one time awaiting their turn to pass through. To facilitate movement in case of blockage of one line or another a number of emergency crossover roads have been put in. These are worked mechanically by ground frames, release of the electric locks being obtained when necessary and appropriate from the Carlisle power box. The actual points are of course electrically locked and detected, and the colour light signalling reading over them can only be cleared when the integrity of the locking and detection is proved. On this journey we had got away from Penrith, and had just topped the 100mph mark below Plumpton, when successively respective signal aspects led up to a RED at Southwaite. We stopped, and our assistant driver called Carlisle on the signal post telephone. Through some temporary defect the signal could not be cleared, although there was no obstruction on the line ahead. I should add that the colour-light signalling controlled from Carlisle had not long previously been brought into service, and this was undoubtedly one of the minor troubles that arise during the 'settling-down' period. On plain line we could have been authorised to pass the signal at danger and then to proceed according to the indications of the next signals ahead. At Southwaite this could not be done, because of the emergency crossover just ahead. The maintenance men working near had to be instructed to 'clip' the points, and only when this was done could we be called on, to pass over the points at dead slow speed, and then to continue normally. It was something like irony that in what seemed a very short distance afterwards we were travelling at 100mph once more! Because of this the last 17·9 miles from Penrith into Carlisle took 28½min, and with the cumulative effect of this and the earlier delays we were 55min late on arrival.

When the accelerated diesel timings were introduced in 1970, the pass-to-stop time from Penrith into Carlisle was 17½min; but as this included 4min recovery time, these trains were expected to run the last 17·9 miles in 13½min, when making up lost time, and the final 13·2 miles from Plumpton were then allowed only 10min. In the schedule in operation in the early part of 1973, before the electric service to Preston was inaugurated, 5min of the extra 10min temporarily inserted in the schedules of the Crewe–Carlisle non-stops was put in between Penrith and Carlisle, giving a generous 22½min for this last section. This recovery time was of course not enough to compensate for the Southwaite delay on my journey. Reverting to the very fast point-to-point time of 1970 however it was rarely necessary to run up to full recovery standard; but the actual times made on one occasion when this was done are interesting to set on record:

Dist miles		*Time from Penrith m*	*s*	*Av speed mph*
0·0	Penrith*	0	00	–
4·8	Plumpton (site)	3	25	84·4
10·5	Southwaite	7	03	94·3
13·0	Wreay (site)	8	41	91·8
17·9	Carlisle	13	15	53·7

In Scotland the diversion of the principal daytime express trains to the G&SW route, from May 1971 limited the chances of studying what the Class '50' locomotives in pairs might have done if nothing more than 'route improvement' and resignalling had been authorised. In the 1970 accelerations the Liverpool and Manchester trains has some very sharp timings with intermediate stops at Lockerbie, Beattock and Carstairs. The 08.15

* Passed at 60mph Max speed 100mph

from Liverpool to Glasgow, for example, was required to run the 25·7 miles from Carlisle to Lockerbie in 20½min, start to stop, and to continue over the 14 miles to Beattock in 12min start to stop. It was made more difficult at that time in that the line maximum speed over this route of Scottish Region was then limited to 80mph. Time had to be made, therefore, by vigorous starts and rapid hillclimbing. For trains having to start afresh from an intermediate stop at the now-closed Beattock station the schedule time was eased by the inclusion of a generous amount of recovery time between Beattock summit and Carstairs. For while the famous Beattock Bank was scheduled to have its 10 miles climbed in 12½min from a dead start no less than 25½min were allowed for the downhill 23·9 miles to Carstairs. The 5min of recovery time inserted on this latter stretch was indeed enough to compensate for those occasions when only one Class '50' locomotive was available. Then one could not expect the bank itself to be climbed in less than about 16min, with a twelve-coach train; but this loss of 3½min could be made good with a clear road down to Carstairs.

With normal rostered engine power the allowance of 12½min, start to pass, for the 10 miles of the Beattock Bank left some margin in reserve. An attained speed of 62–64mph sustained on the 1 in 70 gradient would involve an equivalent drawbar horse-power of about 4,000, compared to the 4,700 edhp represented by a sustained 75mph on the 1 in 75 gradient of Shap. A factor that has appreciably affected the motive power situation during the transition period, particularly so far as the accelerated express passenger trains were concerned, was that although the Class '50' locomotives were designed for working in multiple, none of the other diesel-electric locomotives regularly working over the route could be coupled with them. While the original Type '4' English Electric design, now Class '40' are equipped for working in multiple, the numerous Class '47' are not so that when two Class '50' locomotives were not available, reinforcement, from a locomotive of another class was not possible. Neither could two Class '47's be used as a substitute. Of course it can well be appreciated that the motive power situation was in a state of 'suspended animation' until the decision to electrify was made. As it is, no new first line motive power has been allocated to the West Coast main line since the Class '50' locomotives were introduced. Once the decision to electrify was taken no further diesels could be expected, and it was part of the economic justification for electrification that diesel locomotives made surplus should be transferred elsewhere to avoid the need for purchasing new locomotives.

During this difficult time of transition I had an interesting run on the 11.40 up from Glasgow, not long after the re-opening of the Caledonian line to ordinary daytime traffic, when for a train of thirteen coaches, 432 tons, we were powered by a single Class '47' locomotive, a serious deficiency on a train timed for haulage by two Class '50's. I was riding in the locomotive cab, and consider that we did remarkably well in the circumstances, especially as this class of locomotive is limited to a maximum speed of 95mph. This train was allowed only 105min for the 102·3 miles from Glasgow to Carlisle including 6½min scheduled standing time at three intermediate stops, and with a marked deficiency in tractive power, as compared to that for which the schedule was planned the restarts from these stations were relatively slow. Matters were not made easier by a lengthy stretch of line between Polmadie and Cambuslang subject to a temporary speed restriction, while this was also the occasion when the inexperience of a signalman on the new Motherwell power box panel led to our being stopped unnecessarily at Elvanfoot. This latter check accounted for at least 5min of the 11min lateness with which we arrived at Carlisle.

The lack of engine power as compared to that of the two Class '50' locomotives was apparent in climbing the continuously adverse gradient from the Motherwell start, mostly on 1 in 100, when we took 8¾min to pass Law Junction, 5·3 miles. But excellent time was being made through Upper Clydesdale, with an average speed of 73·7mph for 13 miles, until the unfortunate signal stop at Elvanfoot intervened. No higher speed than 40mph could be subsequently attained on the 1 in 99 up to Beattock Summit. As will be seen from the log the ensuing 23·9 miles to the stop at Lockerbie took only 17min 28sec, with an average of 90mph from Beattock station site to Nethercleugh. Summarising this interesting journey, with 2min lost through the temporary speed restriction between Polmadie and Cambuslang, one minute station overtime at Motherwell, and 5min due to the stop at Elvanfoot there remained only 3min to book against the locomotive – highly creditable in such circumstances.

A run southwards from Carlisle during the time when

diversions over the G&SW line were in operation shows how the slightly relaxed timings could be kept, if conditions were favourable at locations where single-line working was in force. It was on the same service as that concerned in the previous run, but in March 1972 leaving Glasgow at 11.20 and travelling via Kilmarnock and Dumfries. In the schedule of 93min there was inserted a total of 21½min recovery time. There was a heavy slack near Penrith, which caused a loss of 3½min between Carlisle and Shap Summit; but the section of single line working between Tebay and Low Gill was negotiated without the train being actually stopped at either end – a fortunate and unusual experience. Nevertheless, despite the availability of 5½min recovery time between Tebay and Oxenholme a further 2½min had been lost on schedule, and having left Carlisle 2min late the train was still 3½min late on passing Carnforth. The road was clear thereafter and with ample recovery time available the arrival in Preston was 6min early. The abridged log of this very satisfactory run is appended.

Train IM30 : Carlisle–Preston

Load : 13 coaches, 439 tons tare, 465 tons full

Locomotives : Two Class '50' diesels.

Dist miles		*Sch min*	*Actual m*	*s*	*Punctuality min*	
0·0	Carlisle	0	0	00	2	L
13·1	Plumpton	12½	12	46	2¼	L
–			p.w.slack			
17·9	Penrith	16	17	28	3½	L
31·4	Shap Summit	27½	31	03	5½	L
36·9	Tebay	32	37	41	7¾	L
–			single line working			
41·1	Low Gill Jc.		45	56		
50·0	Oxenholme	47½	53	32	8	L
62·8	Carnforth	61	62	37	3½	L
69·1	Lancaster	65½	67	07	3½	L
90·1	Preston	93	84	50	6	E

Recovery times : 5½min Tebay–Oxenholme
5min Oxenholme–Carnforth
11min Lancaster–Preston

Net running time 72min

Brief mention may also be made of a Sunday diversion, in December 1971, of train IM19 the 11.55 Glasgow to Euston via the Settle and Carlisle line, Blackburn and Manchester Victoria. This train consisted of eleven coaches, a gross trailing load of 405 tons, and was worked by two Class '50' diesels. With the restrictions in speed of this route, and the incidence of two moderate checks it was not possible to keep the sharp timing of 45½min from Carlisle to Aisgill summit, 48·3 miles; but with 5min recovery time in the schedule, Blea Moor was passed slightly ahead of time despite a start from Carlisle 5½ min late, 59·5 miles in 55min 58sec. Single line working was in force however between Settle station and Settle Junction, and this, despite a further 5min of recovery time took up all the time that had been regained. The train was 5½min late when passing on to the Ribble Valley line of the former L&YR at Hellifield. No further fast running was possible until the train had negotiated 61¼ miles of difficult connecting lines in Lancashire, and joined the Manchester – London main line at Stockport. This diversion route totalled up to 162 miles from Carlisle to Crewe, instead of 141 miles by the direct line, and the working times made up 211min, an average speed of no more than 40mph. But with the first 71·5 miles from Carlisle to Settle covered in just under 68min, start to stop, the time taken thereafter in covering the remaining 90 miles to Crewe is an adequate commentary on what was involved in these weekend diversions. The aggregate running time from the restart at Settle to arrival in Crewe was a few seconds under 150min.

LM Region: 12.17 Crewe–Carlisle
'The Royal Scot'

Load: 12 coaches, 402 tons tare, 425 tons full
Locomotives: Class '50' diesels Nos 411 and 421

Dist miles		*Sch min*	*Actual m s*	*Speeds mph*
0·0	CREWE	0	0 00	—
3·1	*Coppenhall Junction*	4½	4 58	81
8·8	*Winsford Junction*		8 36	100
11·8	Hartford		10 21	103
16·5	*Weaver Junction*	13	13 11	86 *

—	*Norton Crossing*		—	101
22·1	*Acton Grange Junction*	17	16 37	—
24·1	WARRINGTON	18½	18 07	72 *
27·5	*Winwick Junction*	21½	20 53	78/67 *
29·8	*Golborne Junction*		22 53	—
33·2	Bamfurlong (site)		25 13	94
35·8	WIGAN	27½	27 11	69 *
38·1	*Boars Head* (site)		29 03	75
41·6	*Coppull* (site)		31 48	90
45·5	*Euxton Junction*	39	33 58	103
46·9	Leyland		34 52	
—			sigs	
50·9	PRESTON	44½	39 33	25 *
55·7	*Barton*		44 59	86
60·4	*Garstang*		48 13	91
—			pws	20 *
66·2	Bay Horse		54 44	88
—			—	90
70·9	*Lancaster No 1* (site)		58 05	60 *
71·9	LANCASTER	62	59 05	60 *
75·1	Hest Bank		61 57	82
78·2	CARNFORTH	67	63 58	90
81·4	*Milepost 9½*		66 10	86
85·5	*Milnthorpe*		68 40	103
91·0	OXENHOLME	76	72 25	83/86
92·9	*Milepost 21*		73 48	83
94·9	*Milepost 23*		75 15	81
98·1	*Grayrigg*		77 38	75 *
104·1	TEBAY	89	82 13	90
105·9	*Milepost 34*		83 28	86
107·4	*Milepost 35½*		84 35	75
108·9	*Milepost 37*		85 50	75
109·6	*Shap Summit*	93½	86 35	60 *
112·9	Milepost 41		**90 53**	Stop
			Single line delays	
141·0	CARLISLE	130	186 25	

* Speed restrictions

Scottish Region: 11.40 Glasgow–Carlisle

Load: 13 coaches, 432 tons tare, 460 tons full
Locomotive: Class 47 Diesel No 1842

Dist *miles*		*Sch* *min*	*Actual* *m s*	*Speeds* *mph*
0·0	GLASGOW CENTRAL	0	0 00	—
—			pws	
3·0	Rutherglen		6 10	
—			pws	20
4·9	Cambuslang		10 22	
6·5	Newton		12 40	54½
8·4	Uddingston		14 37	69
—			sigs	
12·8	MOTHERWELL	**18**	**19 40**	
1·0	*Milepost 88½*		2 30	
3·0	*Milepost 86½*		5 28	44
5·3	*Law Junction*		8 38	43
7·6	Carluke		11 29	50/45
11·0	*Milepost 78½*		15 46	51
13·7	*Lanark Junction*		18 12	69
—			sigs	
1·59	CARSTAIRS	**19½**	**21 15**	
3·6	*Leggatfoot*		4 57	53
5·1	*Thankerton*		6 27	68
6·7	*Symington*		8 00	61
10·4	*Lamington*		11 00	83½
15·8	*Abington*		15 08	75
—			**20 52**	Signal
			22 20	stop
23·9	*Beattock Summit*		27 28	40
33·9	*Beattock*		34 46	92/88
39·1	*Wamphray*		38 19	91/88
41·9	*Dinwoodie*		40 09	90
44·9	*Nethercleugh*		42 10	91
47·8	LOCKERBIE	**35½**	**44 56**	
5·7	*Ecclefechan*		7 17	72
9·1	*Kirtlebridge*		9 47	90/84
12·8	*Kirkpatrick*		12 20	90

Scottish Region: 11.40 Glasgow—Carlisle (*Continued*)

15·6	*Quintinshill*		14 21	80 *
17·2	*Gretna Junction*		15 32	85/83
23·8	*Kingmoor*		20 15	84
25·8	CARLISLE	$25\frac{1}{2}$	23 20	

* Speed restrictions

11: THE FINAL PRELIMINARIES

In the last half year before the inauguration of the full electric service to Glasgow, there was ample evidence, even to the ordinary passenger, of the success of the planning that had taken place since the project was authorised. The electrified service from London was extended to Preston at the end of July 1973, and that station then became the changeover point from electric to diesel traction on the Scottish services from London. By then several of the new Class '87' electric locomotives were in traffic, and one could begin to appreciate their outstanding capabilities in acceleration and high tractive power. By the courtesy of the Chief Operating Manager, London Midland Region, arrangements were made for me to ride in the cab of one of the new locomotives from Euston to Crewe. This was not only an exercise in the observation of 'performance' in its narrower aspects, in noting overall times made and in accelerating the load, and maintenance of high speed. In Chapter 7 I referred at some length to the unsatisfactory features of Class '86' performance that had developed with increasing mileage, in respect of comfort of the ride, and adverse effects on the track. In riding a Class '87' locomotive one naturally looked with much interest for the improvements effected by the changes in design.

First of all however reference must be made to the improvement in tractive power characteristics, which are demonstrated theoretically by curves of basic performance. On the 'weak-field' characteristic these locomotives have a continuous power rating of 5,000 horsepower at the rail, providing a tractive effort of 16,000lb at 100mph, 20,000lb at 90mph and 27,000lb at 80mph. In view of the gradients involved in climbing the Shap and Beattock inclines it is naturally interesting to try and evaluate what the full power is likely to result in when climbing such gradients. In still air the tractive resistance of modern BR stock can be taken at about 14lb per ton, at 90mph and about 17·5lb per ton at 100mph. To haul such a train of twelve coaches at 90mph up a 1 in 75 gradient would involve a little over 4,000 horsepower at the drawbar, to which would be needed to add the power to propel the locomotive itself. From this it certainly seems likely that with the day expresses, which load to twelve coaches weighing about 400 tons tare, the Class '87' locomotives should be able to *sustain* speeds of around 90 mph on the steepest inclines, in favourable weather conditions. Of course the adverse climatic conditions frequently prevailing over the route north of Lancaster has been taken into account in planning train schedules – not only in respect of contrary winds, but also in bad rail conditions causing slipping.

Arrangements were made for me to ride locomotive No 87004 on the 11.05 express from Euston, and although this train had not one of the fastest schedules on the line a considerable number of delays were experienced en route that called for running up to the line maximum speeds over each section to regain as much time as possible. A detailed log of the journey is subjoined, and a few of its leading features may be specially mentioned. Before we were clear of the London suburbs a track failure north of Willesden entailed a stop at a colour light signal adjacent to Milepost 6¼. On obtaining authority to proceed, by the signal post telephone, an extremely rapid re-start was made, with speed rising to 75mph in 1¾ miles from rest, and on the continuous adverse gradient of 1 in 335 to 96mph in a further 2 miles. With a gross trailing load of 385 tons this was a notable exposition of the accelerative capacity of the new locomotives. From Harrow, over the continuation of the long rise to Tring, and over the first 4 miles of the subsequent descent speed averaged 97mph. After the slow running entailed by the switch from fast to slow lines at Leighton Buzzard, and the return to the fast lines at Denbigh Hall Junction performance was normal to Rugby, the various minor speed restrictions precluded any spectacular acceleration.

There was another remarkable example of acceleration on leaving Nuneaton, as follows:

Distance from Euston (Miles)		*Time from restart* *m*	*s*	*Speeds mph*
97·1	Nuneaton	0	00	0
98¼	Milepost 98¼	1	48	70

99	Milepost 99	2	25	86
100	Milepost 100	3	05	94

The gradient is falling at 1 in 730 to Milepost 99 and then rising at 1 in 645. In 2·9 miles from rest a speed of 94mph was attained, after which power was shut off to allow speed to drift down to the 70mph limit required through Atherstone station, at the 102½ milepost from Euston. As will be seen from the log the train was subject to considerable delay from permanent way work between Tamworth and Stafford; but with running up to line maximum speed thereafter the train was only 11½min late on arrival at Crewe, after a series of delays costing approximately 26min in running. The net start-to-stop average speeds were 88·7mph from Euston to Rugby, and 81·4mph from Nuneaton to Crewe. The locomotive continued to Preston, with a different crew, but my own observations terminated at Crewe on this occasion.

While the extreme vigour of the acceleration on two occasions during this trip was a manifestation of great power the riding qualities of the new locomotive was a source of constant interest. The 'bouncing' action at any appreciable speed that was so characteristic of the Class '86' locomotives was completely absent. The vertical ride was entirely steady at all speeds, and although there was side oscillation on some curving stretches of line, it was of quite small amplitude, and did not persist. It was altogether a much more comfortable ride, and gave the impression that the locomotive was being as kind to the track as it was to those in the cab. At the same time the riding performance of the Class '86' locomotives never seems to have had any intimidating effect on their drivers. Long experience of steam locomotive operation on a great variety of designs has for long confirmed the view that enginemen will ease up if the riding begins to get dangerous. There is an essential difference between 'rough' and 'unsafe' riding. A run made in the early summer of 1973 on the 12 noon express from Euston to Manchester shows the kind of performance that was frequently obtained with the Class '86' locomotives, despite their bouncing action.

On this run, with a load of eleven coaches, making with passengers, a gross trailing load of 390 tons, Bletchley was passed in 31min 55sec from the start, Rugby in 54min 23sec, Nuneaton in 63min 52sec and Armitage in 78min 46sec. The

LM Region: 11.05 Euston–Crewe

Load: 11 coaches, 363 tons tare, 385 tons full

Locomotive: Class '87', No 87004

Dist miles		*Sch min*	*Actual m s*	*Speeds mph*
0·0	EUSTON	0	0 00	—
2·4	South Hampstead		4 04	65
5·4	Willesden Junction	7	6 20	90
6·3	*Milepost 6¼*		**7 53**	signal
—			9 10	stop
8·1	Wembley		11 37	75
11·4	Harrow		13 44	99
13·3	Hatch End		14 56	95
17·5	WATFORD JUNCTION	14½	17 32	100
21·0	Kings Langley		19 41	96
24·5	Boxmoor		21 50	97½
28·0	Berkhamsted		24 04	89 *
31·7	Tring	23½	26 23	100
36·1	Cheddington		29 01	100
—			crossover	20 *
46·7	BLETCHLEY	33½	41 05	75 max
—			crossover	30 max
52·4	Wolverton		48 24	80
59·9	*Roade* (site)		53 12	100
69·7	*Weedon*		59 25	75 *
75·3	*Welton*		63 05	100
—			sigs	—
82·6	RUGBY	**64**	**69 26**	—
2·4	*Milepost 85*		3 36	78
5·5	*Brinklow*		5 37	99
8·7	*Shilton*		7 35	100
14·5	NUNEATON	**13**	**12 06**	
2·9	*Milepost 100*		3 05	94
5·3	Atherstone		4 40	95/70 *
9·4	Polesworth		7 28	100
12·9	TAMWORTH	10½	9 39	95
—			several	
—			pw slacks	
23·9	*Armitage*		27 46	69/94
27·2	Rugeley		30 00	90

LM Region: 11.05 Euston—Crewe (*Continued*)

30·0	*Colwich*	21½	31 56	—
			pw slack	
36·5	STAFFORD		38 58	20
41·8	Norton Bridge		43 57	90
46·4	*Standon Bridge*		46 47	100/94
50·5	*Whitmore*		49 19	99
56·0	*Betley Road*		52 47	100
			sigs	
61·0	CREWE	53	58 30	

Net times: Euston–Rugby 56min
Nuneaton–Crewe 45min

average speeds from the Euston start to these four places were 87·8, 91·2, 91·3 and 92·4mph respectively, and the 'flying' average over the 118·9 miles from Willesden Junction to Rugeley, covered in 73min 48sec, was 96·7mph. This high average included observation of all the intermediate speed restrictions at Berkhamsted, Leighton Buzzard, Wolverton, Weedon, Rugby and Atherstone. The train turned on to the North Staffordshire line at Colwich in 84min 59sec from leaving Euston, having made a start-to-pass average of exactly 90 miles per hour.

With a high speed train service of the intensity of that to be introduced in May 1974, particularly over a route on which so much has recently been done to raise speed limits on many sections of the line, it is vitally important to check the riding of locomotives and coaching stock, running at the new maximum service speeds. Test runs were arranged from Euston to Glasgow on September 19th, 1973, returning on the following day, and by the courtesy of the London Midland, and of the Scottish Region authorities I was privileged to travel by the train, and to see the various forms of check that were being made. Although some fast running was necessarily involved, it is important to emphasise that these runs were not tests of locomotive capacity. At the time the overhead wires were not erected over the entire route, and the train had to be diesel-hauled between Preston and Kingmoor. As only one Class '50' locomotive could be made available, and the electric locomotive had to be hauled 'dead' over this section, the load had to be arranged so as to be within

* Speed restrictions

the capacity of a single Class '50' diesel to maintain the new electric timings. From Euston therefore the test train consisted of only three vehicles. Immediately behind the locomotive was the new test coach MENTOR, which very appropriate code name is made up from the initials of its function – Mobile Electrical Network Testing Observation and Recording. Then came a Mark III brake-third, used by members of the testing staff not immediately on duty, and finally the civil engineer's track recording car – a modern development of the time-honoured 'whitewash' car, but one that records not only side movement, but 'twist' in the track.

I was very interested to find that the locomotive, which was working through from Euston to Glasgow, was one of the modified Class '86' with the new bogie suspension, and the SAAB resilient wheels – these are now designated 86/2. I was invited to ride on this locomotive for the first stage of the test, from Euston to Crewe, and thus had an opportunity of experiencing the greatly improved riding qualities. The new springing seems to have very successfully taken all the vertical bouncing out of the ride. So far as speed was concerned, a load of only three coaches presented no difficulties so far as traction was concerned, but was nevertheless a test of driving skill, in keeping the speed strictly to the limits imposed by the track. As far as Rugby also, we had problems of another kind. We were not able to leave Euston at our scheduled time of 09.25, and actually got away at 09.33, immediately behind the 09.30 to Liverpool, which calls at Watford. It was hoped that this latter train might have been put slow line as far as Watford, so that we could have got ahead while the stop was being made, but this was not done, and approaching Bushey we sighted adverse signals, and on rounding the curve we saw the other train only just leaving Watford Junction station. She must have made an extremely vigorous start, because although we hung back until we were getting green signals, we were still able to cover the 14·2 miles up to Tring in 9min 50sec. Of course, with a powerful electric locomotive and only three coaches we were able to make some lightning accelerations!

In the early stages of the test some calibration of the locomotive speedometer had to be made. A cross-check on the intercom between the cab and MENTOR showed that the locomotive speedometer was reading about 3mph high at 100mph, so that from Harrow onwards, when this check-up was completed, we took a reading of 103mph on the 'speedo' as our maximum. After Tring the Liverpool train seemed to have eased down, and we got a succession of 'double yellows'. It was important that the testing cars behind us got recordings at maximum permitted speed round the curves at Leighton Buzzard, Wolverton, and Weedon, and so the locomotive was held in, and then *accelerated* to produce 80mph at Leighton, a specially authorised 90, at Wolverton, and after coasting through the Heyfords at 58mph a dash up to 79mph for Weedon. But of course this was not providing the high speed test on plain line that the civil engineer required, and since the train immediately following us was the 09.40 to Birmingham, it was arranged to stop north of Rugby, when we were clear of her path, for 3min to let the Liverpool train get well ahead, and enable us to make a fast and undelayed run as far as Stafford, where there was a severe slack for track repairs in operation. Despite all the checks and deliberate easings we had still taken no more than 63½min from Euston to passing Rugby. We stopped at signal RY299, a point 84·8 miles from Euston.

From the restart we were able to really get going. The accompanying log shows details of our progress, but, of course, apart from the extremely rapid start – 100mph in 1¾ miles from rest! – the running was little different from what one would experience daily over this route with eleven or twelve coach trains. But the speed gave the test cars behind us plenty of data, and the locomotive continued to ride extremely well. At Crewe I went back into the train to log the electric run to Preston from the brake-third. As will be seen from the log we ran to a signal stop just outside Preston station in 35min 27sec from Crewe – a start to stop average of 85·7mph. An interesting feature was the short piece between Winwick and Golborne Junctions, over which there are speed restrictions of 70 and 80mph respectively. Between them there is a length of 1¾ miles, uplifted to 100mph. With full length trains there can be little chance of taking advantage of this latter, on the rising gradients existing throughout; but with only three coaches it was different. Our driver rather overdid the slack at Winwick, coming down to 62mph; but then came a terrific acceleration to 95mph before he again overdid the Golborne slack, by coming down to 69mph. Even so the average speed of exactly 90 mph from Warrington to

Wigan probably counts as something of a record. The 'flying average' over the 45·5 miles from Coppenhall Junction to Farington was 92·5mph.

At Preston a wait of just over an hour was scheduled, to provide a lunch break, and induct us into a further high speed path. Again however we were dogged with delays. There had been a derailment near Barton, which involved temporary single line working on the up line, with pilotmen, and we had to wait until the down Royal Scot had gone ahead. So we were not only late in leaving Preston, but of course experienced further delay in slow running out to Garstang and in crossing over there. In consequence we were 17½min late in passing Lancaster. From there our point-to-point timing allowed 52½min for the 72 miles to Carlisle, and we were able to improve on this slightly. It is difficult to assess just what the 'dead' 86/2 electric locomotive represented in resistance to haulage; but with the dead weight of 177 tons the Class '50' locomotive seemed to make rather heavy weather of the principal gradients. We fell to 75mph at Grayrigg summit, and to 73mph at Shap Summit. Nevertheless the uphill point to point times were kept, with a total of exactly 14min from Oxenholme to Summit, against 15min booked. In view of the late running, however, those on board had hoped for something rather more spectacular.

By the courtesy of the chief civil engineers, first of the London Midland, and then of the Scottish Region, I was able to travel in the track testing car at the rear end of the train throughout from Preston to Glasgow, and to observe how the various irregularities in the track were recorded, and pin-pointed in their location. Of these irregularities however there were remarkably few, particularly seeing that the car itself was loose-coupled to the vehicle next ahead and was thus riding freely, without any of the normal constraint of closely-adjusted screw couplings, or of the modern buck-eye couplers. From Carlisle we continued to be diesel hauled out to Kingmoor and from the further stop there we continued, with electric haulage, to make a most impressive run onwards into Scotland. As the accompanying log shows we ran at, or very close to, the line maximum speed throughout to Motherwell. We covered almost 90 miles in the first hour from the start, and it was certainly a novel experience for me to ride up the Beattock bank at a steady 91mph. From the brief stop at Newton we turned on to the Kirkhill line, and thence round the western side of the Cathcart Circle, to reach Glasgow Central.

On the following morning I rode at first in the saloon, to log in detail the fast run planned non-stop from Glasgow Central to Kingmoor, via the western section of the Cathcart Circle. We left 5min late by booked time, but there was an ample recovery margin in the initial allowance of 24min for the 10 miles to Newton, by this circuitous route, and we entered on to the main line almost exactly on time. We had scarcely got going in true 'electric' style before we were stopped, because of a power points failure south of Motherwell. From the restart we made a fast and undelayed run to Kingmoor, though it was certainly significant of the conditions in which this test was made that the time over the 64·9 miles between Carstairs and Gretna Junction, 41min 30sec, was no more than fractionally faster than that we had made, mostly against the grade, on the previous day. That southbound average of 94mph was however enough to show the striking extent to which route improvement has been carried out; while the near-perfection of the riding of the saloon was in itself ample testimony.

At Kingmoor we changed back to diesel haulage for the next stage of the run, to Preston, and from Carlisle Citadel I was privileged to ride in MENTOR. Before telling of my own impressions however something must be said of the nature and functions of this veritable laboratory on wheels. It is a converted passenger coach, originally built in 1955 and has been adapted for its present use at the Swindon Works of British Rail Engineering. Air and vacuum brakes have been fitted together with B4 modern bogies to enable MENTOR to travel at speeds up to 100mph. The vehicle has been given a flat roof, with a domed observation section in the centre, and carries two pantographs, one of each type at present in use by British Rail. The pantograph is used by electric locomotives to collect current from the overhead wires, and the tests carried out by MENTOR include observation and recording of pantograph performance. Inside the vehicle the accommodation includes a compartment with a table and seating for six which is used as a Conference room, a large Instrument Room, and the Observation Room under the domed section of the roof. This has bench-type seats fitted on a raised dais to enable observers to inspect overhead equipment. Other facilities provided to make MENTOR completely self-contained include a small fitted galley for preparing meals, a toilet, and a generator room housing a 12kW Diesel alternator which provides power for all services within the vehicle, and for the compressor used to raise and lower the pantographs. The generator is also used to charge the vehicle batteries, which include one capable of operating the pantographs should the main power source fail.

The apparatus installed in the instrument room includes an ultra-violet recorder which, for overhead equipment tests, is linked to a specially instrumented pantograph. In this way a wide range of information is collected, and presented in the form of a 'print out' from the recorder. Included in the functions monitored is the force exerted on the pantograph head as it moves along the conductor wire, its rate of acceleration, changes in the wire height, and the amount by which the wire is 'staggered' above the track. The conductor wire does not run in a straight line above the centre of the track, alternative lengths are 'staggered' so that the wire moves across the carbons on the pantograph head as the locomotive proceeds, avoiding excessive wear in any one place. The amount of 'stagger' is critical and specially sectioned carbons are used to indicate its value for all sections of overhead wire tested. This latter facility is only available when the overhead system is dead. All these details, together with the speed of the vehicle, and the location of all line side structures, which are recorded by a photo-electric cell, appear as separate items on the print out produced by the recorder at the rate of 20in per minute. When the overhead system is live the data is transmitted via a radio telemetry link from the pantograph to a receiver inside the vehicle.

I was invited to ride in the observation room under the domed section of the roof, and to look ahead over the flat section of the roof and watch the action of the pantograph on the overhead line. At the time of this test the overhead line had been erected from Carlisle to a point just south of Carnforth, but it was not alive and the testing work was thus conducted under the 'dead' conditions previously mentioned. Our Class '50' diesel did not seem much stronger than on the previous day, and we had not accelerated to more than 86mph by Southwaite where the observers had hoped for 100mph. A signal check to 30mph before Plumpton did not improve matters, while for test purposes the pantograph was lowered at Eden Valley Junction, and not raised again until we were approaching Shap Summit. Despite the check before Plumpton however the booked allowance of 27½min from Carlisle to Summit had been practically observed. Then, with the pantograph up once more, for test purposes, we had quite an exciting descent to Tebay, with a maximum of 106mph. MENTOR was riding beautifully at this speed, and it was most interesting to watch the action of the pantograph on the overhead wire. A temporary speed restriction to 20mph during the descent of the Grayrigg bank caused a loss of 2min in running; but with 3min recovery time in the schedule between Carnforth and Preston, we arrived outside the latter station almost exactly on time.

Just at the time when I was writing this chapter a letter from one of my train-logging friends suggested that with electric haulage the 'norm' for the Preston-Crewe section is likely to be less than 40min, and he sent me details of a run on the 16.05 train from Euston in which the 50·9 miles had been covered in 38¾min by a Class '86' locomotive hauling a twelve-coach train of 398 tons tare. Our schedule on the southbound test journey was 37½min with 2min recovery time between Euxton Junction and Wigan. From this run, which I logged from the track testing car on the rear end of the train, it was quite clear that it is now the speed restrictions rather than anything else that 'call the tune' on this stretch of line. Even with no more than three coaches, and running everywhere up to the permitted line maximum speed, we needed that 2min recovery time to offset the effect of one signal check near the site of the one-time Boars Head station. Our actual time from Preston to Crewe was 37min 56sec. It is certainly a difficult stretch over which to maintain a net average speed of 85mph. I had ridden in the track testing car on this section, and again noted the excellence of the permanent way throughout.

On the final stage of this most interesting round trip, I travelled in the saloon. We had the sharp timing of 106½min for the 158 miles from Crewe to Euston, but got the 'right away' 5min ahead of our booked time. Despite a temporary speed restriction to 20mph on Madeley bank we managed to keep 4½ to 5min ahead until we had passed Weedon. After that the booked point-to-point times were very fast, requiring averages of slightly above 100mph from Bletchley to Tring and Tring to Watford, for example. Having regard to the no-more-than-slight-speed restrictions imposed intermediately these could not be maintained without exceeding the statutory 100mph, and this was not done. In consequence we had dropped back to $3\frac{1}{2}$min ahead of time at Watford, and only won back a fraction by Willesden. One recalled also the days when the drivers of steam locomotives used regularly to romp over the last mile into Euston in about 2min while we were running quietly down to spend nearly 3min on the same stretch. So we took $108\frac{3}{4}$min up from Crewe, or $106\frac{3}{4}$min allowing for the Madeley check. But although the prospect of a new Crewe–Euston 'record' did not materialise the run was eminently satisfactory in its primary object, of providing with consistent precision speeds that showed the riding performance of the track testing car at line maximum, and my warmest thanks are due to the authorities of both the London Midland and Scottish Regions in permitting me to be present on such an important occasion.

I have titled this chapter 'The Final Preliminaries'. This they had to be, so far as the text of this book was concerned. To maintain another tight schedule, that of publication was concerned my dead-line was the end of October 1973. Obviously there will have been many more finishing touches on the line by the time the full electric service to Glasgow opens to the public in May 1974, but I hope what I have written in this chapter will be more than enough to show how thoroughly every aspect of the working has been checked, and re-checked in advance, and that 'Britain's New Railway', as I described the work south of Liverpool and Manchester in my earlier book, will have a major extension of outstanding quality in May 1974.

LM Region: Crewe–Euston

High Speed Test Run
Load: 3 special cars, 97 tons tare
Loco: Class 82/2 No 86003

Dist miles		*Sch min*	*Actual m s*	*Av speed mph*
0·0	CREWE	0	0 00	—
2·1	*Milepost 156*		2 46	—
6·1	*Milepost 152*		5 08	101·3
—			pw slack	(20)
10·1	*Milepost 148*		9 17	
24·5	STAFFORD	17½	18 42	91·8
31·0	*Colwich*	24½	24 01	73·4
41·8	Lichfield	31	31 05	91·9
—			pw slack	(75)
61·0	NUNEATON	43	43 25	93·7
75·5	RUGBY	52½	53 02	90·5
88·4	*Weedon*	61	61 26	92·2
111·4	BLETCHLEY	75	75 55	95·3
126·4	Tring	84	85 15	96·3
140·6	Watford Junction	92½	93 56	98·2
152·7	*Willesden Junction*	100	101 20	98·3
157·1	*Milepost 1*	—	105 48	60·0
158·1	EUSTON	106½	108 40	

Net time 106½min (89mph)

Scottish Region: Kingmoor–Newton

High Speed Test Run
Load: 3 special cars, 97 tons tare
Loco: Class '86/2' No 86003

Dist *miles*		*Actual* *m s*	*Speeds* *mph*
0·0	Kingmoor	0 00	—
4·0	*Floriston*	3 22	100
6·8	*Gretna Junction*	5 01	98
11·1	*Kirkpatrick*	7 52	90
14·8	*Kirtlebridge*	10 19	103
18·2	*Ecclefechan*	12 23	95
23·9	LOCKERBIE	16 03	101/95
26·8	*Nethercleugh*	17 48	102
29·8	*Dinwoodie*	19 38	95
32·6	*Wamphray*	21 18	103
37·8	*Beattock*	24 42	90/88
43·1	*Milepost 45*	28 15	90
45·1	*Milepost 47*	29 34	91
47·1	*Milepost 49*	30 53	91
47·8	*Summit*	31 22	91
50·7	*Elvanfoot*	33 33	88
55·9	*Abington*	37 07	90
61·3	*Lamington*	40 50	89
65·0	*Symington*	43 01	100
66·6	*Thankerton*	43 58	103
70·1	*Milepost 72*	46 06	100
71·7	CARSTAIRS	47 08	90
74·1	*Lanark Junction*	48 48	89
78·8	*Braidwood*	51 58	91
80·0	Carluke	52 48	93
82·3	*Law Junction*	54 17	easing
—	*Garriongill Junction*	—	60
87·6	MOTHERWELL	58 18	96/75
90·1	*Milepost*	60 25	—
		sigs	
92·0	Uddingston	62 38	80
93·9	Newton	65 05	—

LM Region: Rugby–Crewe

High Speed Test Run
Load: 3 special cars, 97 tons tare
Loco: Class 86/2 No 86003

Dist *miles*		*Actual* *m s*	*Speeds* *mph*
0·0	AUTO SIGNAL RY 299	0 00	—
3·3	*Brinklow*	2 36	100
6·6	*Shilton*	4 34	100
8·9	*Bulkington*	5 56	100
12·3	NUNEATON	7 58	102
17·5	Atherstone	11 29	68*
21·7	Polesworth	14 12	100/91
25·2	TAMWORTH	16 29	—
31·5	Lichfield	20 16	100
36·2	*Armitage*	23 04	100
39·5	Rugeley	25 00	91
42·4	*Colwich*	26 55	90
44·7	*Milford*	28 37	80*
—		p.w.s.	20
48·8	STAFFORD	33 59	20
54·1	Norton Bridge	39 40	90
	Standon Bridge	—	100
62·8	*Whitmore*	45 08	100
65·2	*Madeley*	46 35	99
68·5	*Betley Road*	48 33	101
71·5	*Basford Hall Junction*	50 37	—
		sigs	—
73·3	CREWE	55 05	

Net time 51min — 86·5mph

* Speed restrictions

INDEX